AF600228

THE CATHOLIC UNIVERSITY OF AMERICA
CANON LAW STUDIES
NO. 160

THE OBLIGATIONS OF THE TRAVELER ACCORDING TO CANON 14

AN HISTORICAL SYNOPSIS
AND COMMENTARY

BY

REV. JOHN LEO HAMMILL, M.A., J.C.L.
Priest of the Diocese of Ogdensburg

A DISSERTATION

Submitted to the Faculty of the School of Canon Law of the Catholic University of America in Partial Fulfillment of the Requirements for the Degree of Doctor of Canon Law

THE CATHOLIC UNIVERSITY OF AMERICA PRESS
WASHINGTON, D. C.
1942

NIHIL OBSTAT:

Edouardus G. Roelker, S.T.D., J.C.D.

Censor Deputatus

Washingtonii, die 2 mensis iulii, 1942

IMPRIMATUR:

✠ Franciscus Iosephus Monaghan, S.T.D., LL.D.

Episcopus Ogdensburgensis

Ogdensburgi, die 6 mensis iulii, 1942

PRINTED IN THE UNITED STATES OF AMERICA
BY A. M. PHILLIPS, WATERTOWN, N. Y.

To

His Excellency

The Most Reverend Francis Joseph Monaghan, S.T.D., LL.D.

Bishop of Ogdensburg

TABLE OF CONTENTS

INTRODUCTION

CANONISTS and jurists have long been occupied with the determination of the obligations of the traveler, both as regards his place of residence and as regards the place in which he is visiting. The problems thus arising were never more pressing than in our days of modern travel. The historian of Canon Law will find these problems extremely engrossing as he follows the first indeterminate enactments through the beginnings of canonical science in the middle ages until finally juridical principles were developed and a definite canonical discipline regarding the traveler was expressed in canon 14.[1] Comparative jurisprudence finds here valuable illustrations of the analogy between Canon and Civil Law, of their similarity and their differences, and of their mutual influence. Here the canonist has an opportunity to examine the nature of law and to trace its juridical principles in many of their specific applications. Although the Code of Canon Law, promulgated in 1917, did much to clarify the nature and extent of the obligations of the traveler by the principles embodied in canon 14, perplexing problems still remain. The determination of the obligations of the traveler is not only a challenge to the student of law in all of its phases, but eminently practical today.

The present study is confined to the obligations of the traveler according to Canon Law. The term *traveler* has been used generically to signify him who is in the territory of a particular legislator for a brief time. The specific terms of peregrin and vagrant are used only when treating of that period when these terms became clear in the sources, namely in the period after the middle ages. The term *peregrin* refers to

[1] § 1. Peregrini:

1° Non adstringuntur legibus particularibus sui territorii quandiu ab eo absunt, nisi aut earum transgressio in proprio territorio noceat, aut leges sint personales;

2° Neque legibus territorii in quo versantur, iis exceptis quae ordini publico consulunt, vel actuum solemnia determinant;

3° At legibus generalibus tenentur, etiamsi hae suo in territorio non vigeant, minime vero si in loco in quo versantur non obligant.

§ 2. Vagi obligantur legibus tam generalibus quam particularibus quae vigent in loco in quo versantur."—Canon 14.

a traveler who has a domicile[2] or quasi-domicile[3], but is not actually in the territory of either. The consideration of the peregrin in relation to particular law has a double aspect: the peregrin in relation to the laws of the place in which he is at the present, in which he is a stranger; and the peregrin in relation to the laws of his own territory, from which he is absent. In regard to the *laws of his own territory,* the peregrin has been indicated herein as the *absent subject.* In regard to the *laws of the place where he is* at the moment, the peregrin has been indicated as the *stranger.* The term *vagrant* refers to him who has neither domicile nor quasi-domicile.[4]

[2] A person in the place where he possesses a domicile is known as an inhabitant, an *incola.* Cf. canon 91. The notion of domicile dates back to Roman Law. Cf. D (50, 16) 203. It was presupposed in Canon Law as early as the middle ages, and nowhere is it expressly defined or treated in the *Corpus Iuris Canonici.* Cf. Vindex, "Domicilium et quasi-domicilium eorumque effectus in Codice Juris Canonici,"—*Jus Pontificium,* VI (1926), 39. Hereafter this periodical is cited as *Jus Pont.* Domicile, under the Code, is acquired by the double factor of intention and residence, or by mere residence for ten years. It is lost by departure with the intention of never returning. Cf. canons 92, § 1; 95.

[3] A person in the place where he possesses a quasi-domicile is known as an *advena.* Cf. canon 91. The notion of quasi-domicile was not evolved until after the Council of Trent and the discussions occasioned by the *Tametsi* decree regarding the juridical form of marriage. It did not receive its definite formation in law until 1867. Cf. Vindex, "Domicilium et quasi-domicilium eorumque effectus in Codice Juris Canonici,"—*Jus Pont., VI* (1926), 42; Costello, *Domicile and Quasi-Domicile* (The Catholic University of America Canon Law Studies, n. 60, Washington, D. C.: The Catholic University of America, 1930), p. 87. Quasi-domicile, under the Code, is acquired by residence with the intention of staying for the greater part of the year. Cf. canon 92, § 2.

[4] The use of the word *vagrant* to translate the term *vagus* is to be carefully distinguished from the common use of the term in an opprobrious sense in both English and American law. Black states that vagrant is "a general term including in English law the several classes of idle and disorderly persons, rogues, and vagabonds, and incorrigible rogues. In American law, the term is variously defined by statute but the general meaning is that of an able-bodied person having no visible means of support and who lives idly without seeking work, or who is a professional beggar, or roams about from place to place without regular employment or fixed abode . . . "—*Black's Law Dictionary* (3.ed. by The Publisher's Editorial Staff, St. Paul Minn.; West Publishing Co., 1933), p. 1796. The difficulty in obtaining an exact legal term in English to translate the term *vagus* arises from the fact that the concept of a person without domicile is foreign to English and American law. "Everyone has a domicile of origin, which he retains until he acquires another; and the one thus acquired is in like manner retained."—Justice Shaw in Arbington *v.* North Bridgwater, 23 *Pickering Reports,*

Since the primary object of this study is the obligations of the traveler in Canon Law, the unqualified term *law* has been used to designate Canon Law, except where the text or the content clearly refers to Civil Law. In reference to that law enacted by the supreme legislative power of the Church and intended of itself for the whole of Christendom, the term *universal* law has been used.[5] By the term *particular* law, on the other hand, is meant that law which is enacted for the subjects of a determined and limited jurisdiction. Particular law may be enacted

177; cf. Story, *Commentaries On the The Conflict of Laws Foreign and Domestic* (5. ed., Boston, 1857), §§ 45 *a*, 47, 48—Hereafter this work is cited as Story, *On The Conflict of Laws*. The word *vagrant* is used here as the best available translation of *vagus*, with the careful exclusion of the opprobrious sense of the word, and meaning simply one who is without domicile or quasi-domicile.—Cf. canon 91.

[5] Laws made for the entire body of the faithful are generally referred to by three distinct terms: *universal* laws, *general* laws, and *common* laws. *Universal* laws oblige throughout the whole Christian world. They are in contradistinction to *particular* laws, which are of themselves intended for the subjects of a definite particular territory. *General* law refers to those laws generically binding on all of the faithful because of the generic reason that they are subjects of the Church. This term is contradistinguished from *singular* law, which is binding only on those subjects of the Church who bear a specific characteristic, as, for example, a law binding only on clerics. *Common* law regulates the ordinary norm of action. It is in contradistinction to *spcial* law, or law which expresses an exception to the ordinary norm, as, for example, the law of canon 881, § 2, stating that he who enjoys ordinary jurisdiction can hear the confessions of his subjects anywhere, is a *special* law in contrast to the *common* law of canon 201, § 2, limiting judicial jurisdiction to the territory of him who possesses it. —Cf. Michiels, *Normae Generales Iuris Canonici, Commentarium Libri I Codicis Iuris Canonici* (2 vols., Lublin: Universitas Catholica, 1929), I, 13, 14. Hereafter this work is cited as Michiels, *Normae Generales*. It will be noted that canon 14, § 1, 3° uses the term *legibus generalibus* to refer to that law which is binding throughout the entire Christian realm. In using the term *universal* law as the more exact equivalent of this term, there has been no rejection of the accepted terminology of the Code. In fact the terminology of the Code has not been particularly consistent, as is evident by the designation of universal law by the term *generale* in canons 13, §1; 20; 22; 71; 83; etc., and by the term *commune* in canons 46; 153; 172, § 3; 501; 2296. § 1; etc.—Cf. Michiels, *Normae Generales*, I, 324, 325; Van Hove, *Commentarium Lovaniense in Codicem Iuris* Canonici (1 vol. in 5 Toms, Mechlinae, Romae: H. Dessain, 1928-1939—Tom. I, *Prolegomena*, 1928; Tom. II *De Legibus Ecclesiasticis*, 1930; Tom. III, *De Consuetudine, De Temporis Supputatione*, 1933; Tom. IV, *De Rescriptis*, 1936; Tom. V, *De Privilegiis, De Dispensationibus*, 1939), Tom. I (*Prolegomena*) n. 36. Hereafter these works will be cited respectively: *Prolegomena, De Legibus, De Consuetudine, De Rescriptis, De Privilegiis*.

either by the Supreme Legislator of the Church, or by particular legislators, such as bishops or other ordinaries, subordinate to the supreme legislative power of the Holy See.[6] In the present study the legislation of particular legislators will be referred to by the term *particular* law, unless otherwise specified by the text or the context.

From a purely theoretical approach, the problem of the present study is akin to the problem of the determination of the personal or territorial character of law. A law is said to be *personal* when it obliges a subject directly, irrespective of territory, and obliges the subject wherever he is.[7] A law is said to be *territorial* when it obliges its subject by reason of territorial circumstances, indirectly, in and through the territory in which the subject is.[8] Laws are *absolutely territorial* when they bind everyone who is within the territorial limits of the place for which the law is made; *relatively territorial,* when their obligatory force extends only to those who are, by reason of domicile or quasi-domicile, the habitual subjects of that territorial jurisdiction, and actually within its limits.[9] Territorial laws, whether absolute or relative, have no obligatory force as such beyond the jurisdictional limits of the territory for which they are passed.[10] A law that is territorial does not bind the absent subject; while a law that is personal does bind the absent subject. The stranger is bound only by those laws which are absolutely territorial. In this way the obligations of the traveler may be deduced

[6] Cf. canons 329, § 1; 355, § 1; 362; 291, §2; Van Hove, *Prolegomena,* nn. 65,66.

[7] Cf. Van Hove, *De Legibus,* n. 121; Michiels, *Normae Generales,* I, 300.

[8] Cf. Van Hove, *De Legibus,* n. 122; Michiels, *Normae Generales,* I, 300.

[9] Cf. Van Hove, *De Legibus,* n. 122.

[10] Note that this classification of law is based on the consideration of the *cause* of the obligation. It is not to be confused with another classification of law into personal and territorial by reason of *observance.* By reason of *observance,* a law is territorial which prescribes an obligation to the fulfilled, or a faculty to be enjoyed, within a definite place. The law prescribing the *ad limina* visit of local ordinaries is in this sense territorial. By reason of *observance* a law is said to be *personal* when its obligation can be fulfilled, or its faculty enjoyed, anywhere. Thus the law obliging clerics to recite the divine office is in this sense personal. Cf. Van Hove, *De Legibus,* n. 120; Maroto, *Institutiones Iuris Canonici ad Normam Novi Codicis* (3. ed. 2 vols., Romae; Apud Commentarium Pro Religiosis, 1921), I, n. 183—cited hereafter as Maroto, *Inst. Iuris Can.;* Beste, *Introductio in Codicem* (Collegeville, Minn.: St. John's Abbey Press, 1938), pp. 62, 63—cited hereafter as Beste, *Introd. in Codicem.*

from the personal or territorial character of the law being investigated. This, however, is not the approach of canon 14. Canon 14 directly indicates the obligations of the traveler regarding particular and universal laws. The question, therefore, of the personality or the territoriality of law has been of immediate concern only in so far as it was helpful in the determination of the more practical problem, the obligations of the traveler.

The scope and formal object of this study appears from the foregoing specification of terms: to determine the obligations of the traveler, whether he is a peregrin or a vagrant, according to Canon Law, whether it is particular or universal law. The historical sources of the present day obligations of the traveler have been investigated in the first part of this study, especially in view of the ultimate interpretation of canon 14.[11] The second part of this dissertation presents the canonical commentary on canon 14, bringing out the more exact meaning of this canon, both as regards the principles embodied in it and as regards the application of these principles to various specific laws.

Positive law, to a certain extent, is the product of its times; it is the rational norm of human actions. For this reason, the method of approach in the historical part of this study has been first to consider the characteristic historical circumstances of the period under discussion. Since all laws are the same at least in this, that law is an ordinance of reason, there exists an analogy of principles in the different juridical orders. So the principles of Roman Law and Civil International Law have been examined, but only in so far as they historically exerted such an analogous influence upon the higher supernatural order of Ecclesiastical Law. Finally, the canonical legislation has been examined in itself, and in the light of its contemporary interpreters in each period, in order to establish its historical meaning. Such is the fourfold method of the historical approach to the study of canon 14.

In the canonical commentary, the method of canon 18 has been followed in order to establish a more clear understanding of the principles involved in determining the obligations of the traveler. The interpretation thus obtained from the expression of the law itself has been guid-

[11] Cf. canon 6, 2°, 3°, 4°.

ed by the authentic interpretations of the legislator on those points where they have been given, by the interpretations of pre-Code authorities in as far as applicable, and by the intrinsic authority of commentators on the Code itself.

The history of the canonical discipline in regard to the traveler logically lends itself to a triple division. In the first period, until Gratian, the materials for the formation of a definite discipline were presented, without, however, the formation of such a discipline. From Gratian to the Council of Trent, these materials were sifted and the main lines of a definite policy established, without, however, going beyond these concrete enactments to the reason behind the law. After the Council of Trent, the nature of law was considered and juridical principles were applied to the obligations of the traveler in all of their phases.

The canonical commentary, after an introductory chapter outlining the formation of canon 14, follows the main lines of the division of the canon. In each number of the canon, first the general rule is considered in itself, and then in a following chapter, the exceptions to the general rule are treated in detail. A special chapter deals with the difficult concept of public order.

It is with the prospect, then, not only of incidentally obtaining a deeper insight into the history and progress of Canon Law and the factors affecting its development, but primarily of tracing the formation of canon 14 from its sources, of establishing its relation to pre-Code law, and finally of determining, both in principle and in various applications, the obligations of the traveler according to Canon Law today that this dissertation is presented.

PART I

Historical Synopsis

Chapter I

PRE-GRATIAN DEVELOPMENT

"But when Cephas came to Antioch, I withstood him to his face, because he was deserving of blame. For before certain persons came from James, he used to eat with the Gentiles; but when they came, he began to withdraw and to separate himself, fearing the circumcised."[1] This incident related by St. Paul emphasizes the difficulties encountered in tracing the discipline of the Church in regard to the traveler in the early centuries. Just as St. Peter in this instance fitted his policy to the circumstances of the moment without a preconceived plan, so the Primitive Church, pre-occupied with a multitude of newly arising problems, formed her discipline when confronted with each newly arising situation. It is too optimistic to look for a well delineated policy, or to hope to draw definite generalizations from the evidence of the period before the Decree of Gratian.

St. Peter was moved to change his policy by the motive of the good of souls, the consideration of scandal. Such a motive is peculiar to the Church. Hence it is not possible to draw a very close parallel between the legislation of the Church and the secular legislation of the time. The strained relations between the persecuted Church and the Roman government in the first four centuries prevented any whole-hearted adoption of the policy of Rome into the discipline of the Church. The influence of Roman and later Civil Law was felt only at a period later than the IV Century.

The background of this influence will be treated in the first article of this chapter. A following article will deal with the legislation of the councils and the influence of the Capitularies and Penitential Books. A final article will examine the writings of the Fathers and of the Popes.

[1] Gal., II, 11, 12.

Article I. The Influence of Roman and Barbaric Law

§ 1. *The Traveler Under Local Authority in Roman Law*

The general characteristic of Roman Law has been recognized by the authors[2] as one of personality of law. This characteristic attitude whereby Roman citizenship was the basis for the legal obligations and rights underlay the development of the Roman Law of persons, and the division of persons into the various classes such as peregrins, latins, *diditicii*, and citizens.[3] A complete examination into the status of the traveler under Roman Law would require a study of the different historical periods in the development of the Roman legislative system. The influence of Roman Law was exercised upon Canon Law through the works of Justinian. To this period, then, the present study will be briefly confined, in order to interpret those texts of Justinian which established the status of the traveler.

The edict of Caracalla (Circa 211-217, A.D.)[4] practically obliterated the distinction between the stranger, living on the soil of, the Roman Empire, and the Roman citizen. Yet this edict is not to be construed so as to do away with every distinction between the Roman and the non-Roman.[5] As late as Justinian's time the laws of Rome were intended for those of the Roman Empire, the subjects of the Roman domination, and not for the barbarian strangers, even though they were in the Empire for a short time.[6] Along with this gradual exten-

[2] Cf. Meili, *International Civil and Commercial Law as founded upon Theory, Legislation, and Practice* (Trs. and supplemented by A. K. Kuhn, London, 1905), pp. 53-57—cited hereafter as Meili, *International Law*: Baviera, *Il Diritto Internazionale dei Romani* (Modena, 1898), pp. 117, 118—cited hereafter as Baviera, *Il Diritto Internazionale;* D'Angelo, *Jus Digestorum* (2 vols., Romae: Athenaeum Pontificium Seminarii Romani ad S. Apollinaris, 1927), I, 146.

[3] This phase of Roman Law need be no more than alluded to for the present purpose. For a more complete treatment, cf. Leage-Ziegler, *Roman Private Law as Founded on the Institutes of Gaius and Justinian* (2.ed., London: Macmillan, 1937), pp. 54-126—cited hereafter as Leage, *Roman Private Law.*

[4] Cf. Girard, *Textes de Droit Romain* (Paris: Librarie Arthur Rousseau, 1923), p. 204.

[5] Cf. Leage, *Roman Private Law,* pp. 76, 77.

[6] "Cunctos populos, quos clementiae nostrae regit temperamentum . . . "—C (1,1) 1. It was this law which furnished the occasion for the extensive treatment which

sion of the authority of Roman Law went another development in the direction of the recognition of a limited local authority. This development, which took place chiefly during the period of the Republic, is manifested in the development of municipalities and townships of non-Roman origin,[7] and in the government of the provinces through the *jus edicendi*[8] and the constitutions for provincial cities, the *leges provinciae*.[9] Such is the brief outline of the historical background of the texts bearing upon the status of the traveler under local authority, as found in the works of Justinian. At the time of Justinian, the unique source of law was the emperor.[10] Only administrative, judicial, and police powers were participated in an hierarchical order by the magistrates and officers inferior to the Emperor.[11] Thus, in the time of Justinian there was a limited local authority, and certain local variations and regulations to be encountered as one traveled from one city to another. More particularly, the local authority was in evidence in the

the glossators gave to the obligations of the traveler during the middle ages. And rightly so, for their first problem was to establish the extension of Roman Law before they could use it as the norm for the more particular problem of the traveler. Cfr. Lainé, *Introduction au Droit International Privé* (Paris, 1888), I, 105-108—cited hereafter as Lainé, *Introd. au Droit Int. Privé.*

[7] Cfr. Aulus Gellius, *Noctium Atticum Liber XVI* (ed. J. C. Rolfe, *The Attic Nights of Aulus Gellius,* London: Wm. Heinemann, 1928), 13,6. Cf. Toutain, J. "Études sur l'organization du Haut-empire. De la distinction faite par Aulu-Gelle entre les municipes et les colonies des provinces à l'époque impériale," —*Mélanges d'Archéologie et d'Histoire, École Française de Rome,* XVI (1896), 315-329; Poste-Whittuck, *Gaii Institutiones, or Institutes of Roman Law by Gaius* (4.ed., Oxford, 1904), pp. 296, 507; Abbott-Johnson, *Municipal Administration in the Roman Empire* (Princeton: Princeton University Press, 1926), p. 3.—cited hereafter as Abbot-Johnson, *Municipal Administration.*

[8] Cf. Cicero, *Epistola ad Atticum* (ed. Purser, Oxoniensis: *Scriptorum Classicorum Bibliotheca Oxoniensis,* Vol. 2, 1903), 5.21.11, 6.1.15; *Epistolae ad Familiares* (Ed. Capps-Page-Rouse: *The Loeb Classical Library, Cicero, The Letters to His Friends,* London: Wm. Heinemann, New York: Putnam, 1927), 3.8.4., -5.

[9] Willems, *Le Sénat de la République Romaine* (2.ed., 2 vols., Paris, 1885), I, 703-717; Abbot-Johnson, *Municipal Administration,* p. 49.

[10] Cf. Girard, *Manuel Elémentaire de Droit Romain* (8.ed., Paris: Librairie Arthur Rosseau, 1929), pp. 55, 79.

[11] Cf. Wenger, *Institutes of The Roman Law of Procedure* (revised and translated by Fisk, New York: Veritas Press, 1940), pp. 60-70, 258-260. Cited hereafter as Wenger, *Roman Law Procedure.*

matter of procedure, in the establishment of the competent forum. Here the jurisdiction of the local magistrates was restricted to each one's own territory.[12]

The subjects of this local authority were called *municipes* or *incolae.*[13] Subjection to such local authority was based on origin or domicile. Origin was determined by the legal place of birth, the origin of the father of the child of *iustae nuptiae,*[14] or of the mother if there were no *iustae nuptiae.*[15] Domicile, a permanent residence, to be away from which means to be away from home, and to return to which means to return home,[16] was constituted by two elements, permanent residence and the intention of maintaining it.[17] The effects of the law of origin and the law of domicile were to bind the resident to the particular local regulations of the magistrate and to constitute the general forum of the resident even while he traveled away from home.[18] By opposition, the stranger in a local community was not generally subject to the local jurisdiction of the magistrates.[19]

By exception to this general rule, however, competent forum was acquired outside the place of origin or domicile by reason of crime

[12] "*Paulus Libro primo ad edictum* Extra territorium ius dicenti impune non pareatur. idem est et si supra iurisdictionem suam velit ius dicere."—D (2,1) 20. The precise meaning of this text is that the inferior magistrate cannot exercise his judicial power while he is outside of his own territory.—Cf. Wenger, *Roman Law Procedure,* p. 39. This text is especially notable for the extension given it by the application made by Boniface VIII in his decretal *Ut animarum* (c. 2, *de constitutionibus, I,* 2, in VI°) to prove that particular laws were devoid of obligatory force outside the territory of the inferior legislator. Although this extension was unwarranted in Classical Roman Law, Justinian had already begun the expansion of the term *jus dicere* to include the whole power of ruling subjects.—Cf. N (57) 1; N (120) 6, 2; N (5) 3; N (131) 4; Van De Kerkhove, "De notione jurisdictionis in jure Romano,"—*Jus Pont.,* XVI (1926), pp. 49-65.

[13] D (50,1) 29; C (10,40) 7.

[14] D (50,1) 6, 1.

[15] D (50,1) 1, 2; D (50,1) 9; D (50,1) 15, 3; C (10, 40 [39]) 7.

[16] D (50,16) 203; C (10,40) 7.

[17] D (50,1) 20; C (10,40) 2; cf. Sherman, *Roman Law in the Modern World* (2.ed., 3 vols., New York: Baker Voorhis and Co., 1924), II, 33.

[18] D (50,17) 121; D (1,18) 3; D (50,1) 29; C (4,63) 4; C (4,41) 2.

[19] C (10,40) 1; C (10,40) 3; C (10,40) 4; D (1,18) 3. This last fragment, the law *Praeses provinciae,* is often cited by the glossators and the decretalists.

committed by a stranger,[20] by reason of contract,[21] and in general, by reason of litigation over possessions situated in the place.[22] It was from these texts of the Digest, the Code, and the Novels of Justinian that the glossators and decretalists took their inspiration, too frequently confusing that which pertained only to judicial jurisdiction with that which pertained to legislative power.

§ 2. *The Traveler and Barbaric Law*

After the breakdown of the Roman Empire, an era of strict personality of law was to ensue, under the *leges barbarorum*. Each person was bound by the laws of his place of origin, regardless of where he was.[23] The Roman Law was taken up and adopted by the barbarians as the proper law for the Romans, while the barbarians lived according to the consuetudinary law of their own race.[24]

In the later part of this period before Gratian, a contrary system had come into being. By the IX or the X Century, the old nations and tribes, under which race law held sway, were gradually submerged. By amalgamation and intermarriage, new nations had arisen. The systems of feudal subjection and villeinage had changed the free communities

[20] D (47,11) 9—quoted by the medieval authors as the law *Sunt quaedam*; C (3,15) 1—cited as the law *Quaestiones eorum*; C (3,13) 1—cited as the law *Non quidem fuit*; and the Novel *Qua in Provincia*, N (69) 1.

[21] D (5,1) 19, 1; D (5,1) 65; D (5,1) 34; D (21,1) 31; D (21,2) 6; D (22,1) 1; C (13,13) 2; N (19) 1. Cf. Mackintosh, *Roman Law in Modern Practice* (*Tagore Law Lectures*, Edinburgh: Green and Son L'td., 1934), p. 106; Meili, *International Law*, p. 57; Baviera, *Il Diritto Internazionale*, pp. 125-130; D'Angelo, *Jus Digestorum*, I, 147. Yet Chénon limits the application of these texts to mean that only obscure contracts were to be interpreted by local customs, if any existed, or only in *judicia bonae fidei.*—"La loi pérégrine à Rome,"—*Bulletin du Comité des Travaux Historiques et Scientifiques, Section des Sciences Économiques et Sociales* (Paris, 1890), pp. 212-245; cf. Weiss, *Traité Élémentaire du Droit International Privé* (2.ed., Paris, 1890), p. 263, note 6.—cited hereafter as Weiss, *Droit Intern. Privé*.

[22] Cf. D (26,7) 32, 6; D (26,7) 47; D (26,5) 27; C (3,17) 1; C (8,10) 3.

[23] Cf. Angobardus, Bishop of Lyons, *Epistola Regi Ludovico Pio*,—*MPL*, CIV, 116, 117. Meili states that "In order to understand the range of race law, we need only to keep in mind the general influence of the European in the Orient. An inhabitant of a European colony (e.g. of the Dutch or French Indies) could submit himself to European law."—Meili, *International Law*, p. 60.

[24] Cf. Van Hove, *De Legibus*, n. 112.

into a body of military vassals and serving dependents. Instead of national laws, feudal usages became, as Savigny says,[25] the birthright of all, and the traveler was bound by the laws of the place where he was exclusively. But the influence of Roman Law still remained strong in southern France and Lombardy, ready for the development of the free municipal commonwealths which furnished the milieu of the great revival of classical Roman Law, and of the glossators.[26]

Such then is the traditional attitude of Roman Law regarding the traveler, and such its subsequent history. With this brief outline of the historical background of the Civil Law influences upon the canonical legislation, one is now prepared to follow the development of a canonical jurisprudence regarding the same problems, as it grew out of these civil and historical surroundings prior to the rise of the great medieval universities and the Decree of Gratian.

Article II. Pre-Gratian Legislation Regarding the Traveler

The period of the early Church was at first a period of secular prosperity. Communications in the Roman world were at their best. These conditions, as well as the great initial missionary activity and the pressure of persecution, engendered in the early Christians a desire for travel, an impatience with restrictions within local limits.[27] It is not surprising that the problems of the traveler arose during the very lives of the Apostles, as indicated by the worries of St. Peter in Antioch. That there were local divergencies in the second and third Centuries is evident from the controversies over the date for the celebration of Easter, and the differences in the observance of fast days and feasts.[28]

[25] Savigny-Cathcart, *History of Roman Law During the Middle Ages* (1 vol. published, Edinburgh, 1829), I, 164-168. Cited hereafter as Savigny, *Roman Law During Middle Ages.* Cf. also Meili, *International Law,* p. 61; Lainé, *Introd. au Droit Int. Privé,* pp. 62, 63.

[26] Cfr. Savigny, *Roman Law During Middle Ages,* I, 168; Lainé, *Introd. au Droit Int. Privé,* p. 50; Meili, *International Law,* p. 62.

[27] Cf. Fournier-Le Bras, *Histoire des Collections Canoniques en Occident depuis les Fausses Décrétales jusqu'au Décret de Gratien* (2 vols., Paris: Recruil Sirey, 1931), I, 13, note 1. Hereafter cited as *Histoire des Collections.*

[28] Cf. Baronius, *Annales Ecclesiastici* (23 vols. in 37, Bari, 1864-1883), I, 456; Mansi, *Sacrorum Conciliorum Nova et Amplissima Collectio* (53 vols. in 59, Parisiis Lipsiae, Arnhem, 1901-1927), I, 718. This work is hereafter cited as Mansi.

Baronius[29] refers to the early origin of the *litterae formatae*. This was a very important and constant institution relating to travelers in the early Church. These letters of recommendation must accompany the traveler, especially the cleric, if he was to be admitted into active participation in the religious life of the community in which he was visiting. The requirement of these letters of recommendation was a common enactment by the V Century.[30] In connection with the laws requiring letters of recommendation for travelers are the laws requiring the residence of clerics in their parishes. Thus a series of early councils[31] enacted laws limiting the time that a bishop or lesser cleric might be absent from his parish, while the Canons of the Holy Apostles[32] required lesser clerics to get permission for an absence. The Council of Byzacium (379, in Africa)[33] required visiting clerics to reveal the reasons for their presence to the bishop or priests of the place where they were, and other councils[34] legislated absolutely against clerics' leaving the place which they were serving. These local provisions were given universal application by the General Council of Chalcedon.[35]

The Council of Elvira (305)[36] decreed that a person excommunicated by one bishop should not be reinstated by another, and that those, including strangers, who absented themselves from divine services were

[29] *Annales Ecclesiastici*, II, 246-249.

[30] Cf. *Canones Ecclesiae Africanae*, canon 56—Mansi, III, 750; *Canones Apostolorum* (Probably of Syrian origin in IV Century), c. 32—Mansi, I, 31; *Constitutiones Sanctorum Apostolorum*, Lib. II, cap. 58 (probably of Syrian origin in V or VI Century)—Mansi, I, 363; Council of Antioch (341), c. 7—Mansi, II 1323; Synod of Syria (410) c. 9—Mansi, III, 1170; *Canones Synodi Romanorum ad Gallos Episcopos juxta Quaestiones ab Illis Propositas* (402), c. 14—Mansi, III, 1138.

[31] Cf. Council of Sardica (347), c. 15—Mansi, III, 29; Council of Hippo (397?), cc. 29, 34—Mansi, III, 895, 896; Council of Laodicaea (320), c. 40—Mansi, II, 581; Council of Antioch (341), c. 3—Mansi, II 1322; Council of Aachen (Aix-La-Chapelle, 402), c. 71—Mansi, II, 1322.

[32] Canon 15—Mansi, I, 51.

[33] Canon 37—Mansi, I, 51.

[34] Cf. II Council of Milevi (Mila, 416), c. 18—Mansi, IV, 313; Council of Carthage (419), c. 28—Mansi, IV, 415.

[35] Canon 5—Mansi, VII, 376; Schroeder, *Disciplinary Decrees of the General Councils* (St. Louis: Herder, 1937), p. 94—cited hereafter as Schroeder, *Disciplinary Decrees*.

[36] Canon 53—Mansi, II, 11; cf. I Council of Arles (314), c. 16—Mansi, II, 47.

to be excommunicated.[37] Legislation of this type shows the principle in force of a united episcopate, and a respect for the boundaries of local authorities. This definite respect for local authority and subjection to it was made universal in the First General Council at Nicaea,[38] and was clearly set forth in the First General Council of Constantinople, which stated:

> Bishops who are outside their diocese shall not go to Churches that are outside their territorial boundaries, and they shall not disturb the Churches; but according to the canons, the Bishop of Alexandria is to administer the affairs of Egypt only, the bishops of the East shall rule the East only, those of Pontus over Pontus only, those of Thrace over Thrace only. Unless invited, bishops are not to go outside of their dioceses, either for the purpose of ordaining, or for any other act of ecclesiastical administration . . .[39]

The provisions of this canon may be found in the canons of many particular councils.[40]

Canon 4 of the General Council of Chalcedon[41] introduced the subjection of monasteries to the jurisdiction of the local bishops. Schroeder states that this legislation was probably directed against the interference of the disorderly and fanatical Eastern Monks in ecclesiastical affairs. It was occasioned by Barsumas and the Monophysiting monks of Syria who supported Dioscorus and the Robber Synod of Ephesus. Soon, however, exemptions of the monasteries began to be granted by law.[42] The influence of the Celtic monks was great in the development

[37] Canon 21—Mansi, II 9.

[38] Canon 5—Mansi, II 954; Schroeder, *Disciplinary Decrees*, p. 29.

[39] Schroeder, *Disciplinary Decrees*, p. 64. Cf. Mansi, III, 559.

[40] Cf. Council of Hippo, (397?) Statute 21—Mansi, III, 895; Council of Sardica (347), cc. 14, 16, 19—Mansi, III, 28, 29; Synod of Latopoli (Esneh, 367), c. 5—Mansi, III, 147; III Council of Carthage (398), c. 5—Mansi, III, 155; Council of Byzacium (379), c. 21—Mansi, III, 883; Council of Torino (397), c. 7—Mansi, III, 862; Council of Toledo (398) c. 12—Mansi, III, 1013; I Council of Antioch (341), c. 13—Mansi, II, 1324.

[41] Mansi, VII, 376. Cf. Synod of Agde (506), c. 7—Mansi, VIII, 319; Synod of Orleans (511), c. 19—Mansi, VIII, 354; V Council of Arles (554), cc. 2, 3—Mansi, IX, 702. Cf. also Schroeder, *Disciplinary Decrees*, p. 94.

[42] Cf. Schroeder, *Disciplinary Decrees*, p. 94; IV Synod of Toledo (633), c. 51—Mansi, X, 615; Synod of Hereford (674), c. 3—Mansi, XI, 127.

of these privileges of the monasteries. Their first care, after founding a monastery, was to obtain its exemption from the local authority.[43] The monastery of Bobbio was the first to obtain such exemption and direct subjection to the Holy See (628).[44] Interesting problems arise out of the extension given to the term jurisdiction in connection with these exemptions, and since the Code, the problem is still discussed whether these exempt places are juridically outside of the diocese.

During the time from the Council of Chalcedon to the Pontificate of Gregory the Great, except for the brief span of the Gelasian reform,[45] the central power of the Church declined before the turmoil of the barbarian invasions. While the Civil Law was in the confusion of the many personal laws of the *Leges Barbarorum*, Canon Law suffered a similar confusion from a multitude of particular councils. These served, however, to diffuse the previous enactments throughout the Church in the West.[46]

[43] Cf. Fournier-Le Bras, *Histoire des Collections*, I, 65, note 1.

[44] Cf. Schroeder, *Disciplinary Decrees*, p. 94; Jaffé, *Regesta Pontificum Romanorum ab Condita Ecclesia ad Annum post Christum Natum MCXCVIII* (Editionem secundam correctam et auctam auspiciis Gulielmi Wattenback, curaverunt S. Loewenfeld, F. Kalenbrunner, P. Ewald, 2 vols. in 1, Lipsiae, 1885-1888), n. 2016. Hereafter this work is cited according to the initials of its editors, i.e. to the year 590, JK; from 590 to 882, JE; from 882 to 1198, JL.

[45] This reform ended about 523—cf. Fournier-Le Bras, *Histoire des Collections*, I, 7, 73.

[46] For the *litterae formatae*, cf. Synod of Agde (506), c. 38—Mansi, VIII, 331; I Council of Torino (461), c. 12—Mansi, VII, 946; Council of Venice (465), c. 5—Mansi, VII, 952; Synod of St. Patrick (450-456?), cc. 33, 34—Mansi, VI 519; Council of Epaôn (517), c. 6—*Monumenta Germaniae Historica, Legum Sectio III, Concilia, Vol. I, Aevi Merovingici* (Rec. F. Maassen, Hannoverae, 1893), p. 20—hereafter cited as *MGH, Legum Sect. III, I;* V Council of Orleans (549), c. 5—*MGH, Legum* Sect. III, I, 102; Council of Rheims (627), c. 12—*MGH, Legum Sect.* III, I, 204; Council of Hereford (673), c. 5—Mansi, XI, 129; Council of Frankfurt (794), c. 27—*MGH, Legum Sect.*, III, II (Rec. A. Wermenghoff, 1908), 169.

For the laws of residence of clerics, cf. Synod of St. Patrick, c. 24—Mansi, VI, 518; Council of Valenza (524, Spain), c. 5—Mansi, VII, 622; II Council of Lugo (572), c. 7—Mansi, IX, 849; Excerpts of Egbert of York (748), cc. 60, 66—Mansi, XII, 418; Statutes of Boniface (747), statute 1—Mansi, XII, 384; Council of Frankfurt, c. 7—*MGH, Legum Sect.*, III, II, 167; Council of Rouen (1050), c. 3—Mansi, XIX, 752.

Moreover, in the VI Century, explicit enactments were made requiring strangers to observe the order where they were while celebrating divine offices.[47] The Church in France required that the disputed date of the celebration of Easter be observed by all on the established date.[48] Finally, contentious jurisdiction, as we know it today, was restricted to territorial limits by the II Council of Lyons (567-570).[49]

A new influence, that of the Celtic and Germanic laws, was brought into the discipline of the Church from the north in the IX Century. This was the tendency to reach out beyond territorial limits, the tendency of personality of law.[50] The Synod of Pavia (889)[51] generally permitted all members of the Church to use their own laws. The Council of Nantes (895)[52] required parishioners to attend Mass in their own parish Churches on feasts and Sundays. A Synod of Ravenna (877)[53] required the faithful to pay tithes to that church of which they were parishioners, and forbade clerics to solicit offerings outside their own territories. Yet, contrary to the spirit of these enactments, a national synod in Hungary[54] decreed that Italians coming to Hungary on business were to fast in the Monday and Tuesday prior to Ash Wednesday, as did the Hungarians.

The influence toward personality of law from the time of Charle-

For limitations on Episcopal power within territorial limits, cf. Synod of St. Patrick, c. 30—Mansi, VI, 518; I Council of Orange (460), c. 8—Mansi, VI, 437; IV Council of Arles (524), c. 4—*MGH, Legum Sect.*, III, I, 37; III Council of Orleans (538), c. 16 (15)—*MGH, Legum Sect.*, III, 102; Council of Châlon-sur-Saôn (639-654), c. 13—*MGH, Legum Sect.*, III, I, 211; Council of Hereford, c. 2—Mansi, XI, 129; Council of Verno (755), c. 13—Mansi, XII, 581; Council of Rouen, c. 9—Mansi, XIX, 753; Council of Mayence (888), c. 10—Mansi, XVIII-A, 68; Council of Ravenna (997), c. 3—Mansi, XIX, 220; Council of London (1125), c. 10—Mansi, XXI, 322.

[47] Council of Gerona (517, Spain), c. 1—Mansi, VIII, 549; Council of Epaôn (517), c. 27—*MGH, Legum Sect.*, III, I, 25.

[48] IV Council of Orleans (541), cc. 1, 38—*MGH, Legum Sect.*, III, I, 87, 93.

[49] C. 1—*MGH, Legum Sect.*, III ,I, 139.

[50] Cf. Fournier-Le Bras, *Histoire des Collections*, I, 65.

[51] C. 7—Mansi, XVII-A, 92.

[52] Cc. 1, 2—Mansi, XVIII-A, 166. Fournier-Le Bras note that these canons may have been apocryphal—*Histoire des Collections*, I, 259.

[53] Statute 18—Mansi, XVII-B, 340.

[54] Synod of Szabolez (1092), cap. 31—Mansi, XX, 775, 776.

magne resulted especially from the Capitularies of the Frankish Kings and the Penitential Books. The Capitularies of the kings often directly concerned ecclesiastical matters, and, where they were in force, enjoyed authority equal to the canons themselves. Much of the same legislation as that of the councils was repeated in these laws of the kings.[55] The influence of the Capitularies towards attaching law to the person is reflected in the numerous laws which made clerics subject to the laws and authority of their proper bishop wherever they were.[56]

Although the Penitential Books from the Island Church presented the character of personal laws, their influence was diffused over the whole of the Church in northern Europe, though lacking in juridical authority, and by no means permanent. Chiefly catalogues of private penances for various delicts, they were made according to customs, or very often by private authority. Condemned by subsequent councils,[57] their influence was not felt after the end of this period.[58]

The evidence from the canonical legislation issued prior to the Decree of Gratian indicates that a clearly determined territorial division of jurisdiction was firmly established in the Church. Certain laws suggest that a principle of strict territoriality of law was in force. However, the evidence does not warrant the conclusion that the traveler was generally bound by the laws of the place where he was visiting. A definite policy does not appear to have been adopted regarding the traveler.

[55] Cf. *Karoli Magni Capitulare Ecclesiasticum* (789), cap. 1, 3, 41—*MGH, Legum Sectio,* II (*Capitularia Regum Francorum,* ed. A. Boretius, Hannoverae, 1883), I, 54, 60; *Capitulare Francofurtense* (797), cap. 8—*MGH, Legum Sectio,* II, I, 74.

[56] *Capitulare Francofurtense* (797), cap. 6—*MGH, Legum Sect.*, II, I, 73; *Capitulare Aquisgranense* (801), cap. 15—*MGH, Legum Sect.*, II, I, 92; *Capitulare Ticinense* (801, Pavia), cap. 10—*MGH, Legum Sect.,* II, I, 84; *Caroli Magni Selecta Capitula Ecclesiastica* (801), cap 3—Mansi, XIII, 1051; *Capitulare Ium Ludovici Pii* (819), cap. 6—Mansi, XVII-B, 599; *Hlothari Constitutio Romana* (827), cap 5—*MGH, Legum Sect.*, II, I, 240; *Karoli II Conventus apud Pistas* (869), cap. 3, 4, 5—*MGH, Legum Sect.*, II, I, 509.

[57] Cf. II Council of Châlon-sur-Saône (813), c. 38—*MGH, Legum Sect.*, III, II, 281; Council of Tours (813), c. 22—*MGH, Legum Sect.*, III, II, 289; VI Council of Paris (829), c. 32—Mansi, XIV, 559.

[58] Cf. Van Hove, *Prolegomena,* n. 135.

Article III. The Writings of the Fathers and the Popes

§ 1. *Writings of the Fathers*

The outstanding statements on the obligation of the traveler in the whole period before Gratian came at the end of the IV Century from the pen of St. Augustine. Because of the importance placed upon the texts taken from the works of St. Augustine by the decretalists, as well as because of their indication of the contemporary attitude towards the obligations of the traveler, these texts merit a detailed consideration.

Only three texts in the works of St. Augustine have a definite and explicit bearing upon the obligations of the traveler. The first is taken from his treatise *De Doctrina Christiana*:

> Quisquis autem rebus praetereuntibus restrictius utitur, quam sese habent mores eorum cum quibus vivit, aut intemperans, aut superstitiosus est. Quisquis vero eis utitur, ut metas consuetudinis bonorum, inter quos versatur, excedat, aut aliquid significat, aut flagitiosus est.[59]

The second text is from his *Confessions*:

> Quae si omnes gentes fecerunt, eodem criminis diuina lege tenerentur, quae non sic fecit homines ut se illo uteretur modo. uiolatur quippe ipsa societas, quae cum deo nobis esse debet, cum eadem natura, cuius ille auctor est, libidinis peruersitate polluitur. quae autem contra mores hominum sunt flagitia, pro morum diuersitate uitanda sunt; ut pactum inter se ciuitatis aut gentis consuetudine, uel lege firmatum, nulla ciuis aut peregrini libidine uioletur. turpis enim omnis pars uniuerso suo non congruens . . . si enim regi licet in ciuitate cui regnat, iubere aliquid, quod neque ante illum quisquam, nec ipse unquam iusserat, et non contra societatem ciuitatis eius obtemperatur, immo contra societatem non obtemperatur—generale quippe pactum est societatis humanae oboedire regibus suis—quanto magis deus regnator uniuersae creaturae . . .[60]

[59] *MPL*, XXXIV, 15. This text was incorporated in the great canonical collections: cf. Ivo, *Panormia*, II, 195—*MPL*, CLIX, 1126; c. 1, *Quisquis*, D., XLI.

[60] *Corpus Scriptorium Ecclesiasticorum Latinorum* (68 vols., Pragae, Vindobonae,

The third and most explicit text is from his letter to Januarius:

> Alia uero quae per loca terrarum regionesque uariantur, sicuti est, quod alii ieiunat sabbato, alii non, alii quotidie communicant corpori et sanguini dominico, alii certis diebus accipiunt, alibi nullus dies intermittitur, quo non offeratur, alibi sabbato tantum et dominico, alibi tantum dominico—et si quid huiusmodi animaduerti potest, totum hoc genus rerum liberas habet obseruationes nec disciplina ulla est in his melior graui prudentique Christiano, nisi ut eo modo agat, quo agere uiderit ecclesiam, ad quamcumque forte deuenerit. quod enim neque contra fidem neque contra bonos mores esse conuincitur, indifferens habendum et pro morum, inter quos uiuitur societate seruandum est.
>
> Credo te aliquando audisse, tamen etiam nunc commemoro: mater mea Mediolanum me consecuta inuenit ecclesiam sabbato non ieiunare. coeperat perturbari et fluctuari quid ageret. tunc ego talia non curabam, sed propter ipsam consului de hac re beatisimae memoriae uirum Ambrosium. respondit nihil se docere me posse, nisi quod ipse faceret, quia si melius nosset, id potius obseruaret. cumque ego putassem nulla redita ratione auctoritate sola sua nos uoluisse admonere, ne sabbato ieiunaremus subsecutus est et ait mihi: ' Cum Roman uenio, ieiuno sabbato; cum hic sum, non ieiuno: sic etiam tu, ad quam forte ecclesiam ueneris, eius morem serua, si cuiquam non uis esse scandalum, nec quemquam tibi." hoc cum matri renuntiassem, libenter amplexa est. ego uero de hac sententia etiam atque etiam cogitans ita semper habui, tamquam celesti oraculo acceperim. sensi enim saepe dolens at gemens multas infirmorum perturbationes fieri, per quorundam fratrum contentiosam obstinationem uel superstitiosam timiditatem, qui in rebus huiusmodi, neque sanctae scripturae auctoritate, neque uniuersalis Ecclesiae traditione, neque uitae corrigendae utilitate, ad certum possunt terminum peruenire, tantum quia subest qualiscumque ratiocinatio cogitantis aut quia in sua patria sic ipse con-

Lipsiae, 1866—), XXXIII (*Sti. Aureli Augustini Confessionum,* Rec. P. Knöll, 1896), III, n. 15, pp. 56, 57. Cited hereafter as *CSEL*. Cf. MPL, XXXII, 689; Ivo, *Panormia,* II, 195; c. 2, *Quae contra,* D. VIII.

sueuit, aut qui alibi uidit, factum putans, tam litigiosas excitant quaestiones, ut nisi quod ipsi faciunt, nihil rectum existimant.[61]

He insists upon this conformity to the local regulations throughout this whole letter.[62]

The doctrine of St. Augustine stated in these passages has been subject to much controversy among his interpreters. One school of interpreters held that the doctrine of St. Augustine exempted strangers from the observance of local laws and customs, except when bound by the danger of causing scandal. Thus the more explicit doctrine expressed in the letter to Januarius was used to qualify the general doctrine expressed in the treatise *De Doctrina Christiana* and in the *Confessions.*[63]

The opposite interpretation, that the texts of St. Augustine imply the general obligation of the stranger to conform to the customs of the place where he actually was, enjoys ancient authority as well as modern.[64] The first of these texts, taken from the *De Doctrina Christiana,* has for its object the moral counsel to follow the example of prudent Christians as the norm in the use of this world's goods. It does not present juridical evidence of the obligations of the traveler, considered by itself.

The second, from the *Confessions,* is more to the point, and conveys a juridical import. St. Augustine is basing the obligation on authority, whether of the Divine Legislator Himself, or of the human legislator.

[61] *Epistola LIV* (*Ad Inquisitiones Ianuarii*), c. XI, 3, 3—*CSEL,* XXXIV (*Sti. Aureli Augustini Epistolae, Pars II,* Rec. Goldbacher, 1898), pp. 160, 161. Cf. *MPL,* XXXIII, 200, 201; c. *IIIa,* 11, D. XII.

[62] Cf. *o.c.,*c. IV, V—*CSEL,* XXXIV, pp. 164, 165.

[63] Cf. Huguccio of Ferrara, *Summa Decreti,* ad c. 2, D. VIII, v° *Peregrini*—quoted by Onclin, *De Territoriali vel Personali Legis Indole,* Universitas Catholica Lovaniensis. Dissertationes, Series II, Tomus 31 (Gembloci: J. Duculot, 1938), p. 36. Cited hereafter as Onclin, *De Legis Indole.*

[64] Cf. *infra,* p. 27. Among its modern supporters may be cited Onclin, *De Legis Indole,* pp. 20, 187; Van Hove, "La territorialité et la personnalité des lois en droit canonique depuis Gratien (vers 1140) jusqu'à Jean Andrea (†1348),"—*Tijdschrift Voor Rechtsgeschiednis—Revue D' Histoire de Droit,* III (1922), 284-287. Hereafter cited as Van Hove, "La territorialité et la personnalité des lois,"—*TVR,* III (1922).

Nor can he be more general in stating the clear obligation of the stranger. For he says that the offenses against the usages of men are to be avoided according to the diversity of those usages; that the settled way of life in the law or custom of a people is not to be violated by the resident or the visitor.

The third text, from the letter to Januarius, has been the particular point at issue in the controversies. The weakness in this text appears from the fact that it is based on a moral consideration, scandal, rather than upon a juridical one, and that it seems at first glance to pertain only to the customs of fasting.

Speaking of certain customs being of free observance, the context refers this freedom to the fact that matters of faith and morals are not at issue. Beyond this there is a consideration of local discipline. Even if the customs are indifferent from the viewpoint of faith and morals, it does not follow that they may be freely observed or violated as a matter of local discipline. Such seems to be the true thought in this text of St. Augustine. To substantiate this decision, St. Augustine appeals to the authority of St. Ambrose. St. Ambrose lays down a general principle here, and then makes its application to the matter of fasting. After stating the principle and the authority of St. Ambrose, St. Augustine then appeals to the danger of scandal as an added motive for conformity to the customs of the place.

This interpretation is confirmed by a text from the works of St. Jerome. When Lucinus Boeticus planned to sail for Jerusalem from Spain, St. Jerome advised him, on the authority of St. Hippolytus, to follow the traditions of the Church in matters of fasting and receiving the Eucharist, lest he upset the practices of others by contrary habits.[65]

Other texts were occasionally appealed to by the decretalists to give authority for the stand they took on the obligations of the traveler, but these other texts usually had no real connection with the matter. St. Isidore's Book of Etymologies, cited by Gratian,[66] for example,

[65] S. Hieronimi, *Epistola LXXI ad Lucinum,* n. 6—*CSEL,* LV (*Epistolae Sancti Hieronimi,* rec. Hilberg, 1912), p. 6.

[66] C. 5, D. VIII.

merely denies the nature and force of custom, giving no indication whether the traveler is bound or not.[67]

§ 2. *Letters of the Popes*

Much of the same matter which was prescribed in the legislation of the councils was repeated in the letters of the Popes.[68] Clearer evidence of the exemption of the traveler from the observance of local laws may be found in a letter of Pope Leo IX[69] to Michael, Patriarch of Constantinople. In this letter it is pointed out that the priests of the Oriental discipline are permitted to celebrate Mass in their own rite, even while visiting within the territory of the Church of the Latin discipline. That this may be a special concession to promote harmony weakens its force for general application. Gregory the Great, in a letter to St. Augustine, the Apostle of England, explains that a diversity of customs in the Church is not against faith, but rather those customs which are best should be adopted into the discipline of the Church in England.[70] It is argued from this letter, that since St. Augustine was absent from his native church, Rome, the pope was implying that he was not bound to observe the laws and customs of his place of origin. The special purpose of this letter also weakens its force for general application.

An indirect but substantial influence upon the development of the discipline regarding the obligations of the traveler came from Gregory

[67] *S. Isidorii, Hispalensis Episcopi, Etymologiarum Libri* XX, Lib. II, c. 10, n. 2 —*MPL,* LXXXII, 199. Cf. also, Nicholas I, in a letter to Photius, in which he testifies to the diversity of customs, without stating their obligatory force upon the traveler—JF, 2691; and in his *Responsa ad Consulta Bulgarorum,* where he dispenses this Church from the Eastern custom of fasting on Saturdays—*MGH, Epistolae Karolini Aevi,* VI, P. II, Fasc. I (ed. E. Perles, Hannoverae, 1912), n. 99; JE, n. 2812.

[68] Cf. *Epistola Ia Anacleti Papae* (76-78?), III—JK, n. 3; *Epistola Ia Hygini Papae* (152-154?)—JK, n. 35;*Fabiani Papae Epist. IIIa ad Hilarium Episcopum* (238) II—JK, n. 94; *Cornelii Papae Epist. IIa ad Rufum Coepiscopum Orientalem* (251-253?)—JK, n. 115; *Sixti Papae II Epist. IIIa* (257-258?)—JK, n. 133; *Julii Papae I, Epist. IIa, sive Rescriptum Julii* (337), VI, XVI, XVII—JK, n. 196; *Innocentii Papae Epist. ad Florentinum* (401-417?)—JK, n. 317; *Lucii Papae I Epist. ad Galliae atque Hispaniae Episcopos* (253), III, IV—Mansi, I, 876, 877.

[69] Cap. 29, *Epist. C* (1054)—JL, 4302.

[70] Epist. XI, 56—*MGH, Epistolarum Series,* II, I, P. I. (ed. P. Ewald, Berolini, 1887), 331. The editor, after a long discussion on the authenticity of this letter, concludes that it is genuine.

the Great in his amplification of the notion of jurisdiction. The law in the Digest of Justinian, cited as the law *Extra,* which restricted judicial jurisdiction to the territory of the judge, has been noted.[71] By the extension of this term to include the whole scope of jurisdiction, this law *Extra* was misinterpreted as a juridical authority for the restriction of legislative power also to the territory of the legislator. This extension of the notion of jurisdiction took place chiefly within the pontificate of Gregory the Great.[72] The first recorded use of the word jurisdiction in ecclesiastical matters occurs in a letter from Pope Gregory to John of Larissa, Metropolitan of the province of *Prima Justiniana.* Here the Pope rebukes the Metropolitan for removing Adrian, his suffragan, from the See of Thebes, because Adrian and his See had been previously withdrawn from the *jurisdiction* of the Metropolitan by Pope Pelagius.[73] This more extended use of the term jurisdiction persisted during the whole period from Gregory until the Decree of Gratian, especially in connection with the exemption of monasteries from diocesan jurisdiction.[74] Kereckhove was therefore able to conclude that by 1215 the term jurisdiction came to mean the whole public power to rule subjects, legislative and coercive as well as judicial.[75]

In summary, the whole period before the Decree of Gratian does not offer sufficient evidence for a definite conclusion concerning the ob-

[71] D (2,1) 20; cf. *supra,* p. 10, note 12.

[72] Cf. D'Angelo, *Jus Digestorum,* I, 149; Hilling, "Über dem Gebrauch des Ausdrucks iurisdictio im Rechwahrend der ersten Hälfte das Mittelalters"—*Archiv für katholisches Kirchenrecht,* CXVIII (1938), 165-170—hereafter this periodical is cited as *AKKR*; Hilling, " Die Bedeuntung der iurisdictio voluntaria und involuntaria im römischen Recht und im kanonischen Recht des Mittelalters und der Neuzeit,"—*AKKR,* CV 1925), 448-474; Van De Kereckhove, "De notione jurisdictionis apud decretistas et priores decretalistas,"—*Jus Pont.,* XVIII (1938), 10-14.

[73] JE, n. 1211 (592 A.D.). Cf. Hilling: "Es ist einleuchtend, dats hier der Ausdruck iurisdictio in einem viel weiteren Sinne als im römischen Recht gebraucht ist. Der Papst versteht darunter die gesamte Amtsgewalt des Metropoliten der prima Justiniana."—"Die Bedeuntung der iurisdictio voluntaria und involuntaria im römischen Recht und im kanonischen Recht des Mittelalters und der Neuzeit."—*AKKR,* CV (1925), 451.

[74] Cf. JE, nn. 2016; 1846; 2293; 3466; JL, nn. 3791; 4215; 1116; 6504; etc. Cf. Hilling, o.c., *AKKR,* CXVIII (1938), 166.

[75] "De notione jurisdictionis apud decretistas et priores decretalistas,"—*Jus Pont.,* XVIII (1938), 13.

ligations of the traveler. At the most, indications of a policy of territoriality of law may be noted, with trends toward the opposite. A clear and definite policy does not appear in either the legislation or the writings. Subsequent authors were able to draw from its sources, erroneously at times, support for whichever of the two contrary positions they desired to espouse.

Chapter II

DEVELOPMENT FROM GRATIAN TO THE COUNCIL OF TRENT

At the time when the great canonical collection, the Decree of Gratian, was completed in 1140, the explicit treatment of the obligations of the traveler was the object of particular study due to the rise of the medieval universities, especially at Rome and Bologna, and the intensive commercial activity centered about the Italian cities. Each of these free municipal commonwealths had its own statutes. The Classical Roman Law of Justinian was sought as an aid to commerce, and in the solution of the problems of the traveler.

The earliest among the civil jurists of this period held that the traveler was bound to follow the laws of the place where he was.[1] In the XIII Century this doctrine was already abandoned by the predecessors[2] of the famous Bartolus (†1357), whose doctrine stands as the first complete treatment of the problems connected with the obligations of the traveler, and typical of the post-glossators:[3] namely, that the traveler was directly exempted from the statutes of the place where he was, but indirectly bound in matters of contracts, delicts, statutes affecting things located in the place (*ratione rei sitae*), and the formalities of contracts and judicial procedure.[4]

The influence of Bartolus and the post-glossators passed over easily into the doctrines of the canonists through the close cooperation in the schools and universities in the study of the respective systems of law. Particularly is this close cooperation personified in the person of

[1] Cf. Neumeyer, *Die gemeinrechtliche Entwickelung des internationalen Privat-und Strafrechts bis Bartolus* (2 vols., München, Berlin und Leipzig, 1901-1916), II, 58, 59. Cited as *Entwickelung des Privat-und Strafrechts.*

[2] Cf. Meili, *Über das historische Debüt der Doktrin des internationalen Privat-und Strafrechts* (Leipzig, 1899), pp. 37-40; Lainé, *Introd. au Droit Intern. Privé*, pp. 118-122.

[3] Cf. Meili, *Civil and Commercial Law*, p. 66.

[4] Bartolus à Saxaferrato, *Omnia Quae Extant Opera* (11 vols., Venetiis, 1590-1595), VII (1590), ad *l. Cunctos populos*, I, C. I, *De Summa Trinitate et Fide Catholica*, 1, nn. 1-32.

Baldus de Ubaldis (†1400), whose doctrine is mainly that of Bartolus.[5]

Article I. Doctrine in the Decree of Gratian and Its Interpreters

§ 1. *Doctrine in the Decree of Gratian*

Although Gratian made his collection in the setting of the intensive cultivation of Classical Roman Law sources, and the close cooperation of the students of both systems of law, there is no clear cut and scientific policy regarding the traveler indicated in his Decree. Concrete texts formed in view of concrete situations furnished the materials for the chapters of the Decree, and the sources from which the decretists and decretalists developed their theories. Often these texts had little application to the matter as a whole.[6] The only texts which do have evident bearing on the matter, and which the *glossa ordinaria* invokes as indicative of the obligations of the stranger, are the chapters *Quae contra*,[7] *Illa*,[8] and *Quisquis*.[9]

An interpretation of these texts has been presented when treating of them in their original sources.[10] Taken all together, these three texts may easily be interpreted to imply the obligation of the traveler to conform to the customs and laws in force where he is visiting. Only one, the chapter *Quisquis*, may have been used in the Decree of Gratian to demonstrate the obligations of the traveler. The rubrics of this text as it was inserted in the Decree of Gratian, however, do not specify that such was its purpose.[11] The other two texts were, according to the

[5] Cf. Lainé, *Introd. au Droit Intern. Privé*, pp. 281-284.

[6] Cf. c. 10, D. XII; c. 5, C. VII, q. 3; c. 8, C. IX, q. 2; c. 25, C. XXIV, q. 3; c. 15, C. XXV, q. 2; c. 1, C. XXXVI, q. 2; c. 13, D. III, *De Cons.*

[7] C. 2, D. VIII. This text has already been quoted in its source, the *Confessions* of St. Augustine, *supra*, p. 18.

[8] C. 11, D. XII. This text has also been quoted in its source, the letter of St. Augustine to Januarius, *supra*, p. 18.

[9] C. I, D. XLI. This text has been quoted from the *De Doctrina Christiana*, *supra* p. 19.

[10] Cf. The Doctrine of St. Augustine, *supra* pp. 19, 21.

[11] "Pro moribus eorum, cum quibus vivimus, etiam uti debemus alimentis."—*Rubrica* ad c. 1, D. XLI.

rubrics,[12] not intended by Gratian to solve the problem of the obligations of the traveler. Furthermore, none of these texts, either in their sources or in the Decree of Gratian, have uncontested juridical force. The way was thus left open for contrary interpretations, especially with the aid of Roman Law sources.

§ 2. *Doctrine in the Works of the Decretists*

It must not be assumed that an immediate application of these texts was made by the commentators of the Decree of Gratian, the decretists as they are called, to the problem of the obligations of the traveler.[13] The earliest decretists who did treat the problem, like the first glossators, saw in these texts the general obligation of the stranger to conform to the laws of the place where he was. Rufinus (wrote *circa* 1157-1159)[14] presupposes the obligation of the stranger to follow the laws of the place where he is, and states only general exceptions to this general rule. John of Faenza (wrote *circa* 1171), who used the work of Rufinus extensively,[15] held that the judge was to apply the law of the place in settling a trial, and not the law of the defendant or the plaintiff.[61] This same doctrine was explicitly held by Simon of Bisignano,[17] John LeMoyne (†1313),[18] and by both Joannes Teutonicus (Wrote

[12] "Adversus naturale jus nulli quidquam agere licet."—*Rubrica* ad c. 2, D. VIII; "Quod neque contra fidem, neque contra bonos mores esse convicitur, indifferenter est habendum."—*Rubrica* ad c. 2, D. XII.

[13] Neumeyer notes five manuscripts, those of Pocapaglia, first discipie of Gratian, Roland Bandinelli, Stephen of Tournai, and two anonymous manuscripts, which do not treat the question.—*Entwickelung des Privat-und Strafechts*, II, 110.

[14] Cf. *Die Summa Decretorum des Magister Rufinus* (ed. Heinrich Singer, Paderborn, 1902), ad c. 2, D. IX, p. 22.

[15] Cf. Kuttner, *Repertorium der Kanonistik (1140-1234), Prodromus Corporis Glossatorum*, Studi e Testi, 71 (Città del Vaticano: Biblioteca Apostolica Vaticana, 1937), p. 145. Cited hereafter as Kuttner, *Repertorium*.

[16] *Decretum Gratiani Emendatum et Notationibus Illustratum Una cum Glossis* (Venetiis, 1605), *Glossa ordinaria* ad c. 4, D. XII, v° *praesertim*. Cited hereafter as *Glossa*.

[17] Wrote circa 1177—Kuttner, *Repertorium*, p. 149. "Peregrinus tenetur sequi constitutionibus civitatis in quo manet . . . "—*Summa Decreti*, can. 38—cited by Van Hove, "La territorialité et la personnalité des lois,"—*TVR*, III (1922), 288. Van Hove hesitates to accept this text as authentic.

[18] "Viatores tenentur sequi consuetudinem loci ad quem veniunt . . . "—*Apparatus in* VI^{um}—Cited by Neumeyer, *Entweckelung des Privat-und Strafrechts*, II. 125.

circa 1215-1217)[19] and Bartholomew of Brescia (wrote *circa* 1245)[20] in the *glossa ordinaria.*[21]

Still in the late years of the XII Century, Hugh of Pisa (*circa* 1188) interpreted the texts from St. Augustine by limiting the chapter *Quae contra* by the chapter *Illa.* Thus he held that strangers were not bound by the laws of the place where they were except in danger of scandal.[22] This doctrine was transmitted to the XIII Century by Guy de Baysio,[23] and in the XIV and XV Centuries adopted generally by those who were inspired by the Decree of Gratian.[24]

Besides these texts of the Decree of Gratian, many decretists appealed to texts from Roman Law. Joannes Teutonicus, although he interpreted the texts of St. Augustine to mean that the stranger should conform to the laws of the place, adopted as his own position the doctrine that the stranger was not bound by the laws of the place.[25] William Durantis (†1286)[26] appealed to him, as well as to the civilists, Jacobus Balduinus and Albert of Pavia, for authority in using arguments from Roman Law. The laws upon which they based their deductions were the laws *Haeres absens* and *Debitor*, which did not apply to the question.[27]

[19] Cf. Kuttner, *Repertorium,* p. 1.

[20] Cf. Kuttner, *Repertorium,* p. 103.

[21] *Glossa* ad c. 2, D. VIII, v^is^. *aut peregrini;* c. 11, D. XII, v°, *societate.*

[22] "argumentum quod peregrini et scholares debent vivere et judicari secundum consuetudinem civitatis in qua inveniuntur. quod verum est, si volunt habitare vel ut vitetur scandalum . . . "—*Summa Decretorum,* ad c. 2, D. VIII, v° *peregrini*—quoted from Neumeyer, *Entwickelung des Privat-und Strafrechts,* II, 113.

[23] "Serva si aliter faciendo paries scandalum . . . Secundum Huguccionem."—*Rosarium Domini Guidonis Archydiaconi Bononie super Decreto,* c. *Illa,* 11, D. XII, v°. *serva*—quoted from Van Hove, "La territorialité et la personnalité des lois."—*TVR,* III, 290.

[24] Cf. Paludanus, *Locubrationum Opus in IV Sententiarum* (Paris, 1518), Dist. XV, Q. IV, A. III, fol. 69a; St. Antoninus (†1389), *Summa Sacrae Theologiae, Iuris Pontificii, et Caesarei* (4 vols., Venetiis, 1571), II, tit. 6, c. 2, § 2; Panormitanus (Nicolaus de Tudeschis, †1435), *Commentaria in V Libros Decretalium* (5 vols. in 7, Venetiis, 1588) c. 2, X, XIII, *de observatione ieiunii,* 46, n. 6.

[25] Cf. *Glossa,* ad c. 2, D. VIII, v^is^. *aut peregrini, arg. contra.*

[26] *Speculum Iuris* (5 vols., Venetiis, 1575), IV, partic. i.

[27] Cf. *supra,* p. 11.

Another approach to the problem was in the procedural question of which law the judge should apply in settling cases. In this connection, Hugh of Pisa[28] developed his departure from the established position of his day. He held that by freely choosing the judge, the stranger submitted himself to be judged according to the law of the judge, while otherwise the judge should apply the law of the litigants or of the one delegating him. Bartholomew of Brescia[29] held that the judge was to follow the law of the place in cases involving delicts and contracts, but otherwise the law of the parties. This doctrine was generally adopted.[30]

Thus by the end of the period before the collection of the Decretals of Gregory IX, there was a reversal of the original position of the decretists. It was finally generally held that the traveler was not as a rule bound to conform to the laws of the place where he was a stranger. Exceptional cases were pointed out, however, when he was bound by the laws of the place, namely, cases involving contracts and delicts, and when he freely submitted himself to the local jurisdiction.

Article II. Decretals of Gregory IX and their Interpretation

§ 1. *Legislation in the Decretals of Gregory IX*

The leading legislation in the collection of Gregory IX relative to the obligations of the traveler is to be found in the decretal *A nobis*:

> A nobis fuit ex parte tua quaesitum, utrum si quis ita pronunciaverit: "quisquis furtum fecerit, excommunicatus sit": haec

[28] "Alii aliter distinguunt: si litigantes sponte se subiiciunt foro alieni iudicis . . . debeat iudex iudicare secundum suas consuetudines . . . si vero non sponte, sed inviti ei subiiciuntur, tunc ille debebit iudicare secundum consuetudines delegantis vel litigatorum."—quoted by Neumeyer, *Entwickelung des Privat-und Strafrechts,* II, 113.

[29] *Glossa,* ad c. 4, D. XII, v.°, *praesertim.*

[30] Cfr. Innocent IV, *Apparatus Decretalium Innocentii Papae IV* (Venetiis, 1481), in c. *Raynutius,* 16, X, *de testamentis et ultimis voluntatibus,* III, 26; Dominicus a Sancto Geminiano, *Commentaria Propria Diligentissime Castigata in Decretum* (Venetiis, 1504), c. *Que contra,* D. VIII, v.° *examinibus;* Bernard of Pavia (†1213), *Commentarium in Primam Compilationem* (Ratisbonae, 1861), p, 6—cited by Van Hove, "La territorialité et la personnalité des lois,"—*TVR,* III (1922), 299; Guido de Baysio, *Rosarium,* D. 12, c. 4, v°. *alterius*—quoted by Neumeyer, *Entwickelung des Privat-und Strafrechts,* II, 123.

> generalis clausula ad ipsius excommunicatoris subditos referatur, an extendatur ad omnes qui non sunt de iurisdictione illius. Ad quod *utique* dicimus, quod hac sententia non nisi subditi obligantur, nisi forte plus ei contulerit maior et largior auctoritas delegantis.[81]

The original author of this decretal is Clement III (1139).[82] It states that a general sentence of excommunication binds only the subjects of the authority giving the sentence. As may be seen from careful reading of the text, it regards only subordinate authority. It is limited in its scope to the matter of the delict of theft, and expressly refers to a sentence. It is in connection with the extension and meaning of the terms *subject* and *sentence* that it becomes the object of controversy.

The decretal *De illis*, of earlier origin,[83] explicitly states that a traveler from another parish may be punished by excommunication for committing a crime:

> De illis autem, *qui intra parochiam beneficium aut hereditatem habent, et alterius episcopi parochiani sunt*, et de loco ad locum iter faciunt, et ibi rapinas et depredationes peragunt, placuit, ut ab illius loci praelato excommunicentur, nec ante ex parochia illa exeant, quam digne quae perpetrarunt emendent; quorum excommunicatio *seniori eorum* et proprio episcopo significanda est, ne eos recipiat, antequam illuc redeant, ubi rapinam fecerunt, et omnia plene emendent.[84]

And the decretal *Postulasti* further distinguishes between jurisdictions and asserts that the bishop of the place where the delict was committed imposes the penalty, while the bishop of the diocese, where the delinquent has a benefice or office, executes it:

> Postulasti per sedem apostolicam edoceri, utrum sacerdos habens ecclesiam in una dioecesi, et residens in eadem, domicilium vero patrimonii ratione in alia, ibi delinquens, ab eo, in cuius dioecesi

[81] C. 21, X, *de sententia excommunicationis*, V, 39.

[82] JL, n. 17053.

[83] *Karlomanni Capitularia* (884), c. 5, 6—*MGH, Legum Sect.* I (ed. Pertz, Hanoverae, 1835, Leipzig, 1925), I, 552.

[84] C. 1, X, *de raptoribus*, V, 17.

habet patrimonium, pro delicto ibidem commisso debeat iudicari, praesertim in causis, quae officii sui, seu beneficii privationem exposcunt? Ad quod breviter respondemus, quod per episcopum, in cuius dioecesi deliquit, sententia promulgari poterit in eundem; sed ab eo, in cuius dioecesi beneficium obtinet, erit quoad illud huiusmodi exsecutio sententiae facienda.[35]

It may be noted, in seeking harmony between these last two texts and the decretal *A nobis*, that the latter speaks of a general sentence, while the former two speak of a particular inflicting of a penalty.

While there were other decretals, most of which had no application to the problem,[36] cited by the decretalists in reference to the obligations of the traveler, only one more need be pointed out, because it presents the headings under which the chief exceptions to the general exemption of the stranger were grouped, the decretal *Licet ratione*:

> Licet ratione delicti, seu contractus, aut domicilii, sive rei, de qua contra possessorem causa movetur, quibus forum regulariter quis sortitur, episcopus vester apud sedem apostolicum conventus non fuerit, quia tamen, omnium ecclesiarum mater est eadem et magistra, rite compelli potuit ut ibi suis adversariis responderet, nisi pro alia iusta et necessaria causa venisset, quam si tunc allegasset, ius revocandi domum salvum fuisset eidem.[37]

§ 2. *Interpretation Given to the Decretals of Gregory IX*

The position being generally accepted that the stranger was directly exempted from the obligations of the place where he was, the interpreters of the Decretals of Gregory IX developed the exceptions to this position on the ground of indirect obligation. William Durantis[38]

[35] C. 14, X, *de foro competenti*, II, 2. This decretal comes from Innocent III in 1213, in an answer to an enquiry from the Bishop of Beauvais.—Potthast, *Regesta Pontificum Romanorum* (2 vols., Berolini: R. De Becker, 1874-1875), I, n. 4722—cited hereafter as Potthast.

[36] Cf. c. 1, X, *de constitutionibus*, I, 2; c. 1, X, *de consuetudinibus*, I, 9; c. 9, X, *de foro competenti*, II, 2; c. 2, X, *de observatione ieiuniorum*, III, 46.

[37] C. 20, X, *de foro competenti*, II, 2—Potthast, n. 9587. This decretal comes from a response of Gregory IX to the Bishop of Troyes (France) in 1227-34 [?].

[38] *Speculum Iuris*, Lib. V, partic. I, nn. 5-7.

clearly set forth the meaning of the doctrine that the stranger was directly exempt, but indirectly bound by the laws of the place where he was. Direct obligation arises from the proper efficacy of the law. The stranger was exempted from this obligation of the law. Indirect obligation arises from some source outside the law itself, namely delict, contract, or the like. The stranger could be bound by such obligations. Direct obligation arose from domicile. Due to the progress in the doctrine of domicile made by the glossators on Roman Law, the decretalists were able to extend the notion to include the place where one came with the intention of perpetually remaining, or where he actually remained for ten years.[39] Innocent IV held that even a shorter residence, for the greater part of the year, was sufficient to give rise to direct subjection to local laws.[40] The name quasi-domicile was given to such a residence by Anthony of Butrio (†1408) and Dominicus a Sancto Dominiano (†1436).[41]

First among the extrinsic reasons for the subjection of the stranger to local laws was the commission of a delict, according to the almost universal teaching of the decretalists.[42] The difficulty in this position arises from the fact that the decretal *A nobis* states that a general sentence binds only the subjects of the one excommunicating. The easiest way to reconcile this decretal with the generally accepted doctrine was in the wide interpretation of the word subject: all were made subject

[39] Cf. Baldus de Ubaldis, *Commentaria . . . in Codicis Libros* (9 vols. in 7, Venetiis, 1572), I, c. III, 15; Hostiensis (Henry of Susa, †1271), *Commentaria in V Libros Decretalium* (5 vols. in 3, Venetiis, 1581), I, ad c. 9, X, *de foro competenti,* II, 2; Henricus Boich (†1350), *In V Libros Decretalium Commentaria* (Venetiis, 1574), ad c. 9, X, *de foro Competenti,* II, 2, nn. 2, 3.

[40] *Apparatus,* ad c. 15, X, *de foro competenti,* II, 2.

[41] *Commentaria Propria,* ad c. 29, X, *de rescriptis,* I, 3. Cf. Felinus Sandeus (†1503), *Commentaria in Decretalium Libros Quinque* (5 vols., Venetiis, 1620), ad c. 29, X, *de rescriptis,* I, 3, n. 11.

[42] Cf. Innocent IV, *Apparatus,* ad c. 21, X, *de sententia excommunicationis,* V, 39; Godfrey of Trani (†1245), *Summa Decretalium, de sententia excommunicationis,* V, 39, n. 11—quoted by Neumeyer, *Entwickelung des Privat-und Strafrechts,* II, 134, nota 1; Hostiensis, *Commentaria,* ad c. 21, X, *de sententia excommunicationis,* V, 39; Durantis, *Speculum Iuris,* IV, partic. I, n. 9; Panormitanus, *Commentaria in V Decretalium,* ad c. 21, X, *de sententia excommunicationis,* V, 39, n. 7; Boich, *In V Libros Decretalium Commentaria,* ad c. 3, X, *de eo, qui mittitur in possessione rei servandae,* II, 15, n. 7.

to the legislator by reason of crime committed (*ratione delicti*).[43] However, such an interpretation defeats the purpose of the decretal. Tancred[44] commenting on this decretal as it appeared in the *II Compilation*[45] said that the stranger was bound only when the legislator expressly so stated, as for example, by adding the words "in my diocese." Thus, and for this Tancred is to be noted, the real reason for the obligation of the stranger is to be found in the will of the legislator expressed in the statute. Innocent IV, partly rejecting the solution given by Tancred, distinguished between a sentence and a law. A sentence is inflicted for a delict already committed; a law regards future actions. A true law, general enough in its extension, and applying to the subordinates of the legislator, binds all, outsiders and residents alike. Strangers are made subject to it by reason of delict.[46] The reason for the distinction between a sentence, which could always bind strangers, and the law, which could bind strangers only when the proper elements of the law were present, was supplied by Bernard of Montmirat.[47] This position of Innocent IV was accepted as the more common doctrine by the subsequent authors before the Council of Trent.[48]

[43] Cf. Godfrey of Trani, *Summa Decretalium*, V, *De sententia excommunicationis* 39, n. 11—Neumeyer, *Entwickelung des Privat-und Strafrechts*, II, 134, nota 1.

[44] "Si vero dixerit 'si quis furtum fecerit in paroechia mea,' tunc ratione delicti omnes, qui ibi delinquerunt, ligantur illa sententia ratione prius dicta."—*Glossa ad Compilationem II*—quoted from Neymeyer, *Entwickelung des Privat-und Strafrechts*, II, 139. This Gloss is dated by Kuttner at about 1210—*Repertorium*, p. 327.

[45] C. 10, II, *de sententia excommunicationis*, V, 18—*Antiquae Collectiones Decretalium cum Antonii Augustini Episcopi Ilerdensis Notis* (Ilerdae, 1576), pp. 123, 124.

[46] *Apparatus*, ad c. 21, X, *de sententia excommunicationis*, V, 39.

[47] "Et est ratio diversitatis in sententiis et statuto, quia lex fit cum deliberatione, sine iuris ordine et causae cognitione . . . Sed sententia debet fieri cum causae cognitione."—*Abbatis Antiqui Super V Libros Decretalium Lectura*—quoted from Van Hove, "La territorialité et la personnalité des lois,"—*TVR*, III (1922), 311, note 2. Kuttner demonstrates that the *Abbas Antiquus* was Bernard of Montmirat. He wrote this work in 1261.—"Wer war der Dekretalist 'Abbas antiquus'?"—*Zeitschrift der Savigny-Stiftung für Rechtsgeschichte*, LVII (1937), 471-487.

[48] Cf. Angelus Clavensis (†1484-5), *Summa Angelica de Casibus Conscientialibus cum Additionibus . . . Jacobi Ungarelli, necnon Augustino Patavino* (Venetiis, 1510), v°. *Excommunicatio*, n. 10; v° *Statutum*, n. 1—cited hereafter as *Summa Angelica*; Panormitanus, *Commentaria*, ad c. 21, X, *de sententia excommunicationis*, V, 39, n. 7; Sandeus, *Commentaria*, ad c. 21, X, *de sententia excommunicationis*, V, 39, n. 1.

Another indirect reason for the obligation of the stranger to follow the laws of the place is found regarding contracts and the solemnities of juridical acts. By the time of William Durantis[49] the most common position, out of a variety of possibilities considered, was that both the customs and the statutes of the place where the contract was made regulated its solemnities.[50] Panormitanus[51] distinguished between the solemnities of the contract, which were regulated by the law of the place where the contract was made, and the execution of the contract, which was regulated by the law of the place where it was to be performed.

This principle, known as the principle of *locus regit actum*, received further applications to the contract of marriage and to testaments.[52] In making testaments, the law of the place where the will was drawn up made it valid for all of the personal property disposed, no matter where that property was. The application of this principle to procedure was an important contribution of the younger Bernard of Compostella (*circa* 1261).[53]

A final reason for indirect subjection to the laws of the place was the ownership of real property located in that place (*ratione rei sitae*). Not only was this a means of proceeding against the outsider who had departed from the place where he had committed an injury,[54] but, as

[49] *Speculum Iuris*, II, partic. I, § *Feriarum*, v°. *sed pone*.

[50] Cf. Innocent IV, *Apparatus*, *in rubricam*, X, *de consuetudinibus*, I, 4; Panormitanus, *Commentaria*, ad c. 2, X, *de foro competenti*, II, 2, n. 30; Boich *In Decretales*, ad c. 2, X, *de consuetudinibus*, I, 4, n. 3.

[51] *Commentaria*, ad c. 20, X, II, *de foro competenti*, 2, n. 30.

[52] Cf. Boich, *In Decretales*, ad c. 3, X, *de testamentis et ultimis voluntatibus*, III, 26, n. 10.

[53] " . . . aut loquitur de consuetudine quae attenditur circa factum iudicis vel processum, et tunc ista consuetudo non dicitur litigantium, sed fori iudicis."—*Lectura in Ium Librum Decretalium*, Tit. I, 4, super *rubrica*—quoted from Neumeyer, *Entwickelung des Privat-und Strafrechts*, II, 120.

[54] "Potest procedi in res eius ad missionem in possessionem rerum quas ibi habet, sed non contra personam ad excommunicationem . . . quia ibi in re habet iurisdictionem et ideo in ea potest dicere ius missionis in possessionem . . . sed in personam non potest ius dicere."—Godfrey of Trani, *Apparatus*, X, II, *de foro competenti*, 2, n. 3—quoted from Neumeyer, *Entwickelung des Privat-und Strafrechts*, II, 142, nota 1.

Innocent IV[55] pointed out, a means of subjecting an outsider to the authority of him who had jurisdiction over the place where the property was located.

While these indirect obligations of the stranger to observe the laws of the place met with the general approval of the decretalists, two other questions caused much controversy. The first of these was the effect of ignorance as an excusing cause from the obligation of the traveler.[56] The second of these problems, the obligation of the absent subject to observe the laws of his proper territory, is of present interest. Tancred had already insinuated that this obligation depends upon the will of the legislator. This position was explicitly adopted by Innocent IV[57] and Bernard of Montmirat (*Abbas Antiquus*).[58] Others held the position made famous by Hostiensis that the inferior legislator had no jurisdiction to bind his subjects outside of his territory.[59]

ARTICLE III. THE *Liber VIus* AND ITS INTERPRETATION

§ 1. *Legislation in the* Liber VIus

The basis of the doctrine on the obligations of the traveler in the Sixth Book of Decretals, compiled by the authority of Boniface VIII, is found in the decretal *Ut animarum*. In this decretal Boniface VIII intended to give an authoritative solution to the controverted questions concerning both ignorance and the obligations of the absent subject.[60]

[55] *Apparatus*, ad c. 13, X, *qui filii sint legitimi*, IV, n. 17; cf. Panormitanus, *Commentaria*, ad c. 9, X, *de foro competenti*, II, 2, n. 11; Sandeus, ad c. 14, X, *de foro competenti*, II, 2, n. 12.

[56] Cf. Bernard of Parma (†1263), *Decretales Gregorii Papae IX, una cum Glossa Restitutae* (Romae, 1582), *glossa* ad c. 21, X, *de sententia excommunicationis*, V, 39, v^{is}. *non nisi subditi;* Hostiensis, *Commentaria*, ad c. 21, X, *de sententia excommunicationis*, V, 39, v^{is}. *ad quod dic.*

[57] *Apparatus*, ad c. 21, X, *de sententia excommunicationis*, V, 39.

[58] "Statutum generale episcopi subditos tantum ligat . . . etiamsi subditus extra diocesim furtum committat. Secus autem si dixisset: quisquis furtum commiserit in mea dioecesi . . ."—quoted from Van Hove, "La territorialité et la personnalité des lois,"—*TVR*, III (1922), 322.

[59] Cf. Hostiensis, *Commentaria*, ad c. 21, X, *de sententia excommunicationis*, V, 39.

[60] Cf. *Liber Sextus Decretalium Bonifacii Papae VIII, Clementis Papae V Constitutiones, Extravagantes tum Viginti Ioannis Papae XXII, Haec Omnia cum Suis*

Hence the decretal may be divided into two parts:

A. Ut animarum periculis obvietur, sententiis per stauta quorumcumque ordinariorum prolatis ligari nolumus ignorantes: dum tamen eorum ignorantia crassa non fuerit aut supina.

B. Statuto episcopi, quo in omnes, qui furtum commiserint, excommunicationis sententia promulgatur, subditi eius, furtum extra ipsius dioecesim committentes, minime ligari noscuntur, quum extra territorium ius dicenti non pareatur impune.[61]

The text of the first part is general in its extension, referring to strangers and inhabitants alike. It does not pertain specifically to the obligations of strangers, although it does have frequent application in their regard.

The text of the second part of the decretal refers only to particular law. As an authoritative clarification of the controversy arising out of the decretal *A nobis,* it is confined to the terminology of the latter, to a general excommunication on account of theft. The reason given for the legislation, the defect of jurisdiction on the part of the superior issuing the sentence, warrants its general application to all particular laws in general, and not just to penal statutes. This reason, allegedly based on a fragment of the Digest of Justinian ascribed to Paulus, is a misapplication of the Roman Law. For this law states that a judge has no jurisdiction outside of his territory, not that a subject is not bound by legislative power when he is outside the territory.[62] It is true that a great factor in this misinterpretation of the Roman Law *Extra* was the extension of the term jurisdiction under the pontificate of Gregory the Great to include all public power, legislative as well as judicial.[63]

Finally it should be noted that the effect of this part of the decretal *Ut animarum* was not to leave the traveler free from the obligation of all law. He still remained bound by universal law, and the indirect ob-

Glossis Suae Integritati Restituta (Venetiis, 1591), *Glossa* in c. *Ut animarum,* 2, *de constitutionibus,* I, 2, in VI°. Hereafter this gloss is cited as *Glossa.* The author of this gloss is Joannes Andreae.

[61] C. 2, *de constitutionibus,* I, 2, in VI°.

[62] Cf. *supra,* p. 10, note 12.

[63] Cf. *supra,* pp. 22, 23.

ligations of the particular laws of the place where he actually was. It expressly stated that the absent subject was not bound by the penal laws of his own territory.

§ 2. *Interpretation of the Decretal* Ut Animarum

The decretal *Ut animarum* canonized the position of Hostiensis and rejected that of Innocent IV. It was but natural for such early decretalists as John LeMoyne (*Joannes Monachus*, †1330)[64] to interpret this decretal according to its letter, exempting the subject only from penal statutes. Pietro D'Ancharno (†1330)[65] was more explicit, stating that a judge could apply the penalty of excommunication to an absent subject, but he had to follow the laws of the place where the delict was committed.[66]

Those decretalists who placed the obligation of the absent subject implicitly upon the will of the legislator allowed the decretal *Ut animarum* to influence them to except penal laws from this general position.[67]

Noting that the basis of this decretal was the Roman Law *Extra*, from the Digest, the common doctrine of this period[68] held that the traveler was exempt from all of the laws of his own territory because of the defect of jurisdiction on the part of the legislator. This general position, however, was qualified so that the subject, the object of his action, and the act itself had to be simultaneously outside of the territory before he would be exempt from the law.[69] Upon this same qualification of the decretal, laws of residence were interpreted to be

[64] Ad c. 2, *de constitutionibus*, I, 2, in VI°, 2—quoted by Onclin, *De Legis Indole*, p. 113.

[65] *Super VI° Decretalium Acutissima Commentaria*, ad c. 2, *de constitutionibus*, I, 2, in VI°—quoted by Onclin, *De Legis Indole*, p. 114.

[66] Cf. Hostiensis, *Commentaria*, in c. 1, X, *de raptoribus*, V, 17.

[67] Cf. Petrus Ancharnus, *Commentaria in V Decretalium*, ad c. 21, X, *de sententia excommunicationis*, V, 38, n. 6—quoted by Onclin, *De Legis Indole*, p. 118; Joannes de Lignano (†1358), *Tractatus . . . in Utraque Facultate . . . Iurisconsultorum, De Censura Ecclesiastica*, § 9, nn. 22-35—cited in Onclin, *l. c.*

[68] Cf. Joannes Andreae, *Glossa* ad c. 2, *de constitutionibus*, I, 2, in VI°.

[69] Cf. Sandeus, *Consilia seu Responsa* (Lugduni, 1553), *cons.* 182; Dominicus de Sancto Geminiano, *Lectura Super Sexto Libro Decretalium*, ad c. 2, *de constitutionibus*, I, 2, in VI°; c. Onclin, *De Legis Indole*, p. 123.

binding upon subjects outside of their own territory. Antonius of Butrio (†1408-1409)[70] taught that the omission of a positive act to be placed within the territory amounted to an act committed within the territory for it took effect there.

Finally, the proponents of this position considered its extension to places physically within the diocese, but enjoying the privilege of exemption from the jurisdiction of the local bishop. Joannes Andreae[71] held that subjects of the local bishop were sufficiently outside the territory, when they were within the confines of such exempt places, to be excused from the laws of their proper local ordinaries. Others held that this privilege of exemption was personal, and therefore not to be extended to strangers; that exempt places were not juridically outside the territory.[72] The doctrine of Joannes Andreae became commonly accepted, and exempt places were considered outside the territory.[73]

As a result of the collections in the *Corpus Iuris Canonici* and the interpretation given to them by the decretalists, the indefiniteness of the concrete laws before the Decree of Gratian was cleared up and a definite policy was developed, which first held for the obligation of the traveler to observe the laws of the place where he was a stranger. Later this view yielded to another which finally became the more common position. It held that the traveler was directly exempt from the obligation of the laws of the place where he was visiting, and from the laws of his place of domicile or quasi-domicile. The obligations of the vagrant and the obligations of the universal law did not as yet receive explicit treatment. Indirect obligations arising from delicts, the solemnities of acts, and real property could bind the traveler to observe the laws of the place where he was. On the other hand, to enjoy freedom

[70] *Commentaria Super VI° Libro Decretalium*, ad c. 2. *de constitutionibus*, I, 2, in VI°, n. 7—quoted by Onclin, *De Legis Indole*, p. 125.

[71] *In Sextum Librum Decretalium Novella Commentaria* (Venetiis, 1581), ad c. 2, *de constitutionibus*, I, 2, in VI°, n. 5.

[72] Cf. Fredricus de Senis (†1343), *Consilia et Quastiones*, cons. 2, n. 4—cited by Onclin, *De Legis Indole*, pp. 120-121.

[73] Felinus Sandeus, *Commentaria*, ad c. 2, *de constitutionibus*, I, 2, in VI°; Lancelottus, *Institutiones Iuris Canonici Quibus Ius Pontificum Singulari Methodo Libris Quatuor Comprehenditur* (Lugduni, 1579), I (*De Ecclesiasticis Constitutionibus*), fol. 7b.

from the obligations of the laws of his own territory, he had to be entirely outside of the territory, as regards himself, his act, and the object of his act. Thus the omission of a positive obligation was reputed as an act having effect within his own territory. The reason assigned for the exemption from the laws of the place of residence was the defect of jurisdiction on the part of the legislator. Tancred and his followers, Pietro D'Ancharno, Joannes de Lignano, and to an extent Innocent IV, are notable in this that they placed the obligations of the traveler upon the will of the legislator. Finally, it should be noted that thus far the basis of the doctrines proposed was always the authority of previous positive law, whether Canon Law or Roman Law.

Chapter III

DEVELOPMENT FROM THE COUNCIL OF TRENT TO THE CODE

The emphasis of the medieval authors was centered upon the authority of existing laws, both of the *Corpus Juris Civilis* and of the *Corpus Juris Canonici.* The period after the Council of Trent was characterized by a shift in emphasis from authority to a philosophical basis for the doctrines on the obligations of the traveler. The intense cultivation of the antiquities during the Rennaisance period brought with it a more critical approach to the ancient sources. The repudiation of authority resulting from the Protestant Revolt stressed the appeal to reason, not only among those hostile to the Church, but, as a consequence, among its defenders. Reason was the only common ground, the only avenue of approach for the Catholic apologists. Out of this spirit of the times came a new method in the science of Canon Law, a method based on arguments from reason and the principles of jurisprudence.

Article I. Legislation from the Council of Trent to the Code

§ 1. *Influence of Civil Law on the Obligations of the Traveler*

The new spirit of the Rennaisance resolved itself in the civil world into a political nationalism. The feudal system, weakened by the crusades and their effects, and by the centralizing tendencies of lesser monarchs, yielded to the establishment of small states. Though the period of development varied widely in different countries, by the time of the Council of Trent, each village enjoyed its own legislative power and made its own statutes different from those of the villages around it. Thus the strict territoriality of law in force in France and the Low Countries gave way to a situation somewhat like that of Italy in the middle ages.[1] Into this milieu Molinaeus (†1575)[2] propagated the doctrine of Bartolus, which was adapted and named the "Theory of

[1] Cf. Mancini, "Les règles générales du droit international privé,"—*Journal du Droit International Privé et de la Jurisprudence Comparée* (Paris, 1874 —), I (1874), 221-239. This periodical is hereafter cited as *JDIP*.

[2] Cf. Meili, *International Law*, p. 71; Lainé, *Introd. au Droit Intern. Privé*, I, 269.

Statutes." To clarify the growing confusion among the followers of Bartolus, D'Argentré (†1590)[3] of Brittany invented the "New Theory of Statutes." According to this theory, laws were considered to be territorial by their very nature, binding on all in the territory, aliens and citizens alike. But certain laws, which regarded the status of persons, were necessary and rare exceptions to this rule. Hence, statutes could be divided into real statutes, binding all in the territory, and personal statutes, binding on citizens even though outside their proper states. In the XVII Century, Huber[4] and the two Voet brothers[5] introduced the "New Theory of Statutes" into the Low countries, with the modification that if the sovereign recognized the personal statutes of another nation, it was due entirely to his benevolence. In the XIX Century this doctrine proposed by Huber and the Voets, of the strict territoriality of law modified by the benevolent will of the sovereign state recognizing the personal statutes of another state, was adopted by American[6] and English jurists.[7] Thus the doctrine of the strict territoriality of laws, based on the very nature of law, was very widespread in its influence by the XIX Century. Its influence upon the development of Canon Law was particularly felt during the XVII and XVIII Centuries, and the School of Würzburg reflected it significantly.

In the XIX Century, Savigny[8] developed a system founded upon an international common interest, supposed to exist between nations of the same general culture, and elaborated from the principles common to all of them. Although this system had great influence upon the codes of the Teutonic countries,[9] its influence was not noticed in the development of Canon Law.

[3] Cf. Lainé,*Introd. au Droit Intern. Privé*, II, pp. 94-112.

[4] *Praelectionum Juris Civilis Tomi Tres Secundum Institutiones et Digesta Justiniani* (3 vols., Maceratae, 1838-1839), II (1838), 55.

[5] Cf. Voet, J., *Commentarium ad Pandectas* (ed. quinta Veneta, 7 vols., Bassani, 1827-1828), III (1827), 49.

[6] Cf. Story, *On the Conflict of Laws*, pp. 27-35; Phillimore, *Commentaries upon International Law* (4 vols., London, 1854-1861), IV, 250.

[7] Cf. Westlake, *A Treatise on Private International Law* (London, 1858), p. 386.

[8] *System des heutigen römischen Rechts* (8 vols., Berlin, 1840-1849), VIII, 27, 108. A brief synopsis of this doctrine is clearly presented by Meili, *International Law*, pp. 91, 92.

[9] Cf. Meili, *International Law*, p. 92.

Another doctrine, of considerable importance to the canonist, the doctrine of the Italian School under the leadership of Mancini, was being developed in this same period. It represented a trend back to the personality of law, whereby the traveler, as a rule, is not bound by the laws of the place where he is, and bound by the laws of his own domicile.

Mancini stated, as a fundamental premise, that the proper juridical order consisted in the harmony of private individual freedom with the exercise of social power. Social power, expressed in public law, is the guarantee of the public order and the sovereignty of the state. Its limits are set by the inoffensive freedom of the individual. The qualities and traits, the needs and customs, the spontaneous and constant tendencies, the national characteristics of a people are manifested in their exercise of individual freedom. The laws of the juridical private order protect and correspond to these individual liberties.

When an alien comes into a state, he brings as part of his physical and psychological being these national characteristics of his fatherland. His free and spontaneous tendencies, his needs and first reactions are the expression of the customs and tradition of his people and of the geographical conditions of his land. To disregard this national characteristic, to misunderstand this difference between the alien and the citizen is to do the former an injustice, violently to restrain his individual inoffensive liberty. The nationality of the stranger demands in strict justice an inviolable respect for his patrimony of private rights. These private rights are divided into two classes. Certain of them pertain to the personal status, the domestic relations of the alien. These are his necessary private rights, independent of his own will, and which he cannot renounce even if he wanted to. In these he is obliged to follow the laws of his own domicile. His remaining private rights, those concerning his goods, his right to contract, and the like, are voluntary private rights. Regarding these he can choose to conform to the laws of the place where he is, or, within the limits of his inoffensive individual freedom, he can regulate his acts according to his own national laws.

He is bound to follow the laws of the place where he is only when the freedom of his activity becomes offensive to the public order. Public order embraces the conditions in which all should submit to the political sovereignty, the conditions necessary for the prosperity of social life. And here in the consideration of public order, which Mancini identified with public law, is the only expropriation of the individual rights of the alien by the state, because the state is a human necessity.[10] Thus the private law of the place did not bind the stranger, it was personal. In many matters, except those affecting the status of persons, the alien was not bound to observe the laws of his domicile either. He did have to observe the public law of the place, however, because it secured public order; it was territorial.[11] Inspired by these doctrines, a number of authors[12] on International Private Law turned their efforts to the determination of the meaning of public order. Their theories are treated in detail when the term public order as it appears in the Code of Canon Law is interpreted.[13] The influence of this doctrine upon Canon Law was effective through the work of Pacelli in the XX Century while the Code was being prepared.[14] The importance of this influence is such that it must, in the testimony of Van Hove[15] and Le Picard,[16] be correctly realized before the canonical doctrine of the obligations of the stranger can be fully understood.

§ 2. *Canonical Legislation and its Official Interpretation*

The period after the Council of Trent is characterized by an approach to the obligations of the traveler through judicial principles and reason rather than through the authority of previous legislation. The appeal to authority, when it was made, was always to the authority of

[10] Cf. Mancini, "Règles générales du droit international privé,"—*JDIP*, I (1874), 284-304.

[11] "A nos yeux le droit *civil privé* est personnel et national, et, comme tel, doit accompagner la personne même en dehors de sa patrie; le *droit public*, au contraire, est territorial: il plane sur le territoire et sur tous ceux qui l'habitent, indigènes ou étrangers sans distinction."—Mancini, *o.c.*, 297.

[12] Cf. Fiore, "De la limitation de l'autorité des lois étrangères et de la détermination des lois d'ordre public,"—*JDIP*, XXXV (1908), pp. 353, 354.

[13] Cf. *infra*, pp. 143, 144.

[14] Cf. *infra*, pp. 72-74.

[15] "Leges quae ordini publico consulunt,"—*Ephemerides Theologicae Lovanienses*, I (1924), 156. Hereafter this periodical is cited as *ETL*.

[16] "La notion d'ordre public en droit canonique,"—*Nouvelle Revue Théologique*, LV (1928), 361. Hereafter this periodical is cited as *NRT*.

the legislation in the *Corpus Juris Canonici,* or of the works of Justinian. It will be necessary, therefore, to delay only long enough at this point to indicate the leading examples of subsequent legislation, and the constant trends of the official interpretations of it.

The Council of Trent established more clearly parochial rights in regard to the administration of the sacraments and the conducting of funeral rites.[17] Questions arose, however, concerning these parochial rights in regard to strangers in the parish. The custom had been inaugurated in some places of yielding these rights over strangers to the cathedral parish of the city. The Sacred Congregation of the Council[18] finally decided that the right of administering the sacraments to strangers belonged to the pastor of the parish in which they were visiting. Unless they themselves had provided otherwise, they were also to be buried by the pastor of the parish in which they died.

To abolish the abuse of vagrant clerics, the Council of Trent enacted legislation so that no cleric was to be allowed to celebrate Mass or administer the sacraments unless he presented letters of recommendation, from his own bishop, to the bishop of the place where he was visiting.[19] This emphasis upon the ancient institution of the *litterae formatae* restricting the freedom of traveling clerics, and submitting them to the vigilance of the local authority was repeated in subsequent declarations from the Holy See.[20]

The Tridentine reformation of monasteries and exempt places furnished indications of the official doctrine on certain important points regarding the obligations of the absent subject. The Council of Trent[21]

[17] Sess. XXV, *de ref.*, c. 13—Mansi, XXXII, 189.

[18] S. C. Concilii, *resolutio,* 24 mar. 1888—*ASS,* XXI (1888), 105. Note that it was within the exclusive competence of the Sacred Congregation of the Council, after consulting the Supreme Pontiff, to give authentic interpretations of the decrees of the Council of Trent.—Sixtus V, Const. "*Immensa,*" 22 ian, 1587—*Bullarum Diplomatum et Privilegiorum Sanctorum Romanorum Pontificum, Taurinensis Editio,* (24 vols., Augustae Taurinorum, 1857- 1872), VIII (1883), n. CXVII. Cited hereafter as *Bull. Rom. Taur.*

[19] Sess. XXIII, *de ref.*, c. 16—Mansi, XXXII, 146.

[20] Cf. S. C. De Prop. Fide, decr., 28 iul. 1626—*Jus Pontificium de Propaganda Fide,* II (ed. R. de Martinis, Romae, 1909), n. 35; S. C. Concilii, decr., 14 nov. 1903—*ASS,* XXXVI (1903), 356.

established that the institutions and places of regulars were entirely exempt. Notwithstanding this exemption, the censures and interdicts of the ordinary of the place, as well as the feast days ordered by him were to be observed by all, even by exempt regulars.[22] This legislation of the Council of Trent establishing clearly the privilege of exemption was constantly repeated and further determined especially as regards limitations of the privilege in favor of episcopal jurisdiction in matters pertaining to diocesan subjects.[23] Clement X, in the constitution "*Superna*," giving regulations concerning regulars who have taken up the office of confessor, stated that they could absolve those coming from another diocese. However, he added this limitation: unless they knew that the penitents came from another diocese with the fraudulent intention to evade the reservations of that other diocese.[24] This law was not abrogated until the instruction of the Holy Office in 1916[25] promulgated the law now in force in canon 900, 3°.[26]

Not only is the limitation of reservations to the territory of the one reserving the cases interesting in the legislation of the constitution "*Superna*," but also the effect of fraud is a point of no little importance in the influence which the constitution had upon later doctrine. The importance of this effect of fraud as an exception to the rule that diocesan laws did not have obligatory force outside the diocese is best studied in the history of the famous *Tametsi* decree of the Council of

[21] Sess. XIV, *de ref.*, c. 5—Mansi, XXXIII, 105; Sess. XXV, *de reg. et monial.*, c. 9—Mansi, XXXIII, 176.

[22] Sess. XXV, *de reg. et monial.*, c. 12—Mansi, XXXIII, 177.

[23] Cf. S. Pius V, const. "*Etsi mendicantium,*" 16 maii 1567, § 1, n. 17, § 2. n. 17 —*Fontes*, n. 121; S. C. Ep. et Reg., *Pistorien.*, 21 nov. 1591—*Fontes*, n. 1449; *Nanneten.*, 8 iul. 1642—*Fontes*, n. 1767; Gregory XV, const. "*Inscrutabili,*" 5 febr. 1622, § 4—*Fontes*, n. 199; Clemens XII, const. "*Admonet nos,*" 11 aug. 1735, §§ 1, 3 —*Fontes*, 297; Benedictus XIV, const. "*Firmandis,*" 6 nov. 1744, §§ 2-16—*Fontes*, n. 347; Leo XIII, const. "*Romanos Pontifices,*" 8 maii 1887, § 7—*Fontes*, n. 582; S. C. Ep. et Reg. *Rhedonen.*, 27 febr. 1863—*Fontes*, n. 1987; S. C. De Relig., *Vicentina*, 3 aug. 1915—*Fontes*, n. 4424.

[24] 21 iun. 1670, § 7—*Fontes*, n. 246. Cf. Clemens VIII, decr. "*Sanctissimus,*" 26 maii 1593—*Fontes*, n. 177; S. C. C., *Caven.*, 22 iun. 1619—*Fontes*, n. 2413; decr. 21 sept. 1624, § 1—*Fontes*, 2454.

[25] S. C. S. Off., instr. 16 iul. 1916—*ASS*, VIII (1916), 315.

[26] Cf. *infra*, pp. 121-125.

Trent.[27] The Council of Trent stipulated that the new decree on the form of marriage should take effect within thirty days in those parishes where it was published.[28] Since it was not published in every parish, questions immediately arose whether those going out of a parish where it was in force to a parish where it was not promulgated remained subject to the canonical form of marriage; or whether he who came from a place not subject to it to a place where it was in force would become bound by the decree.

This latter question was settled on the principle that contracts were regulated by the law of the place where they were entered into.[29] The former question provoked a number of declarations from the Holy See. The basic response was given by the Sacred Congregation of the Council[30] to a series of questions submitted by the Archbishop of Cologne. The Archbishop asked three questions: whether those who went from a place subject to the *Tametsi* to a place not subject to it could contract a valid marriage if they did not observe the Tridentine form; whether a clandestine marriage in such circumstances would be valid if the sole intention of the parties was to evade the prescriptions of the decree *Tametsi;* finally whether, by changing their domicile to the place not subject to the *Tametsi* with the sole intention of evading its prescriptions, they could validly contract a clandestine marriage.

To the first two questions, the Sacred Congregation responded that the marriages would not be legitimate if contracted in fraud. The marriage in the third case would not be valid unless a true domicile were set up. At the insistence of the Archbishop of Cologne, Urban VIII, in the Brief "*Expone nobis*,"[31] confirmed this response in the following year. Benedict XIV[32] again confirmed this decision, drawing attention to the fact that it was the norm invariably used by the Sacred Congregations in this matter. In this same document, he established that

[27] Sess. XXIV, *de ref. matr.*, c. I—Mansi, XXXIII, 153.

[28] "Decernit insuper ut huiusmodi decretum in unaquaque parochia suum robur post triginta dies habere incipit a die primae promulgationis in eadem parochia factae numerandos."—Sess. XXIV, *de ref. matr.*, c. 1—Mansi XXXIII, 153.

[29] S. C. Concilii, *Brixinen.*, 28 ian. 1899—*ASS*, XXXII (1889-90), 350-355.

[30] S. C. C. (ad Archiep. Colonien.), 5 sep. 1626—*Fontes*, n. 447.

[31] 14 aug., 1627—*Bull. Rom. Taur.*, XIII (1868), n. CCLVII.

[32] Litt. ap. (ad Archiep. Goanum), "*Paucis abhinc*," 19 mar. 1758—*Fontes*, n. 447.

one month's residence was sufficient to set up a presumption of the intention to acquire a quasi-domicile, and sufficient to render one subject to the laws governing the form of marriage in the place. From these official interpretations it was made clear that the marriage of peregrins, from a territory where the *Tametsi* was in force, contracted in the territory not under the *Tametsi* were invalid if fraud entered in, that is, if the sole purpose for which the parties left their territories was to evade the law. Equally clear was the validity of those marriages contracted in a place where the parties acquired a true domicile or quasi-domicile. Outside of these cases, the validity of clandestine marriages of peregrins from places subject to the canonical form was still disputed.

Wherefore, the Holy Office issued an instruction in 1893[83] declaring that the *Tametsi* bound all in the territory because it was territorial, and all proper subjects of the territory under the Tridentine form, wherever they were, because personal. In 1899 the Curia of Paris[84] sought the confirmation of the Sacred Congregation of the Council for a decision in favor of the nullity of a marriage contracted clandestinely by parties who had left a place not subject to the *Tametsi* to contract in a place where it was in force. The Sacred Congregation confirmed this decision on January 28, 1899.[85] In this decision, confirmed by the Sacred Congregation of the Council, the general rule was established that laws were territorial by their nature. However, fraud was pointed out to be an exception to this general rule, and was defined as the evasion of the law by departure from the territory when such departure was itself forbidden in the law. Likewise, it was declared to be the general rule that strangers were not subjects to the laws of the place where they were visiting, except when those laws regulated contracts. This same argumentation was confirmed in a decision submitted by the Curia of Paris to the Sacred Congregation of the Council in 1903.[86] It is noteworthy that the authority for the principles deduced in these cases was sought in pre-Tridentine legislation, the Decretals and Roman Law.[87]

[83] (Ad Archiep. S. Francisci), 14 dec., 1893—*ASS*, XXVI (1893), 256.

[84] Cf. *ASS*, XXXII (1899), 346-418.

[85] S.C.C., *Parisien. matrimonii*, 28 ian. 1899—*ASS*, XXXII (1899), 419.

[86] S.C.C., *Parisien. matrimonii*, 18 iul. 1903—*ASS*, XXXVI (1903-04), 225.

[87] The arguments were based upon the Roman Law *Haerens absens*, D (5,1) 19,

From these official interpretations, and from the official confirmations of cases decided concerning the decree *Tametsi,* the obligations of the peregrin were juridically established after the Council of Trent. The question of the vagrant, who had neither domicile nor quasi-domicile, was also settled in the litigations over the *Tametsi* decree. The Curia of Cracow declared a marriage of a vagrant null, because he did not observe the Tridentine form in force where he contracted marriage. The decision was reversed in the second instance in Lublin. After an appeal by the plaintiff in the case, the Sacred Congregation of the Council upheld the decision of the first instance for the nullity of the marriage on the grounds that vagrants are subject to the laws in force wherever they are.[88]

In 1907 the Sacred Congregation of the Council, by order of Pope Pius X, issued the decree *Ne Temere*[89] setting all future difficulties concerning clandestine marriages. It made universal the requirement of the juridical form of marriage. Moreover, it established that the marriages of vagrants were to be witnessed by the bishop of the place, or the pastor with the bishop's permission, or a priest delegated by either.

From this history of the official interpretations of the *Tametsi,* the post-Tridentine law concerning the obligations of the traveler is quite completely revealed. Travelers were generally not bound by the laws in force where they were, or in force in their own proper territory. Although personal laws were admitted possible, laws were by their nature considered territorial. Strangers were bound by laws regulating contracts entered into in the place. When the legislator expressly prohibited departure from the territory with the intention to evade the law, such evasion was fraud; and in such circumstances the subject still remained bound by the law. Vagrants were considered bound by all the laws in force where they actually were.

Except for some indications in the Council of Trent, and the official

which dealt with judicial competence rather than subjection to law, and upon the decretal *Romana,* c. 1, *de foro competenti,* II, 3, in VI°. which also deals with judicial competence in cases involving contracts.

[88] S.C.C., *Cracovien. seu Varsavien. matrimonii,* 27 iun. 1886—*ASS,* XIX (1886) 238.

[89] S.C.C., decr. 2 aug. 1907—*ASS,* XL (1907), 528.

documents of the Holy See, most of the legislation regarding the obligations of the traveler was sought in the decretals and in Roman Law. On the eve of the promulgation of the Code of Canon Law, the Sacred Consistorial Congregation[40] published a declaration regarding proper ecclesiastical dress. In this regard, clerics traveling outside of their own territories could conform to the customs of their own territory or to the customs of the place in which they were traveling, just as the laws of fasting and abstinence of the territory were to be followed by visitors. From this last declaration of the Holy See before the promulgation of the Code, the post-Tridentine legislation regarding the traveler was complete, and the juridical obligations of the traveler were pointed out in their main aspects. A general principle, however, was not established in legislation before the Code.

Article II. Doctrine Regarding the Obligation of the Stranger

§ 1. *Doctrine that the Stranger is Bound by All the Laws of the Place of his Temporary Residence*

Just as the early commentators of the *Corpus Juris Canonici* held the position that the stranger was bound to observe all the laws of the place in which he was traveling, a similar position, based upon arguments from reason, enjoyed much popularity early in the period from the Council of Trent to the Code of Canon Law. The first post-Tridentine defenders of this position, such as Emanuel Sa (†1596),[41] Navarrus (†1586-1587)[42] and Covarruvias (†1577),[43] approached the question from the viewpoint of a moralist, treating the obligations of fasting and attending Mass, without explicitly indicating that such obligations were in any way exceptional to the general rule.

It was for Suarez (†1617)[44] to demonstrate the general principle

[40] S. C. Consist. declar., 31 mart. 1916, nn. 2, 3, 31—*Fontes*, n. 2093.

[41] *Aphorismi Confessariorum ex Variis Doctorum Sententiis Collecti* (ed. novissima, Lugduni, 1669), v°. *festum*, n. 9; v°. *Jejunium*, n. 1. Hereafter this work will be cited as *Aphorismi.*

[42] (Martin Azpilcueta) *Enchiridion sive Manuale Confessariorum et Poenitentium* (Wirceburgi, 1593), c. XIII, n. 5.

[43] *Commentarii in Bonifacii VIII Librum VI* (*Opera Omnia*, 2 vols., Coloniae, 1579), *Pars* I, *Relect.* c. *Alma mater* . . . , in VI°, § 10, n. 3.

[44] *Opera Omnia* (26 vols., Parisiis: Vivès, 1856-1866), XIII (*De Virtute Religio-*

of the subjection of the stranger to all of the laws in force in the place where he was traveling. He based this doctrine upon the intrinsic relation of legislative power to the territory in which it was to be exercised. Laws are made for the territory, and become the law of the state, or the law of the territory.[45] The other defenders[46] of this position followed the argumentation of Suarez closely. The basis for this position therefore can be conveniently studied in the arguments set forth by Suarez, noting in the course of the examination the contributions of the other authors, and thereby indicating further the extrinsic authority enjoyed by this position during the course of the centuries.

Suarez sought his legal authority in Roman and Decretal law. These sources have already been examined and found inconclusive for either of the conflicting accepted opinions. The fundamental reason for the strict territoriality of law whereby the stranger is bound by all of the

nis, 1859), II, c. XIV, nn. 2, 7; V (*De Legibus*, 1856), III, c. XXIII, nn. 2, 3. These two works will hereafter be cited as *De Virtute Religionis* and *De Legibus*.

[45] "Propria ratio est, quia lex generaliter fertur pro tali territorio."—*De Legibus*, III, c. XXIII, n. 3.

[46] Cf. Vasquez (†1604), *Commentarium ac Disputationes in Iam IIae Sancti Thomae* (ed. noviss., 4 vols., Lugduni, 1631), III, Disp. 174, c. III, nn. 28-30; Filliucius (†1622), *Quaestionum Moralium de Christianis Officiis in Casibus Conscientiae Tomi Duo* (2 vols., Lugduni, 1633-1634), I (1634), Tr. X, Pars I, c. VI, n. 198—cited hereafter as Filliucius, *Quaestiones Morales*; Pontius (†1629), *De Sacramento Matrimonii Tractatus* (2. ed., Bruxelles, 1627), Lib. V, c. IX, n. I; Arriaga (†1622), *Disputationes Theologicae in* [*Summam*] *Divi Thomae* (8 vols., Antverpiae, 1643-1655), IV (*De Legibus*, 1648), Disp. XV; Sylvius (†1649), *Commentarii in Totam Primam Secundae S. Thomae Aquinatis* (2 vols., Venetiis, 1726), II, in Q. XCVI, A. V, Quaer. IV—cited hereafter as *In Iam IIae*; Zoesius (†1627), *Commentarius in Jus Canonicum, sive ad Decretales Gregorii IX* (Venetiis, 1757), I, Tit. II, n. 31—cited hereafter as *In Jus Canonicum*; Reiffenstuel (†1703), *Theologia Moralis* (7. ed., 2 vols., Mutinae, 1714), I, Tr. II, Dist. II, Q. III, n. 25; Leurenius (†1723), *Forum Ecclesiasticum in quo Jus Canonicum Universum . . . in iis, quae Utrique Juri Canonico et Civili Communia sunt, Explanantur* (5 vols. in 3, Venetiis, 1729), I, Tit. II, Q. CXIX, n. 5—cited hereafter as *Forum Ecclesiasticum*; Billuart (wrote in 1757), *Summa Sancti Thomae* (ed. nova, 9 vols. in 8, Parisiis [no date]), II. Diss. IV, A. VIII, § IV; *Theologia Dogmatica, Polemica, Scholastica, et Moralis in Alma Universitate Wirceburgensi, Tomus Tertius, Auctore Ignatio Neubauer* (2. ed., Lutetiae Parisiorum, 1852), III, c. IV, A. IV, n. 161—cited hereafter as *Theologia Wirceburgensis*.

laws of the locality where he is traveling, is, according to Suarez,[47] derived from the very nature of law. He arrived at this conclusion by the consideration of the causes and the subject of law.

The final cause of law is the good government of the community. The good government of the community requires that strangers conform to the laws and customs of the territory. This necessary conformity cannot be juridically provided by an appeal to the natural obligation of avoiding scandal. This obligation comes from the virtue of charity; it therefore furnishes a motive for law, not its juridical force. The consideration of scandal furnishes the sufficient reason why the bishop has power to oblige all who are in his territory to obey his laws. Strangers are subject to the local legislator because it is his duty to safeguard the public peace and regulate the normal activity within his territory. The followers of Suarez[48] adopted this argumentation frequently without variation. Schmier (†1728)[49] added that the inhabitants feel more keenly the burden of their laws when they see strangers exempted from those obligations which weigh so heavily upon them. The School of Würzburg,[50] admitting the distinction of the post-glossators between territorial and personal statutes, maintained that laws were territorial by their nature because the legislator obtains his jurisdiction by reason of the territory over which he is superior.

A consideration of the efficient cause of law, the legislator, also furnished Suarez[51] with an argument for the juridical obligation of the stranger to obey all of the laws of the territory in which he was visiting. Since the legislator has the duty to preserve the good order of the territory over which he governs, and to preserve its morals, he must be endowed with sufficient jurisdiction to accomplish this duty, the

[47] *De Virtute Religionis,* II, c. XIV, nn. 10, 11; *De Legibus,* III, c. XXIII, nn. 3, 6.

[48] Cf. Lessius (†1623), *De Justitia et Jure, Ceterisque Virtutibus Libri Quatuor* (4. ed., Antverpiae, 1617), IV, c. 2, dub. vii, n. 50—cited as *De Justitia;* Zoesius, *In Jus Canonicum,* I, tit. 2, n. 33; Sylvius, *In* Iam *IIae,*Q. XCVI, A. V, Quaer. 4; Billuart, *Summa Sancti Thomae,* II, Diss. IV, A. VIII, § iv; Reiffenstuel, *Theologia Moralis,* I, Tr. II, Dist. III, Q. III, n. 25.

[49] *Jurisprudentia Canonica Civilis seu Canonicum Universum* (Venetiis, 1754), I, Tr. I, c. V, § iv, n. 180. Cited as *Jurisprudentia.*

[50] *Theologia Wirceburgensis.* III, n. 161.

[51] Cf. *De Legibus,* III, c. XXIII, n. 3.

jurisdiction to enact laws binding upon strangers. As a matter of fact, bishops are accustomed to punish strangers for not obeying their laws.[52] This argument from the exercise of legislative power was developed with examples by the followers of Suarez.[53] Schmier[54] adduced the argument that the legislator, who has the right either to permit or to refuse entrance into his territory to the stranger, justly admits him into the territory on condition that he shall observe the laws of the territory.

Further proof of the obligation on the part of the stranger to observe all the laws in force in the territory was developed by a consideration of the subject of the law.[55] Subjection in the one implies jurisdiction in the other. Strangers, it is true, are the permanent and absolute subjects of the laws of their proper territories. However, there is a transitory and relative subjection of strangers to the jurisdiction of the legislators of the place where they are traveling. Regarding the deeds he intends to perform in the territory, and regarding those things peculiar to the place where he is, the stranger can be truly said to be relatively subject to the local legislator, regardless of how brief his passage through the territory may be. Indeed, just as a brief absence suffices to withdraw him from the actual jurisdiction of his proper ordinary, in the same proportion he becomes subject to the laws of the place to which he has withdrawn. There should be a proportion between the benefit and the burden.[56] As Schmier[57] pointed out, since the stranger enjoys the benefits and privileges of the place in which he is visiting, so he should share its burdens by observing its laws. Suarez[58] concludes his defense with two observations. If not subject to the particular laws of the place where he is, the traveler would, to the detri-

[52] Cf. *De Virtute Religionis,* II, c. XIV, n. 11; *De Censuris* (*Opera Omnia,* vol. XXIII, 1861), Disp. V., Sect. V, nn. 7-8.

[53] Cf. *Theologia Wirceburgensis,* III, § II, n. 161; Zoesius, *In Jus Canonicum,* I, Tit. II, n. 33; Sylvius, *In Iam IIae,* Q. XCVI, A. V, Quaer. IV.

[54] *Jurisprudentia,* I, Tr. I, c. V, § IV, n. 174.

[55] Cf. Suarez, *De Legibus,* III, c. XXIII, n. 4; *De Virtute Religionis,* II, c. XIV, n. 18.

[56] Cf. *De Virtute Religionis,* II, c. XIV, n. 14; *De Legibus,* III, c. XXIII, n. 4; *R. J.* 55 in VI°.

[57] *Jurisprudentia,* I, Tr. I, c. V, § IV, n. 171.

[58] *De Virtute Religionis,* II, c. XIV, n. 15.

ment of his soul, not be subject to anyone except the universal legislator, or bound by any but the universal laws of the Church. Moreover, in Civil Law, the traveler is bound by the laws in force where he is visiting. The Church is a more juridically perfect society than the state. By analogy, then, the same power of binding strangers exists in the Church.

The application of the doctrine of Suarez to the universal laws of the Church and to the obligations of the vagrant followed logically and without difficulty from his general position that the stranger was bound by all of the laws in force where he was traveling. The obligation of the law begins to urge when the stranger is in the territory during the time specified in the law for its fulfillment. A negative obligation, which binds at all times (*semper et pro semper*), must be complied with at the moment when the stranger enters the territory. A positive obligation does not bind the stranger unless he has remained in the territory during the whole time allowed in the law for its fulfillment.[59]

The arguments advanced by Suarez and his followers justify the conclusion that the stranger can be bound by the laws of the place where he is, but not the universal conclusion that he is bound by all the local laws. His doctrine was popular in the XVII Century, and found many supporters of weighty authority in the XVIII Century. But in the XIX Century it was practically abandoned, being supported only by the School of Würzburg and Bouquillon (†1902),[60] who developed his doctrine in the United States where the principle of strict territoriality of law was in vogue among the civil jurists.

§ 2. *Doctrine that the Stranger is Not Generally Bound by the Laws of the Place where he is Traveling*

The doctrine of the later decretalists, namely, that the traveler is not directly bound to observe the laws of his place of temporary residence, had as one of its first defenders after the Council of Trent, Dominicus

59 Cf. *De Virtute Religionis,* II, c. XIV, nn. 18-22.

60 *Theologia Moralis Fundamentalis* (2. ed., Brugis, 1890) nn. 148-150.

Soto (†1560),[61] the moralist. Bartholomew Medina (†1580)[62] stated the defect of jurisdiction on the part of the legislator as the reason why the stranger is not bound by the laws of the place where he is. Azor (†1603-1608)[63] enumerated as sources of jurisdiction, delict, real possessions, contract, and domicile, and concluded that outside of these the legislator has no jurisdiction over the stranger. The great moralist and canonist, Thomas Sanchez (†1610)[64] along with his contemporary, Paul Laymann (†1635)[65] were the first to give a complete and comprehensive treatment of this doctrine. Their treatment will be followed in the exposition of the defense of this doctrine, noting upon occasion the contributions of other moralists and canonists who, in increasing numbers, defended the same position.

The direct source of the obligations of particular law and subjection to local jurisdiction was considered to be domicile or quasi-domicile. Domicile was acquired by permanent residence, either established by ten years of actual residence, or by arrival in a territory with the intention of remaining there permanently. Quasi-domicile was acquired by residence in a place for the greater part of the year.[66] Those persons who were in a territory for less than the greater part of the year were not directly bound by the local laws.

The juridical authority for this position was also chiefly sought in

[61] *Commentarium in Quartum Sententiarum* (2 vols., Venetiis, 1569), I, in IV, D. XVIII, Q. IV, A. II, § *Est hic tamen.*

[62] *Expositio in Iam IIae Angelici Doctoris D. Thomae Aquinatis* (Venetiis, 1590), Q. XCVIII, A. VI, *ad ultimum argumentum Cajetani,* p. 517.

[63] *Institutionum Moralium Pars Prima* (2. ed., Brixiae, 1617), V, c. XI, col. 496.

[64] *De Sancto Matrimonii Sacramento* (Antwerpiae, 1626), III, Disp. XVIII; *Opus Morale in Praecepta Decalogi* (2 vols., Parmae, 1723), I, Tr. IV, *De Legibus,* c. XII. Hereafter cited as *De Matrimonio* and *Opus Morale.*

[65] *Theologia Moralis in V Libros Distributa* (ed. Prima Patavia, 5 vols. in 2, Patavii, 1733), I, Tr. IV, cap. XI. Cited hereafter as *Theologia Moralis.*

[66] Cf. Sanchez, *De Matrimonio,* III, Disp. XVIII, n. 9; Laymann, *Theologia Moralis,* I, Tr. IV, c. XI, nn. 1, 2; Schmalzgrueber (†1735), *Jus Ecclesiasticum Universum* (5 vols. in 12, Romae, 1843-1845), I, Pars I, Tit. II, Q. VI, n. 42. For the historical development of this concept, cf. Costello, *Domicile and Quasi-Domicile,* pp. 1-26.

the legislative sources before the Council of Trent.[67] The fundamental point upon which the whole defense of this position depends is the defect of jurisdiction on the part of the legislator. A brief survey of the arguments proposed by the main defenders[68] of this doctrine will bear this out.

[67] Cf. Sanchez, *De Matrimonio,* III, Disp. XVIII, nn. 6, 7; Laymann, *Theologia Moralis,* I, Tr. IV, c. XI, n. 6; Diana (†1663), *Resolutiones Morales* (8. ed., Lugduni, 1635), Pars I, Tr. X, *De ieiunio,* Res. II; Schmalzgrueber, *Jus Ecclesiasticum Universum,* I, Pars I, Tit. II, Q. VI, n. 2; St. Alphonsus De Ligorio (†1787), *Theologia Moralis* (nova ed., 2 vols., Vesuntione, 1828), I, Tr. II, dub. II, n. 156; Engel (†1674), *Collegium Universum Juris Canonici* (9. ed., Venetiis, 1760), I, Tit. II, § III, n. 33; Böckhn (†1752), *Commentarius in Jus Canonicum Universum* (5 vols. in 3, Salisburgi-Parisiis, 1776), I, Tit. II, § III, n. 54—cited as Böckhn, *In Jus Canonicum.*

[68] Cf. Sanchez, *De Matrimonio,* III, Disp. XVIII, n. 7; *Opus Morale,* I, Tr. IV, c. XII, n. 38; Laymann, *Theologia Moralis,* I, Tr. IV, c. XI, n. 4; Diana,*Resolutiones Morales,* Pars I, Tr. IX, Res. II; De Lugo (†1660), *Disputationes Scholasticae et Morales* (nova ed., 8 vols., J. B. Fournials, Parisiis: Vivès, 1868-1869), VIII, Lib. VI, dub. XXII, n. 5—cited as De Lugo, *Disputationes Morales*; Coninck (†1633), *Commentarium in Universam Doctrinam D. Thomae, De Sacramentis et Censuris* (2. ed., 2 vols., Antverpiae, 1619), I, Q. 74, A. VIII, dub. 3, n. 111—cited hereafter as Coninck, *De Sacramentis et Censuris;* Bonacina (†1631), *Operum de Morali Theologia* (3 vols., Venetiis, 1687), II, Disp. I, Q. I, punct. VI, n. 36; Pirhing (†1678-1681 ?), *Jus Canonicum Nova Methodo Explicatum* (5 vols. in 4, Dilingae, 1674-1678), V, Tit. XXXIV, Sec. II, n. 29; I, Tit. II, Sec. I, § VI, n. 55—cited as Pirhing, *Jus Canonicum*; Gibalini (†1671), *Scientia Canonica* (7 vols. in 2, Lugduni, 1670), IV, Q. VI, § IX. n. 14; Felix Cajetanus Veranus (†1713), *Juris Canonici Universi Commentarius* (3 vols., Monachii, 1703), I, Tit. II, § IX, n. 14; Lacroix (†1714), *Theologia Moralis, Postremo vero Multis Locupletata et Studiosis Proposita a R. P. Francisco Antonio Zacharia* (3 vols., Ravenna-Venetiis, 1771), I, c. II, dub. III, n. 685—cited hereafter as Lacroix, *Theologia Moralis*; Cozza (†1729), *Tractatus Dogmatico-moralis de Jejunio Ecclesiastico in Tres Partes Distributus* (Romae, 1724), Pars III, dub. I, n. 11—cited hereafter as Cozza, *De Jejunio*; Pichler (†1736), *Jus Canonicum Secundum Quinque Decretalium Titulos Gregorii Papae IX* (2 vols., Venetiis, 1741), I, Tit. II, § V, n. 54—cited hereafter as Pichler, *Jus Canonicum*; Böckhn, *In Jus Canonicum,* I, Tit. II, § III, n. 51; Salmanticenses (1655-1724), *Cursus Theologiae Moralis* (6 vols., Venetiis, 1728), III, Tr. XI, c. III, punct. V, § 1, nn. 58, 61; De Ligorio, *Theologia Moralis,* I, Tr. II, dub. II, n. 156; Zallinger (†1813), *Institutiones Iuris Ecclesiastici* (5 vols., Romae, 1823), I, Tr. II, § 151, II; Santi (†1885),*Praelectiones Juris Canonici Juxta Ordinem Decretalium Gregorii IX* (2 vols., Ratisbonae, Neo Eboraci et Cincinatii, 1886), I, Tit. II, n. 34—cited as *Praelectiones Juris Canonici*; Aertenys (†1896), *Theologia Moralis Secundum Doctrinam S. Alfonsi de*

Although, as Saurez maintained, laws are territorial by their nature, Sanchez held that they are not so strictly territorial that a brief visit in the territory is sufficient to render the traveler obliged to observe them. A brief presence in the territory is considered in law as no presence at all.[69] As a matter of fact, a bishop cannot, outside of necessity, exercise voluntary jurisdiction, such as the administration of the sacraments other than Penance and Holy Eucharist, assist at marriages, grant dispensations, and the like, in favor of strangers.[70] Barbosa (†1649)[71] and Bargilliat (†1926),[72] again in the XX Century, state that the jurisdiction of particular legislators is restricted by its nature to the proper subjects of the legislator. The reason to support this statement that only the members of the community are subject to the particular legislator was first developed by Laymann,[73] and improved by Böckhn.[74] A community is a kind of a mystical and permanent body, drawn together for the sake of mutual help in attaining a common objective. Hence the moral bond, uniting them, has a permanence and stability peculiar to itself. A passing stranger does not enter into this stable and permanent union; he is not concerned with the particular objective of the community. Therefore he does not become subject to the laws promoting this union, or to the authority maintaining this moral bond. Génicot[75] and Lehmkuhl (†1917)[76] used this argument in the XIX Century.

Ligorio (7. ed. aucta et emendata, 2 vols., Paderbornae, 1906), I, n. 167—cited as Aertenys, *Theologia Moralis;* Tanquerey (†1932), *Synopsis Theologiae Moralis et Pastoralis* (3. ed., 2 vols., Neo-Eboraci, Cincinnati, Chicagiae, 1907), II, n. 290 (d) —cited as Tanquerey, *Theologia Moralis.*

[69] *Opus Morale,* Lib. I, c. XII, n. 38. Cf. D (32, 1) 78.

[70] Cf. Sanchez, *Opus Morale, l.c.*; *De Matrimonio,* Lib. III, Disp. XXIII, n. 11; Gibalini, *Scientia Canonica,* Lib. IV, c. VIII, Q. VI, § V.

[71] *Collectanea Doctorum tam Veterum quam Recentorum, in Jus Pontificium Universum* (5 vols. in 4, Lugduni, 1656), in c. 2, X, *de observatione ieiuniorum,* III, 46, n. 6; in c. 21, X, *de sententia excommunicationis,* V, 39, n. 2—cited hereafter as *Collectanea Doctorum.*

[72] *Praelectiones Juris Canonici* (24. ed., 2 vols., Parisiis, 1907), I, Tr. I, A. III, n. 65.

[73] *Theologia Moralis,* I, Tr. IV, c. XI, n. 1.

[74] *In Jus Canonicum,* I, Lib. I, Tit. II, § III, n. 52, *ratio* iii.

[75] *Theologia Moralis Institutiones* (2 vols., Lovanii, 1896), I, Tr. III, n. 96.

[76] *Theologia Moralis* (11. ed., 2 vols., Friburgi Brisgoviae, 1910), I, Tr. II, A. III, § 3, n. 235.

The argument from the elimination of the various titles of jurisdiction, domicile and quasi-domicile, real possessions, delicts, and contracts was further developed by Cozza[77] and Busembaum (†1668),[78] whose followers, Ballerini and Palmieri,[79] presented it in the XIX Century. Finally, arguments from equity were appealed to by Gonzales-Tellez (†1649).[80] He pointed out that the stranger could easily be presumed ignorant of the particular statutes of a territory in which he had just arrived. Moreover, it would be insisting on too great a burden to require a traveler to observe all of the various laws of the different territories through which his journey might lead him.[81]

Proceeding against the main argument of Suarez, that the good government of a territory required that the stranger observe all the laws locally in force, it was pointed out that the good government of the territory was sufficiently provided for by the natural obligation of avoiding scandal and certain other indirect obligations admitted by Sanchez and his followers. In fact, the examples of the actual exercise of jurisdiction over strangers are only examples of special cases directed against scandal or the like.[82] The argument from the proportion which should exist between the benefits received and the burden supported is valid only when there is a necessary and intrinsic relation between the benefit and the burden.[83] Finally, Böckhn[84] noted that the statement

[77] *De Jejunio,* Pars III, dub. I, n. 11.

[78] *Medulla Theologiae Moralis* (2 vols., ed. ult., S. Congr. de Prop. Fide, Tornaci, 1865), I, Tr. II, c. II, dub. III.

[79] *Opus Theologicum Morale in Busembaum Medullam* (3. ed., 7 vols., Prati, 1898-1893), I, Tr. III, c. II, dub. III, n. 361.

[80] *Commentaria Perpetua in Singulos Textus Quinque Librorum Decretalium Gregorii IX* (5 vols. in 4, Venetiis, 1649), V, Tit. 39, c. 21, n. 4.

[81] Cf. Cozza, *De Jejunio,* Pars III, dub. I, n. 9; Coninck, *De Sacramentis et Censuris,* I, Q. 74, A. VIII, dub. 3, n. 111.

[82] Cf. Sanchez, *Opus Morale,* I, Tr. IV, c. XII, n. 38; Laymann, *Theologia Moralis,* I, Tr. IV, c. XI, n. 5; Schmalzgrueber, *Jus Ecclesiasticum Universum,* I, Pars I, Tit. II, § VI, n. 42; Pichler, *Jus Canonicum,* I, Tit. II, § V, n. 54; Böckhn, *In Jus Canonicum,* I, Tit. II, § III, n. 54; Salmanticenses, *Cursus Moralis,* III, Tr. XI, c. III. punct. V, § I, n. 61.

[83] Cf. Sanchez, *Opus Morale,* I, Tr. IV, c. XII, n. 38; Laymann, *Theologia Moralis,* I, Tr. IV, c. XI, n. 5; Cozza, *De Jejunio,* Pars III, dub. I, n. 16, Böckhn, *In Jus Canonicum,* I, Tit. II, § III, n. 52.

[84] *In Jus Canonicum,* I, Lib. I, Tit. II, § III, nn. 52, 54.

that the legislator admits the traveler into his territory only on condition that the latter shall observe the local laws is a gratuitous statemen contrary to the complete enumeration of the four titles of jurisdiction.

Thus the position which opposed that of Suarez, and which was first completely developed, upon the basis of the defect of jurisdiction, by Sanchez and Laymann, became increasingly more common until it was almost the unanimous doctrine of the XIX and XX Centuries before the promulgation of the Code of Canon Law. Like that of Suarez, it was based upon the nature of law itself. Law, however, was not considered, by these authors, to be strictly territorial. Because strangers were not members of the community, the local legislator had no direct jurisdiction over them. They were not directly subject to local laws.

§ 3. *Applications of the Doctrine of Sanchez to Exceptional Obligations of the Stranger, to Universal Law, and to the Vagrant*

In coming to the conclusion that the stranger was not directly bound by the laws of the place where he was visiting, Sanchez and his followers left room for certain juridical obligations, certain quasi-exceptions to their rule, whereby the stranger would be bound by certain laws because of an extrinsic and accidental consideration. In these cases of indirect and extrinsic titles of subjection, the legislator could not only make laws directly comprehending the stranger, but, when the case was clear, the stranger was bound by the law anyway.[85] These cases of indirect obligations were classed under the headings of contracts, delicts, real possessions, similarity of laws in both territories, and the special good of the territory.

In the matter of contracts, Laymann[86] held that the stranger could avail himself of the local laws or not as he wished. The remainder of the partisans of this general view, following Sanchez,[87] unanimously

[85] Cf. Pichler, *Jus Canonicum,* I, Tit. II, § V, n. 55; Bonacina, *Operum de Morali Theologia,* II, Disp. I, Q. I, punct. VI, n. 36.

[86] *Theologia Moralis,* I, Tr. IV, c. XI, n. 5.

[87] Cf. Sanchez, *Opus Morale,* I, Tr. IV, c. XII, n. 36; *De Matrimonio,* III, Disp. XVIII, n. 10; Coninck, *De Sacramentis et Censuris,* I, Q. 74, A. VIII, Dist. III, n.

held that the law of the place regulated the solemnities of contracts which were entered into in the territory. Equally unanimous was the doctrine that the laws respecting real property bound all those whose actions in any way were connected with it juridically: thus the maxim of the *lex rei sitae* was accepted both as a norm for determining judicial competence and a title of subjection to local laws.[88] The obligation of the law directly falls upon the thing, and indirectly upon the person, whether he is an inhabitant or a visitor.

Less unanimity was enjoyed by the views holding for other indirect obligations. When the law of the place imposed the same obligations as that of a particular law in his own proper territory, the stranger was still obliged to observe it according to the early proponents of the doctrine of the direct exemption of the traveler.[89] They could find no cause for exemption in this case, since the same obligation existed in both the proper territory and the territory where the stranger was traveling. However, this position was later shown to be inconsistent, and was rejected universally before the Code. The obligation of the laws of his own territory did not bind the traveler beyond his own territory. And there was no title, from the fact that the law was similar to one in his own territory, by which the legislator could bind the traveler in the territory where he was visiting.[90]

116; Bonacina, *Operum de Morali Theologia,* II, Disp. I, Q. I, punct. VI, n. 38; Barbosa, *Collectanea Doctorum,* in c. 21, X, *de sententia excommunicationis,* V, 39, n. 2; Pichler, *Jus Caninicum,* I, Tit. II, § V, n. 54; De Ligorio, *Theologia Moralis,* I, Tr. II, dub. II, n. 156; Ferraris (†1763), *Prompta Bibliotheca Canonica, Iuridica, Moralis, Theologica, necnon Ascetica, Polemica, Rubricistica, Historica* (ed. novissima, 9 vols., Romae, 1885-1889), V (1889), v°. *lex,* Art. III, n. 34—cited hereafter as *Prompta Bibliotheca*; Ojetti (†1932), *Synopsis Rerum Moralium et Iuris Pontificii Alphabetico Ordine Digesta* (Romae, 1909), v° *peregrinus,* p. 381. Cited hereafter as *Synopsis.*

[88] Cf. Laymann, *Theologia Moralis,* I, Tr. IV, c. XI, n. 7; Bonacina, *Operum de Morali Theologia,* II, Disp. I, Q. I, punct. IV, nn. 38, 51; Pirhing, *Jus Canonicum,* II, Tit. II, Sec. I, § v, n. 55.

[89] Cf. Laymann, *Theologia Moralis,* I, Tr. IV, c. XII, n. 3; Sanchez, *De Matrimonio,* III, Disp. XVIII, n. 3; Pirhing, *Jus Canonicum,* II, II, Tit. II, Sec. I, § IV, n. 34; Salmanticenses, *Cursus Moralis,* Tr. XI, c. III, n. 69; De Ligorio, *Theologia Moralis,* I, I, Tr. II, dub. II, n. 156.

[90] Cf. Diana, *Resolutiones Morales,* Pars I, Tr. X, Res. XV; Böckhn, *In Jus Canonicum,* I, I, Tit. II, § III, n. 54; Pichler, *Jus Canonicum,* I, Tit. II, § V, n. 54;

Considering the decretal *A nobis,* it was generally accepted that the term *ratione delicti* applied only to determine judicial competence when the delinquent was already bound by the penal law in question.[91] The question then naturally arose: when is the stranger bound by penal laws? The general answer to this question was that strangers are not bound by penal laws, both because of the lack of jurisdiction on the part of the particular legislator, and because of the probable ignorance on the part of the stranger.[92] Those penal laws which did bind the stranger were to be determined by the other titles of indirect subjection.

The unanimous opinion of the moralists and canonists, who held the stranger directly exempt from the laws of the place where he was, recognized an indirect obligation binding the stranger to comply with those laws whose observance was *especially* necessary for the public good of the place; whose violation would bring special harm to the social order.

Sanchez[93] expresses this indirect obligation negatively, saying that the stranger is not bound unless his transgression results in harm to the community. Laymann[94] presented it positively, stating that the stran-

Gury (†1866), *Compendium Theologiae Moralis* (ed. Romana, 2 vols., Romae, 1872), I, Tr. *De Legibus,* Pars I, c. II, Art. II, n. 95, 6°; Ballerini-Palmieri, *Opus Theologiae Moralis in Busembaum Medullam,* I, Tr. III, c. II, dub. III, n. 362; Génicot, *Theologia Moralis,* I, Tr. III, c. II, n. 96.

[91] Cf. De Lugo, *Disputationes Morales,* VIII, Lib. VI, dub. XXII, nn. 5, 6; Barbosa, *Collectanea Doctorum,* in c. 21, X, *de sententia excommunicationis,* V, 38, n. 2; Pirhing, *Jus Canonicum,* I, Tit. II, § V, n. 54; Böckhn, *In Jus Canonicum,* I, Tit. II, § III, n. 52; Zallinger, *Institutiones Juris Canonici,* I, Tr. II, § 153.

[92] Cf. Engel, *Collegium Universum Juris Canonici,* V, Tit. XXXIX, § II, n. 34; Bonacina, *Operum de Morali Theologia,* I, Disp. I, Q. I, punct. XI, n. 20; Busembaum, *Medulla Theologiae Moralis,* VIII, c. I, dub. 3, resp. II; Santi, *Praelectiones Iuris Canonici,* V, Tit. XXXIV, n. 18; Ballerini-Palmieri, *Opus Theologiae Moralis in Busembaum Medullam,* VII, n. 50; Bargilliat, *Praelectiones Juris Canonici,* II, n. 1552.

[93] " . . . nisi legum transgressio cederet in damnum illius oppidi."—*De Matrimonio,* III, Dist. XVIII, n. 14.

[94] "Leges quae specialiter feruntur ad bonum et utilitatem talis reipublicae vel ad pacificam communicationem cum incolis . . . "—*Theologia Moralis,* I, Tr. IV, c. XII, n. 4.

ger is bound by laws which are made especially for the good and utility of the republic or for peaceful communication with the inhabitants.

Sanchez[95] appeals to the authority of Bartolus and the civilists for his position. Examples of these laws were most frequently taken from cases common to Civil Law, such as taxes and customs, prohibition to bear arms, local prices for commodities, and forbidden commerce.[96] Bonacina states that it would be unjust to allow the stranger to cause harm in the territory through which he is passing.[97]

The positive approach of Laymann was destined to become the more favored one. Cajetanus Felix[98] classes such laws as laws immediately concerning the public good. When the activity of the stranger falls within the extension of such laws, it falls on matter directly pertaining to the local authority. Thus, though directly exempt, the stranger becomes subject to the local legislative power by reason of the matter upon which his acts fall. Other authors used the arguments of Suarez to demonstrate the reason for this exceptional obligation of the stranger, the correlation of the benefit and the burden to be supported, and the implied condition of the observance of such laws for permission to enter the territory.[99] Pirhing notes that these laws must have the *special* good of the territory, its *special* utility and tranquillity, the *special* peaceful commerce of the territory at stake before the stranger is obliged to observe them.[100] This positive approach, with emphasis upon the *special* necessity of these laws for the public good, the *tranquillity* and *security* of the community, was the common manner of expressing this exceptional obligation in the XIX Century.[101]

[95] *De Matrimonio,* III, Dist. XVIII, n. 14.

[96] Cf. Gibalini, *Scientia Canonica,* IV, Q. VI, § V; La Croix, *Theologia Moralis,* I c. II, dub. III, n. 685; Pichler, *Jus Canonicum,* I, Tit. II, § V, n. 54; De Ligoro, *Theologia Moralis,* I, Tr. II, c. II. dub. III, n. 160; Coninck, *De Sacramentis et Censuris,* I, Q. 74, A. VIII, dub. 3. n. 116.

[97] *Operum de Morali Theologia,* II, Disp. I, Q. I., punct. VI, n. 53.

[98] *Juris Canonici Universi Commentarius,* I, Tit. II, § IX, n. 9.

[99] Cf. Engel,*Collegium Universum Juris Canonici,* I, Tit. II, § III, n. 32; Böckhn, *In Jus Canonicum,* I, Tit. II, § III, n. 32.

[100] *Jus Canonicum,* II, Tit. II, Sect. I, § IV, n. 34.

[101] Cf. Santi, *Praelectiones Juris Canonici,* Lib. I, Tit. II, n. 34; Gury, *Compendium Theologiae Moralis,* I, Pars I, c. II, A. II, n. 95; Ballerini-Palmieri, *Opus Theologiae Moralis in Busembaum Medullam,* I, Tr. III, n. 202; Sabetti, *Compendium*

Notable is the recurrence to examples taken from Civil Law, as though the more tangible material conditions of such laws in the secular realm furnished norms for analogical application in the supernatural realm of the Church. It was during this later period, it will be recalled, that the civil jurists were occupying themselves with a similar problem under the leadership of Mancini. They had characterized these laws as laws of social necessity, social conservation, laws necessary for the security of the place and public order.[102] That these efforts of the civil jurists of the XIX Century went unnoticed by the canonists and moralists is hard to suppose. The terms of the civilists themselves began to appear in the canonical and moral books. De Angelis (†1881)[103] and Tanquerey, who depended upon the notes of Many for this point,[104] speak of the obligation of the stranger to submit to those statutes made in view of the common security of the place, and of the public order.[105] Marc[106] speaks of the obligation imposed on all in the territory because of public security and the public order. Bargilliat, in an edition just prior to the Code,[107] holds the stranger bound to obey laws necessary for public order.

Thus those who followed Sanchez in directly exempting the stranger from the obligations of the local laws, considered him obliged to observe those laws which were *especially* necessary for the public good, the *security* of the place, or as a few XIX Century authors expressed it, which were necessary for the *public order* of the territory.

After treating the obligation of particular law, the question arises whether this same exemption of the stranger applied to the obligation

Theologiae Moralis (3.ed. ab auctore recognita ad normam Conc. Plen. Balt. III atque recentiorum Congr. Rom. decretorum, Neo-Eboraci et Cincinnati, 1888), Tr. III, c. IV, n. 80; Génicot, *Theologiae Moralis Institutiones*, I, n. 96; Ojetti, *Synopsis*, v°. *peregrinus*, p. 381; Lehmkuhl, *Theologia Moralis*, Tr. II, A. III, § III, n. 235.

[102] Cf. *supra*, p. 43.

[103] "Et responsio est non teneri [peregrinum], quia non est subditus, nisi leges positae sint pro *securitate* locorum, quia superior debet attendere ne *ordo publicus* detrimentum capiat."—*Praelectiones Juris Canonici* (4 vols. in 8, Romae-Parisiis, 1877-1887), I, Tit. II, n. 13.

[104] Cf. Van Hove, "Leges quae ordini publico consulunt,"—*ETL*, I (1924), 155.

[105] *Synopsis Theologiae Moralis et Pastoralis*, II, n. 290 (d).

[106] *Institutiones Morales Alphonsianae* (2 vols., Romae, 1885), I, n. 204.

[107] *Praelectiones Juris Canonici* (ed. 1907), I, Tr. I, c. IV, n. 65.

of universal law if it was in force in the place where the traveler actually was, but not in force in his proper territory. The decretalists did not expressly treat this problem. Sanchez in his earlier work, *De Sancto Matrimonii Sacramento,*[108] held that it did apply, because of the fiction that he who was present only for a brief time was as though not present at all. He later abandoned this position, however, since the fiction cannot be supported. The abrogation of the law in the place of domicile or quasi-domicile is a limitation on the exercise of the universal legislative jurisdiction and an exception to the universal law. It is therefore to be interpreted strictly. Fictions, on the other hand, are not juridical unless expressed in the law. Therefore the abrogation of the universal law is not to be extended to the traveler going from a place where it is abrogated to a place where it is in full force. The stranger is bound by all of the universal laws in force in the place where he is traveling.[109] This position was practically unanimously adopted before the Code.[110]

The preceding determinations of the obligations of the stranger applied to him who had a domicile or quasi-domicile elsewhere. It finally remained to investigate the obligations of him who had no domicile or quasi-domicile, the vagrant.

Sanchez[111] held that the same principles developed in regard to the peregrin did not apply to the vagrant. The vagrant was bound to observe all of the laws in force where he happened to be, for not having a domicile or quasi-domicile, he could obtain the benefits of a proper territory only in that place where he actually was. In matters involving judicial jurisdiction, vagrants could be cited wherever they were. By analogy, then, they should be considered bound by the laws in force where they were. And, if they were not bound by the laws of the place

[108] III, Disp. XVIII, n. 7.

[109] Cf. *Opus Morale,* I, Tr. IV, c. XII, n. 39.

[110] Cf. Laymann, *Theologia Moralis,* I, Tr. IV, c. XII, n. 3; Bonacina, *Operum de Morali Theologia,* II, Disp. I, Disp. I, Q. I, punct. VI, n. 55; Busembaum, *Medulla Theologiae Moralis,* I, Tr. II, c. II, dub. III, Schmalzgrueber, *Jus Ecclesiasticum,* I, Pars. I, Tit. II, Q. VI, n. 42; Böckhn, *In Jus Canonicum,* I, Lib. I, Tit. II § III, n. 5; Ferraris, *Prompta Bibliotheca,* V, v°. *Lex,* A. III, n. 48; Ojetti, *Synopsis,* v°. *peregrinus,* p. 381; Lehmkuhl, *Theologia Moralis,* I, n. 233.

[111] *De Matrimonio,* III, Disp. XVIII, n. 16.

where they were, they would be exempt from every particular law, and, to the detriment of their souls, subject only to the Holy Father in matters of voluntary jurisdiction.[112] This position found supporters even up to the Code.[113]

Laymann[114] inclined towards the application of the same principles to the vagrant as to the peregrin, with, however, considerable hesitation. Böckhn[115] demonstrated that there was no juridical basis for the distinction between the principles of the obligations of the vagrant and of the peregrin. The spiritual welfare of the vagrant was sufficiently provided for by universal law and the indirect obligations of particular law. There was the same defect of jurisdiction on the part of the particular legislator, and the vagrant was no more a member of the community than the peregrin. His was the common opinion of the XVII Century and gained in supporters until the promulgation of the Code.[116]

Thus the position which was almost unanimous before the Code, the position of Sanchez and Laymann, was developed and applied to indirect obligations and to specific questions such as the obligation of universal law and the obligation of the vagrant. There was final unanimity among its interpreters on all of these applications except the obligation of the vagrant, which remained a disputed point until the question was settled in the Code.

[112] Cf. *Opus Morale*, Lib. I, Tr. IV, c. XII, n. 25.

[113] Cf. Diana, *Resolutiones Morales*, Pars I, Tr. IX, Res. II; Cozza, *De Jejunio*, Pars III, dub. II; D'Annibale (†1896), *Summula Theologiae Moralis* (3. ed., 3 vols., Romae, 1891), I, n. 205; Noldin (†1922), *Summa Theologiae Moralis* (3 vols., Oeniponte, 1905), II, n. 125.

[114] *Theologia Moralis*, Lib. I, Tr. IV, c. XII, n. 7.

[115] *In Jus Canonicum*, II, Tit. II, § III, n. 55.

[116] Cf. La Croix,*Theologia Moralis*, Lib. I, c. II, dub. III, n. 685; Pichler, *Jus Canonicum*, Lib. I, Tit. II, § V, n. 55; Busembaum, *Medulla Theologiae Moralis*, I, Lib. I, Tr. II, c. II, dub. III, De Ligorio, *Theologia Moralis*, I, Lib. I, Tr. II, c. II, dub. II, n. 156; Schmalzgrueber, *Jus Ecclesiasticum Universum*, I, Pars I, Tit. II, Q. VI, n. 42; Gury, *Compendium Theologiae Moralis*, I, Tr. *De Legibus*, A. II, Q. III, n. 94; Marc, *Institutiones Theologiae Moralis*, I, n. 204; Génicot, *Theologiae Moralis Institutiones*, I, n. 96; Bargilliat, *Praelectiones Juris Canonici*, I, n. 66; Ojetti, *Synopsis*, v°. *vagus*, p. 620; Lehmkuhl, *Theologia Moralis*, I, n. 235; Tanquerey, *Theologia Moralis*, II, n. 291.

ARTICLE III. DOCTRINE REGARDING THE ABSENT SUBJECT

§ 1. *Doctrine of the General Exemption of the Absent Subject from the Particular Laws of His Own Territory*

Although the doctrine concerning the traveler was keenly contested in regard to his obligation towards the laws of the place where he was, the fundamental position taken by both sides was that the nature and purpose of law had in view only the territory for which it was made. When the traveler was considered in relation to the place which he had left, the place of his domicile or quasi-domicile, the controversy ceased. Since the law of a territory was made only for the good government of that territory, then those who were absent from the territory were outside of the purpose of the law and the extension of its obligation. Thus the two positions which were examined in the previous article converge in the considerations of this article.

Soto[117] and Bartholomew Medina,[118] however, held that the traveler was bound by the laws of his place of residence, for while physically absent, he was still reputed to be a citizen of his proper territory, and still remained an inhabitant of the place. Navarrus,[119] Emanuel Sa[120] and Covarruvias[121] rejected this position, subjecting the traveler to the laws which were in force where he actually was, according to their interpretation of the teaching of St. Augustine, and of the decretal *Ut animarum.*

The jurisprudential arguments were first completely developed by Suarez[122] and Sanchez.[123] The legislator could not bind the traveler outside of his territory, for legislative jurisdiction is limited to the territory

[117] *Commentarium in Quartum Sententiarum,* Dist. XVIII, Q. IV, A. II, § *Est hic tamen.*

[118] *Expositio in Iam IIae Angelici Doctoris D. Thomae Aquinatis,* Q. XCVIII, A. VI, *ad ult. arg. Cajetani.*

[119] *Enchiridion sive Manuale Confessariorum et Poenitentium,* c. XIII, n. 5; c. XXIII, n. 120.

[120] *Aphorismi,* v°. *festum,* n. 8; v°. *jejunium,* nn. 4, 5.

[121] *Commentarii in Bonifacii VIII Librum VIum,* Pars I, *Relect.* c. *Alma Mater,* § 10, n. 3.

[122] *De Legibus,* III, c. XXIII, n. 4.

[123] *De Matrimonio,* III, Disp. XVII, n. 18; *Opus Morale,* I, Tr. IV, c. XII, n. 26.

for which it is exercised. Laws of themselves and directly regard the territory for which they are made. A particular legislator has under his government only the territory entrusted to him. Therefore the statutes of an inferior legislator are made only for the peace and benefit of that territory.[124] Pirhing states that the statutes of particular legislators do not bind outside of their territories to avoid confusion in the order of jurisdiction.[125] Leurenius bases the territorial limitation of particular laws upon their stability and perpetuity, for they must have a corresponding perpetual and stable sphere of activity.[126] Arriaga applies the argument deduced from the corporate nature of the community. The common bond of a community consists in the community of living, by which all living in the same place, seek, in mutual and proximate interdependence, their common good. To withdraw from this proximity and community of life is to withdraw from the necessity of mutual dependence and from the common bond and special obligations arising therefrom.[127]

The reason for the exemption of the traveler from the obligations of the laws of his own territory was also derived from the territorial nature of law, whether this is derived from the limitation of the power of the legislator, or from the final cause of the law.[128]

§ 2. *Special Applications of This Doctrine*

The development of the principle in the decretals *A nobis* and *Ut animarum* presented a difficulty in the application of the exemption of

[124] Cf. Saurez, *De Legibus,* III, c. XXIII, n. 4; *De Virtute Religionis,* II, c. XIII, n. 2; Sanchez, *Opus Morale,* I, c. XII; Laymann, *Theologia Moralis,* I, Tr. IV, c. XI; Zoesius, *In Jus Canonicum,* I, Tit. II, n. 31; Bonacina, *Operum De Morali Theologia,* II, Disp. I, Q. I, punct. I, n. 59; Barbosa, *Collectanea Doctorum,* I. n. c. 2, *de constitutionibus,* I, 2, in VI°, n. 10; Schmier, *Jurisprudentia,* I, Tit. I, c. V. § IV, n. 160; Schmalzgrueber, *Jus Ecclesiasticum Universum,* I, Pars I, Tit. II, 2. VI, n. 41.

[125] *Jus Canonicum,* V, Tit. XXXIX, Sect. II, n. 29.

[126] *Forum Ecclesiasticum,* I, Tit. II, Q. CXIV, n. 1.

[127] *Disputationes Theologicae in* [*Summam*] *Divi Thomae,* IV, Disp. XV, Sec. II, nn. 7-8.

[128] Cf. Billuart, *Summa Sancti Thomae,* II, Disp. IV, A. VIII, § IV, dic. 1°; De Angelis, *Praelectiones Juris Canonici,* I, Tit. II, n. 1; Santi, *Praelectiones Juris Canonici,* I, Tit. II, n. 33; Ballerini-Palmieri, *Opus Theologiae Moralis in Busembaum Medullam,* I, n. 177.

the absent subject to the penal laws of his own territory. However, this difficulty was solved by the use of the distinction, received from the middle ages, between precepts and laws. A precept directly affects the person, and therefore can bind outside of the territory. A law takes its effect in and through the territory. It cannot bind outside of the territory. If the particular laws do not bind outside of the territory, then neither can the censures attached to them be incurred outside of the territory.[129]

The doctrine of the decretalists was again applied to the question of juridical absence from the territory. When the subject, although physically absent, caused harm in his own territory by the violation of its laws, he was considered by a fiction to be morally present. Thus an affirmative precept requiring something done in the territory bound the absent subject, because its violation affected the territory. It was required that the person, the act, and the object of the act be simultaneously outside of the territory before the subject was considered exempt from the obligation.[130]

Just as in the middle ages, the question arose whether the exempt places of religious were juridically outside the diocese. Though physically within the diocese, these places did not come completely under episcopal jurisdiction. The first reaction was to consider diocesan subjects exempt from diocesan law while within the exempt places of regulars.[131]

Suarez[132] required complete exemption from episcopal jurisdiction before such an exempt place could be considered sufficiently outside

[129] Cf. Suarez, *De Censuris*, Disp. V, Sect. V, nn. 10, 15; Zoesius, *In Jus Canonicum*, I, Tit. II, n. 31; Lessius, *De Justitia*, IV, c. II, dub. VII, n. 50; Schmier, *Jurisprudentia*, I, Tr. I, c. V, § IV, n. 193; Böckhn, *In Jus Canonicum*, I, Tit. II, § III, n. 45.

[130] Suarez, *De Legibus*, III, c. XXII, n. 8; Leurenius, *Forum Ecclesiasticum*, I, Tit. II, Q. CXIV, n. 2; Barbosa, *Collectanea Doctorum*, V, Tit. XXXIX, c. XXI, n. 2; Santi, *Praelectiones Juris Canonici*, I, Tit. II, n. 33; De Angelis, *Praelectiones Juris Canonici*, I, Tit. II, n. 13; Bargilliat, *Praelectiones Juris Canonici*, I, n. 65.

[131] Cf. Sa, *Aphorismi*, v°. *excommunicatio*, n. 12; Laymann, *Theologia Moralis*, I, Tr. IV, c. XI, n. 5; Zoesius, *In Jus Canonicum*, I, Tit. II, n. 32; Bonacina, *Operum de Morali Theologia*, II, Disp. I, Q. I, punct. VI, n. 65.

[132] *De Censuris*, Disp. V, Sect. V, n. 6.

the diocese to exempt the diocesan subject from episcopal laws. Such exemption would be had, for instance, when a whole town, or parish, was completely (*pleno iure*) withdrawn from episcopal power and subjected directly to the Holy See or to another ordinary. The monasteries and churches of exempt religious are not in this sense completely (*pleno iure*) exempt. The exemption of regulars is personal. The exemption of their monasteries and grounds is not because of the places themselves, but because of the persons in them. Therefore this exemption is not to be extended to diocesan subjects within those grounds.

Though the opinion of Suarez enjoyed the support of great authority,[133] continuous support was given to the solidly probable opinion that subjects of diocesan law were exempted from its regulations even in those places, such as the monasteries of regulars, which were exempted from the local jurisdiction by reason of the persons to whom they belonged.[134]

After considering what constituted juridical absence, the question arose whether a person departing from the territory with the fraudulent intention of evading the law could enjoy the benefit of exemption from it. To leave the territory for a motive other than the evasion of the law was always recognized as within the rights of the subject, and in that case he was not bound by the laws of his own territory. Suarez[135] held that even with the express intention to evade the law, the absent subject was not bound by its obligation when the law itself did not forbid departure with the motive of evading it. This would not be a case of fraud, but of the legitimate use of one's rights. No one, according to the rule of law,[136] commits fraud who uses his legitimate

[133] Cf. Filliucius, *Quaestiones Morales*, II, Tr. XXVII, c. VII, n. 149; Pirhing, *Jus Canonicum*, I, Tit. II, § VII, n. 58; Leurenius, *Forum Ecclesiasticum*, I, Tit. II, Q. CXIV, n. 4.

[134] Cf. Diana, *Resolutiones Morales*, V. Tr. I, Resolutio CII; Laymann, *Theologia Moralis*, I, Tr. IV, cap. XI, n. 5; Salmanticenses, *Cursus Moralis*, II, Tr. X, c. I, punct. IX, n. 114; De Ligorio, *Theologia Moralis*, I, Tr. II, cap. II, dub. II, n. 157; Ballerini-Palmieri, *Opus Theologiae Moralis in Busembaum Medullam*, I, Tr. III, c. II, dub. II, n. 347.

[135] *De Virtute Religionis*, II, c. XIII, n. 4; cf. Filliucius, *Quaestiones Morales*, II, n. XXVII, c. VII, n. 113.

[136] R. J. *Nullus*—D (50, 17) 55.

right. Lessius,[137] however, held that such evasion of the law did amount to fraud, and absence with the intention to evade the law did not exempt the subject from it.

Singular importance was attached to this question in connection with the *Tametsi* decree on the juridical form of marriage.[138] Many early authors considered as valid those marriages which were contracted by parties who left a place under the *Tametsi* decree with the sole purpose of contracting clandestinely in a place where it was not in force. Indeed, the derogation of a universal law was considered as a territorial privilege of benefit to all in the territory.[139] Since the *Tametsi* decree was a disabling law, and since subjects of the universal legislative power in the Church remained subject to it everywhere, Sanchez considered it probable that the *Tametsi* decree bound inhabitants of the territory where it was in force wherever they were.[140] However, he more strongly approved the opinion that the *Tametsi* did not bind anyone outside of the territory where it was in force, and finally adopted this position without reserve.[141]

After the pronouncements of the Holy See in the XVII Century, the majority of authors defined fraud as that departure from the territory to evade the law which was forbidden in the law itself. Aside from an express prohibition to leave the territory, they could find no juridical reason why a subject should still be bound by a law of his own territory just because he left the territory to evade it.[142] Perhaps due to

[137] *De Justitia* IV, c. II, dub. VII, n. 60.

[138] Cf. *supra*, p. 46.

[139] Cf. Laymann, *Theologia Moralis*, I, Tr. IV, c. XI, n. 9; Filliucius, *Quaestiones Morales*, I, Tr. X, Pars I, c. VI, n. 199; Pontius, *De Sacramento Matrimonii Tractatus*, V, c. IX, nn. 2, 3; Barbosa, *Pastoralis Sollicitudo, sive De Officio et Potestate Episcopi Tripartita Descriptio* (4 vols. in 2, Lugduni, 1628), Pars II, Alleg. XXXII, n. 153.

[140] *De Matrimonio*, III, Disp. XVIII, Q. VI, nn. 28-30.

[141] Cf. *Opus Morale*, I, c. XII, n. 26.

[142] Cf. Reiffenstuel, *Ius Canonicum Universum* (5 vols. in 7, Parisiis, 1864-1882), IV, Tit. III, nn. 123-128; Böckhn, *In Jus Canonicum*, I, Tit. II, § III, n. 48; Schmalzgrueber, *Jus Ecclesiasticum Universum*, I, Pars I, Tr. II, § VI, n. 41; De Ligorio, *Theologia Moralis*, I, Tr. II, n. 157; Feije (†1894), *De Impedimentis et Dispensationibus Matrimonialibus* (3. ed., 2 vols., Lovanii, 1885), n. 338; Benedict XIV (Prosperus Labertinus, †1758), *Institutiones Ecclesiasticae Prosperi Lambertini*,

the influence of the civil jurists who were advocating the "New Theory of Statutes," a number of authors, following De Luca (†1683)[143] held that laws could be personal as well as territorial. Laws which directly referred to the status of persons were by their nature personal. The *Tametsi* decree was such a law referring to the status of persons, and therefore it was personal. The Holy See authoritatively confirmed this doctrine in 1893.[144]

Although this distinction between territorial and personal laws did not end all controversy, it was admitted quite generally in regard at least to universal laws.[145]

In brief summary, it can be stated that at the end of the period intervening between the Council of Trent and the promulgation of the Code, the almost unanimous doctrine, confirmed by authoritative statements from the Holy See, was that laws were of their nature territorial. The traveler was normally bound by neither the particular laws of his own territory nor the particular laws of the place in which he was visiting. Certain exceptional obligations, such as laws regarding contracts, real possessions and the special good of the territory, indirectly bound the stranger to observe the laws of the place where he was traveling. When he was juridically absent from the territory, he was not bound by its laws. Juridical absence applied to both physical and moral absence. The possibility of personal laws was not admitted before the late part of the XIX Century. The traveler was considered bound by all of the universal laws in force in the place where he happened to be. Finally, agreement had not been reached concerning the status of a traveler within the places of exempt religious, or concerning the obligations of the vagrant.

*Postea Benedicti XIV^i^* (ed. ab Ildephonsus a S. Carlo, Romae, 1747), Inst. XXXIII, c. IV, n. 4; *De Synodo Dioecesana* (2. ed., Parmae, 1764), II, Lib. XIII, c. IV, n. 10.

[143] *Theatrum Veritatis et Iustitiae* (16 vols. in 9, Coloniae, 1706), VII, Disc. 143, n. 43; D'Annibale, *Summula Theologiae Moralis*, I, n. 204; *Theologia Wirceburgensis*, III, Tr. *De Legibus*, c. IV, A. IV, § 2, nn. 157-162.

[144] Cf. *supra*, p. 47.

[145] Cf. Santi, *Praelectiones Juris Canonici*, IV, Tit. III, n. 80; Gasparri, *Tractatus de Matrimonio* (3. ed., 2 vols., Parisiis-Lugduni, 1900), n. 985.

PART II

Canonical Commentary

Chapter IV

DOCTRINE ADOPTED BY THE CODE

The doctrines commonly held in the interval between the Council of Trent and the promulgation of the Code regarding the obligations of the traveler were based entirely upon what their proponents considered the nature of law, derived chiefly from the final cause of the law. When the possibility of personal laws was officially recognized in 1893, it was still because of the nature of law that these laws had extra-territorial force; because they directly affected the person of the subject.

Article I. Doctrine of the XX Century

However, another basis for the determination of the obligations of the traveler had been suggested in the middle ages by Tancred and a few others,[1] namely the will of the legislator. This solution lay unnoticed until the XVII Century when Castropalao (†1633),[2] following John de Sales (†1612),[3] suggested it anew. His only supporter until the XX Century was William Herincx (†1678).[4] The point upon which these authors centered their doctrine was the obligations of the traveler in relation to the laws of his own territory. They noted that the decretal *Ut animarum,* based upon the Roman Law *Extra,*[5] applied to judicial or contentious jurisdiction rather than to voluntary jurisdiction, of which legislative power participates. Moreover, since the

[1] Cf. *supra,* p. 33.

[2] *Opera Omnia in Septem Tomos Divisa* (7 vols. in 3, Lugduni, 1682), I, Pars I, Tr. III, Disp. I, punct. XXIV, § V, n. 22.

[3] *Tractatus de Legibus in Iam IIae S. Thomae,* Q. XCVI, Tr. XIV, Disp. XIV, Sect. VII, n. 90—cited in Castropalao, *o.c., l.c.*

[4] *Summa Theologiae Scholasticae et Moralis in Quatuor Partes Distributa* (2.ed., 4 vols. in 3, Antverpiae, 1680), II, Pars II, Tr. III, Q. XI. Cited hereafter as *Summa Theologiae.*

[5] Cf. *supra,* p. 10, note 12.

jurisdiction exercised in imposing precepts is essentially the same as that exercised in enacting a law, they were unable to understand why the superior had the power to make a personal precept but not the power to enact a personal law. Therefore, they concluded, since it is within the power of the legislator to make personal laws, the ultimate basis of the obligations of the traveler is the will of the legislator. With the will of the legislator as their ultimate foundation, these authors continued to make the same determinations of the obligations of the traveler which the followers of Suarez made.[6]

This doctrine did not receive full treatment until the XX Century, while the Code of Canon Law was actually in preparation. The penetrating analysis of Eugenio Pacelli,[7] presently reigning Holy Father, Pope Pius XII, presented a new demonstration that nothing in the nature of law by itself gives basis for its territorial restriction. The definition of law, given by St. Thomas Aquinas[8] as "an ordinance of reason for the common good promulgated by him who has care of the community," gives no intrinsic restriction of the obligation of law to the territory. The final cause of law requires only that it be given to a community capable of receiving it. Such a community may exist itself independently of territorial restrictions, as, for instance, a religious order. Moreover, the object of law is primarily the subjects, and not the territory. Law, according to St. Thomas, has for its object the proper governing of human acts.[9] Thus from the intrinsic causes of law and from its final cause, there is no reason for the territorial nature of law.[10] The arguments of John de Sales and William Herincx show that there is no territorial limitation on law from its efficient

[6] Cf. Castropalao, *Opera Omnia,* I, Pars I, Tr. III, Disp. I, punct. XXIV, § III, nn. 2-10; Herincx, *Summa Theologiae,* II, Pars II, Tr. III, Q. XI, § III, n. 132. Cf. *supra,* pp. 49-53; 65-70.

[7] *La Personalità e la Territorialità delle Leggi Specialmente nel Diritto Canonico* (Roma, 1912). Cited as *La Personalità delle Leggi*. Due to the actual impossibility of obtaining a copy of this work, its doctrine will be presented from the summary given by Onclin, *De Legis Indole,* pp. 311-315.

[8] *Summa Theologica,* Ia IIae (*Opera Omnia,* 34 vols., Parisiis: Apud Ludovicum Vivès, 1880-1889, vol. III, 1889), Q. XC, A. IV, c.

[9] *Summa Theologica,* Ia IIae, Q. XC, A. I, c.

[10] Pacelli, *La Personalità delle Leggi,* pp. 13, 14—cited by Onclin, *De Legis Indole,* pp. 311, 312.

cause. The added obligations placed upon strangers by the laws of their proper territory aid the good government of the territory where they are more frequently than such obligations conflict with the local laws. Finally, the arguments of the Italian School of International Law, following Mancini[11] give reasons for the extra-territorial extension of the obligation of law: laws are accommodated to the subject according to his national characteristics, the habits and characteristics acquired through the customs and environment of his home. Hence many laws should bind the subject wherever he goes just as these personal characteristics follow him wherever he goes.[12] There is, then, nothing exclusively territorial about the nature of law; it can bind the subject outside of the territory if such be the will of the legislator.[13]

Whether the absent subject is bound by the laws of his proper territory or not cannot be discovered from the nature of law, but either from the content of the law or the will of the legislator expressed in the law. Some laws are exclusively territorial because of their content, such as laws regulating burials, formalities of acts, and the like. These bind only in the territory and all those who are in it.[14] Other laws, because of their content, have extra-territorial obligatory force. Examples of these laws are found in those cases commonly referred to by the authors when they evolved the fiction of moral presence. Such a fiction is purely arbitrary and without juridical foundation.[15] The extra-territorial obligation of law has special application in the Church because of the spiritual purpose of ecclesiastical legislation; the sanctification of souls. This consideration must still be provided for by the legislator when his subjects leave his territory.[16] The legislator has

[11] Cf. *supra*, p. 42.

[12] Cf. Pacelli, *La Personalità delle Leggi*, pp. 15-19—cited by Onclin, *De Legis Indole*, p. 313.

[13] "Non è sempre esclusivamente territoriale, giacchè a sua efficacia non è sempre necessariamente ristretta nei confini del territorio, ma puo, dipendentemente dalla sua speciale natura e dalla voluntà del legislatore, espendersi e vincolare il suddito anche oltre quei limiti, puo essere cioè al tempo stesso territoriale e personale."—Pacelli, *La Personalità delle Leggi*, p. 17—quoted from Onclin, *De Legis Indole*, p. 313.

[14] Pacelli, *La Personalità delle Leggi*, p. 20—Onclin, *De Legis Indole*, p. 314.

[15] Pacelli, *o.c.*, pp. 22-24—Onclin, *o.c.*, p. 314.

[16] Pacelli, *o.c.*, pp. 20, 21—Onclin, *o.c.*, p. 314.

therefore the power to make laws, normally territorial, obligatory upon his subjects outside of the territory; or to bind strangers by laws which normally would not bind them.[17] Finally, since as a matter of fact the laws of the Church have been generally limited to the territory and to the habitual subjects of the legislator, they are to be presumed such unless clear evidence indicates otherwise. Obligations binding the stranger or the absent subject are to be demonstrated.[18]

Wernz, writing after the appearance of this treatise (†1914),[19] was in full accord with the position of Pacelli relative to the nature of law regarded in itself. He disagreed, however, with the statement that there was a juridical inconsistency in limiting legislative power to the territory of the legislator while the power to make precepts was extended extra-territorially. The proper reason for this distinction is to be found in the will of the legislator.[20] Indeed there is no more juridical inconsistency in limiting the power to make laws to the territory and not limiting the power to make precepts than there is in limiting judicial power to the territory and not limiting voluntary jurisdiction. In fact, such is the express intention of the decretal *Ut animarum*.[21]

Although in effect agreeing with the conclusions of Pacelli, Wernz subscribed to the position of Sanchez, on the basis that such was the positive will of the universal legislator. Strangers, including vagrants, were not bound by the law of the place where they were, unless it was universal law, or because of the exceptions given by the authors examined in the second article of the previous chapter. Those who were both physically and morally absent from their own territory were not bound by its laws.[22]

[17] Pacelli, *o.c.*, p. 15—Onclin, *o.c.*, p. 313.

[18] Pacelli, *o.c.*, p. 15—Onclin, *o.c.*, p. 313.

[19] *Ius Decretalium ad Usum Praelectionum in Scholis Textus Canonici Sive Iuris Decretalium* (3.ed., 6 vols. in 8, Prati, 1913-1915), I (1913), nn. 107, 135. Cited hereafter as Wernz, *Ius Decretalium*.

[20] "A. [uctori] est assentiendum, si p. 11 sq. contendit vim mere territorialem non ex natura rei esse propriam legis, sed auctores allegati contrarium non videntur tenere, qui potius assignant congruam rationem positivae voluntatis legislatoris."—*Ius Decretalium*, I, n. 107, nota (95).

[21] Wernz, *Ius Decretalium*, I, n. 135, nota (225).

[22] Wernz, *Ius Decretalium*, I, n. 107.

Article II. Formation of Canon 14

On November 13, 1904, the work of the codification of Canon Law was begun under the inspiration of Pius X, and committed to a council of Cardinals presided over by the then Archbishop Gasparri.[23] It is interesting to note that Pacelli, the future Pius XII, was one of the two secretaries of this body of consultors.[24] Others of the authorities, whose doctrines have just been examined, numbered among the consultors were Wernz, Ojetti, Palmieri, and Many.[25] The influence of these consultors upon the ultimate formation of the canons can only be conjectured by the number of times each canon was presented for their consideration before it was finally adopted.[26]

In 1912, at the time when Pacelli's treatise was being presented to the public, a provisional schema of the first book, the *Normae Generales,* was submitted for the approval of the bishops of the whole world. In this schema, the canon which dealt with the obligations of the traveler, canon 12, stated:

> Peregrini non adstringuntur legibus particularibus sui territorii a quo absunt, nisi transgressio in patria noceat aut leges sint personales; lex autem praesumitur territorialis, nisi aliud constat.[27]

Thus the possibility and existence of personal or extra-territorial laws was recognized, and the doctrine of the territorial nature of laws was abandoned. This provisional schema of the future law on the obligations of the traveler resembled the doctrine of Pacelli in a most striking manner. The presumption, however, was preserved in favor of the common doctrine based upon the decretal *Ut animarum,* and held ever since the Council of Trent: the presumption that laws were territorial, unless otherwise demonstrated.

[23] Pius X, Motu Proprio, "Arduum sane," 19 mar. 1904—ASS (1904) XXXVI, 549.

[24] Cf. Van Hove, *Prolegomena,* n. 359.

[25] Cf. Maroto, *Inst. Iuris Can.*, I, n. 155.

[26] Cf. Maroto, *Inst. Iuris Can.,* I, n. 158.

[27] Cf. Maroto, *Inst. Iuris Can.,* I, n. 183, p. 181. nota 1.

In 1914, even this presumption was abandoned, and in doubt, laws were to be presumed personal. The provisional draft of canon 8, § 2 stated:

> Lex non praesumitur territorialis, sed personalis, nisi aliud constet.[28]

By this presumption, the traveler was not bound by the laws of the territory where he was staying, but bound by the laws of his proper territory, unless otherwise demonstrated. This doctrine approaches even more closely the doctrine of the Italian School of International Law following Mancini.

However, the general presumption of canon 12 in the 1912 schema was finally adopted in the Code of Canon Law, when it was promulgated in 1917.[29] The practical application of this general presumption to the obligations of the traveler is found in canon 14 of the Code of Canon Law.

The first paragraph of this canon treats of the obligations of the traveler in the sense of the peregrin, he who has a domicile or quasi-domicile elsewhere. The first number of this paragraph states:

> Non adstringuntur legibus particularibus sui territorii quandiu ab eo absunt, nisi aut earum transgressio in proprio territorio noceat, aut leges sint personales.

It asserts only as a presumption the doctrine based upon the decretal *Ut animarum*, and accepted almost universally before the Code. It departs from the traditional doctrine, and follows the doctrine of Pacelli in the implication that this presumption is based upon the positive will of the legislator, and in the recognition of the power of the legislator to enact personal laws. Hence, in interpreting the presumption, the traditional doctrine will be of much value, but must be modified by the new doctrine of the XX Century.

The second number of this paragraph treats of the obligations of the traveler in relation to the laws of the place in which he is a stranger. It states:

[28] Maroto, *Inst. Iuris Can.*, I, n. 183, p. 181, nota. 1.

[29] Cf. canon 8, § 2.

> Neque [adstringuntur] legibus territorii in quo versantur, iis exceptis quae ordini publico consulunt, vel actuum solemnia determinant.

This number definitely abandons the doctrine of the early decretalists and of Suarez. It asserts the doctrine held by Sanchez, and canonizes the term public order, probably adopted from the Italian School of International Law by De Angelis, Tanquerey and Marc. The doctrine of Sanchez and of the International Law jurists will be valuable in its interpretation.

The third number of this paragraph treats of the obligation of universal laws:

> At legibus generalibus tenentur, etiamsi hae suo in territorio non vigeant, minime vero si in loco in quo versantur non obligent.

This number states the common opinion of the followers of both Suarez and Sanchez.

Finally, the second paragraph of this canon treats of those who have neither a domicile nor a quasi-domicile, vagrants:[30]

> Vagi obligantur legibus tam generalibus quam particularibus quae vigent in loco in quo versantur.

This paragraph decides the controversy among the canonists and moralists before the Code by adopting the position held by Sanchez and Suarez, and rejecting that held by Laymann and his supporters. Vagrants are bound by all of the laws in force where they actually happen to be visiting.

Such, then is the interesting story of the formation of canon 14, and its relation to the pre-Code legislation and doctrine. It is the object of the second part of this dissertation to apply the norms of interpretation thus established in order to define more concretely the exact nature and extent of the obligations of the traveler according to the present legislation of the Church.

[30] Cf. *supra*, p. 2, note 4.

Chapter V

THE ABSENT SUBJECT AND THE PARTICULAR LAWS OF HIS OWN TERRITORY

The first number of § 1 of canon 14 establishes the discipline regulating the obligation of the absent subject to observe the particular laws of his own territory. The solution of this problem has been more easily found in Canon Law than in Private International Law.[1] In Private International Law, the problem resolves itself into the conflict of laws of two sovereign states.[2] In Canon Law the problem concerns the particular laws pertaining to different particular societies which are hierarchically subordinate to one universal and completely autonomous authority, namely the Holy See.[3] Thus in departing from the almost unanimous position of the pre-Code authorities, the Code was able to give a practical solution to the problem of the obligations of the absent subject by recognizing the extra-territorial force of particular laws.[4] The theoretical justification for this position was fully developed by Pacelli when he demonstrated that not only is law neither territorial nor personal of itself, but also that the good of souls and the proper government of the ecclesiastical society occasionally require the enactment of particular personal laws.[5] Commentators since the Code have done no more than recast his arguments or give a brief summary of them.[6] This chapter is concerned with an interpretation and analysis of the positive discipline as established in the Code.

[1] Cf. Michiels, *Normae Generales*, I, 307.

[2] Cf. Onclin, *De Legis Indole*, p. 314.

[3] Cf. canons 218; 227; 228; 291, § 1; 329.

[4] Hence, Onclin states: "Codex tamen non intendit solvere quaestionem philosophiae iuris, utrum natura sua lex particularis ad territorium restringitur an non . . . Itaque de natura legis particularis non habetur in Codice declaratio doctrinalis et generalis, sed solummodo solutio practica pro legislatoribus particularibus in Ecclesia."—*De Legis Indole*, pp. 325-326.

[5] Cf. *supra*, pp. 72-74.

[6] Cf. Maroto, *Inst. Iuris Can.*, I, nn. 183, 200; Van Hove, *De Legibus*, n. 124; Toso, *Ad Codicem Iuris Canonici Commentaria Minora* (5 vols., Romae: Marietti-Tiferni Tiberini: ex officina Typogr. Vinciana), I (2.ed., Tiferni Tiberini: ex officina Typogr. Vinciana, 1921), 22, 23—cited hereafter as Toso, *Comm. Minora*, I; Michiels, *Normae Generales*, I, 308-310; Cicognani, *Ius Canonicum Primo Studii Anno in Usum*

Article I. What Particular Laws Are Included in Canon 14, § 1, 1°

To determine the exact extension of the application of canon 14, § 1, 1° the question of whether all particular laws are included within its scope or not must be considered. Particular laws are of several kinds by reason of their author: laws of the universal legislator, whether of an oecumenical council or of the Holy See, which are enacted for a particular territory only; laws of particular legislators, whether local or religious ordinaries, plenary or provincial councils; and unwritten laws or customs which have developed in a particular territory only. Particular laws can be considered also from the viewpoint of whether they are intended for a community which has territorial limits, or for a community which has no reference to territorial boundaries, such as religious orders. The present article considers which of these various types of particular laws are included in canon 14, § 1, 1°.

§ 1. *Particular Laws of Territorial Communities*

The general wording of canon 14, § 1, 1° implies that all particular laws, no matter who their author is, come within its scope. The formation of canon 14 and of canon 8, § 2 clearly indicates that the particular laws of the universal legislator are included in the term *legibus particularibus*.[7] Historically, the question of the obligations of the traveler concerned chiefly the statutes and legislation of local ordinaries.[8] By logical inference, therefore, canon 14, § 1, 1° refers also to the particular laws of plenary and provincial councils. This application of canon 14, § 1, 1° to all of the various kinds of particular laws

Auditorum Excerpta (2 vols.; vol. I, Romae: Ex Officina Typographica Ausonia, 1925; vol. II, Romae: Ex Schola Typographica "Pio X," 1925), II, 78-80—cited hereafter as Cicognani, *Ius Canonicum;* Claeys Bouuaert-Simenon, *Manuale Juris Canonici ad Usum Seminariorum* (3.ed., 3 vols., Gandae et Leodii: J. De Meester et Fils, 1930), I, 88—cited hereafter as *Manuale Iuris Can.*; Deschepper, "De territorialitate et personalitate legum episcopalium,"—*Collationes Brugenses,* XXIII (1923), 200, 201. This periodical is cited hereafter as *Coll. Brug.*

[7] The presumption that laws are territorial was originally attached to the canon dealing with particular laws. Finally it was applied to all laws in canon 8, § 2. Cf. *supra* p. 76.

[8] Cf. *supra*, pp. 26, 29, 35.

for territorial communities enjoys the unhesitating support of the commentators since the Code.[9]

§ 2. *Custom or Unwritten Laws*

Custom is defined as unwritten law introduced by repeated acts of the community with the consent of a competent ecclesiastical superior.[10] The attention of St. Augustine was drawn to particular customs rather than to particular laws in the texts so famous in the discussions of the obligations of the traveler.[11] The decretalists and canonists before the Code applied the same principles to customary law as they did to written law when solving the problems of the absent subject.[12] Nor does there appear any reason to depart from this historically accepted application of the same principles and presumptions of written law to custom in the matter of the obligations of the traveler.[13]

[9] Berutti unequivocally states: "Leges quaelibet particulares hic considerantur quae pro determinata dioecesi, seu provincia, seu regione statutae sint sive ab ordinario loci, sive a Concilio provinciali aut plenario, sive etiam a Romano Pontifice vel a Concilio Oecumenico . . "—*Institutiones Iuris Canonici* (Vol. I, Taurini-Romae: Marietti, 1936), I, n. 61. Cf. Michiels, *Normae Generales*, I, 310; Maroto, *Inst. Iuris Can.*, I, n. 183; Chelodi-Bertagnolli, *Ius De Personis Iuxta Codicem Iuris Canonici* (2.ed., Tridenti: Libr. Edit. Tridentum, 1927), n. 65—cited as *Ius De Personis;* Claeys Bouuaert-Simenon, *Manuale Iuris Can.*, I, n. 92; Toso, *Comm. Minora*, I, 33; Cicognani, *Ius Canonicum*, II, 77; Van Hove, *De Legibus*, n. 124; Beste, *Introd. in Codicem*, p. 63; Onclin, *De Legis Indole*, p. 327; Deschepper, "De indole personali legum episcopalium— *Coll. Brug.*, XXIII (1923), 220, 221; Leroux, "Le sujet des lois ecclésiastiques,"—*Revue Ecclésiastique de Liège*, XVI (1924-1925), 336—hereafter this periodical will be cited as *REL.*

[10] Cf. Van Hove, *De Consuetudine*, n. 2; Michiels, *Normae Generales*, II, 83.

[11] Cf. *supra*, pp. 18, 19.

[12] Cf. c. 3, D. VIII; c. 4, D. XII; Ioannes Andreae, *Commentaria Novella, in rubrica, de consuetudine*, I, 4, in VI°; Bernardus Papiensis, *Summa*, Tit III, *De consuet.*, § 5—ed. Lasperyers, p. 6; Suarez, *De Legibus*, Lib. III, c. XVI, nn. 6, 9; Wherle, *De la Coutume dans le Droit Canonique* (Paris: Recueil Sirey, 1928), pp. 249-250.

[13] Cf. Van Hove, *De Consuetudine*, n. 247; Guilfoyle, *Custom* (The Catholic University of America Canon Law Studies, n. 105, Washington, D. C.: The Catholic University of America Press, 1937), pp. 92, 93: "Since custom and *lex* (qua law) are not essentially different and since the one is presumed territorial, it seems that the other should enjoy the same presumption."; Vindex, "Domicilium et quasi-domicilium eorumque effectus in Codice Juris Canonici,"—*Jus Pont.*, VI (1926), 112.

§ 3. *Particular Statutes, Rules, and Laws of Communities without Territorial Determination*

In treating the discipline regarding the absent subject, the question arises concerning the particular laws and regulations of societies existing without reference to territorial limits. Religious communities are the classical example of such societies. The application of canon 14, § 1, 1° is restricted to those rules, statutes, and laws which are derived from provincial chapters and major superiors of clerical religious institutes enjoying jurisdiction and legislative power.[14] When it is clear that the particular legislators of clerical religious institutes are actually using their legislative power, and not their dominative power, their enactments have the force of law.[15] Such statutes are then particular laws enacted for a definite territory. There appears no reason why the discipline established in canon 14, § 1, 1° does not apply to such particular laws.[16] However, local chapters and superiors of religious communities are presumed to use their dominative power, rather than their legislative power, when issuing statutes and precepts. The normal relationship of subject to religious superior is based on the quasi-contract of the former's admission into the society rather than upon the title of jurisdiction arising from domicile or quasi-domicile.[17] Moreover, the special purpose of the religious society is the personal sanctity of the members of the community. The superiors generally indicate the means to this end by the use of dominative power.[18] Finally, only

[14] Cf. Coronata, *Institutiones Iuris Canonici ad Usum Utriusque Cleri et Scholarum* (5 vols., Taurini: Marietti, 1933-1939; Vols. I et II, 2.ed., 1939, Vol. III, 1.ed., 1933, Vol. IV, 1.ed., 1933, Vol. V, 1.ed., 1936), I, n. 509—cited hereafter as *Inst. Iuris Can.;* Schaefer, *De Religiosis ad Normam Codicis Iuris Canonici* (3.ed., Roma: Typis Polyglottis Vaticanis, 1940), n. 151, 1—hereafter cited as *De Religiosis.*

[15] Cf. Coronata, *Inst. Iuris Can.*, I, n. 505; Larraona, "De potestate dominativa publica in iure canonico,"—*Acta Congressus Iuridici Internationalis,* IV (Romae: Apud Custodiam Librariam Pont. Instituti Utriusque Iuris, 1937), 166, 167. Hereafter this work is cited *Acta Congr. Iuridici,* IV.

[16] Cf. Van Hove, *De Legibus,* n. 208.

[17] Cf. Coronata, *Inst. Iuris Can.*, I, n. 505; Teodori, "Peregrini quoad leges servandas,"—*Consultationes Iuris Canonici,* I (Romae: Apud Custodiam Librariam Pon. Instituti Utriusque Iuris, 1934), 18—hereafter this work is cited as *Consult. Iuris Can.*, I; Larraona, "De potestate dominativa publica in Iure Canonico,"—*Acta Congr. Iuridici,* IV, 161, 175, 177, nota (99).

[18] Cf. Michiels, *Normae Generales,* I, 134.

the religious of clerical religious institutes have jurisdiction and legislative power. The other religious institutes have only dominative power[19] and consequently cannot make particular laws.

For these reasons, therefore, the rules and particular prescriptions of local religious communities and provinces are not to be included under the general prescriptions of canon 14, § 1, 1°.[20] A claim for exemption from them because of absence from the territory according to canon 14, §1, 1°, must be established by showing that the legislator had true jurisdiction and intended to use it in making the regulation, or by showing that the rule or precept was territorial in effect.

Article II. Meaning of Juridical Absence from the Territory

Canon 14, § 1, 1° normally exempts the absent subject from the obligation of observing the particular laws of his own territory when he is absent from it. The term *absent* here means juridical absence, for physical absence is not the only condition that might give rise to this exemption.

§ 1. *Juridical Absence of a Diocesan Subject in the Exempt Places of Religious*

There are within the territorial limits of dioceses and provinces places juridically withdrawn from the territorial jurisdiction of the ordinary of the place, namely, the places of exempt religious.[21] Whether the subject of diocesan or provincial laws can be said to be juridically absent from his territory when he is within such an exempt place

[19] Cf. Schaefer, *De Religiosis,* n. 105, 1; Chelodi-Bertagnolli, *Ius De Personis,* n. 250; Larraona, "De potestate dominativa publica in Iure Canonico,"—*Acta Congr. Iuridici,* IV, 170, 171.

[20] Cf. Van Hove, *De Legibus,* n. 208; Michiels, *Normae Generales,* I, 308; Teodori, "Peregrini quoad leges servandas,"—*Consult. Iuris Can.,* I, 18; Beste, *Introd. in Codicem,* p. 63; Cocchi, *Commentarium in Codicem Iuris Canonici* (8 vols., Taurinorum Augustae: Marietti, 1932-1940), I (5.ed., 1938), n. 99—cited hereafter as *Comm. in Codicem;* Wernz-Vidal, *Ius Canonicum* (7 Tom. in 8 vols., Romae: Apud Aedes Universitatis Gregorianae 1923-1938), I (1938), nn. 152, 154; Deschepper, "De territorialitate et personalitate legum episcopalium,"—*Coll. Brug.,* XXIII (1923), 200; Jone, *Gesetzbuch des Kanonischen Rechtes* (3 vols., Paderborn: Ferdinand Schöningh, 1939-1941), I, 28.—Hereafter cited as Jone, *Kanonischen Rechtes.*

[21] Cf. canon 615.

situated in his diocese or province, and therefore generally exempt from the obligation of the particular laws in force in his own territory, has been a much controverted question since the time of Joannes Andreae.[22]

The privilege of exemption from episcopal jurisdiction is either full, or active exemption, or it is partial, or passive exemption. By full or active exemption, the entire place is withdrawn from the jurisdiction of the diocesan ordinary, and placed under the jurisdiction of the religious prelate.[23] Passive exemption, on the contrary, directly affects the members of the religious institute, and only indirectly, by reason of the exempt members, does it affect the places where they are.[24] A place enjoying active exemption, such as an abbey *nullius*, is admittedly outside the surrounding diocese in the juridical sense, and a diocesan subject who is within such a place is admittedly juridically absent. The partial or passive exemption of religious communities which do not enjoy jurisdiction clearly cannot constitute their houses and churches places juridically outside of the diocese, and a diocesan subject does not enjoy the favor of canon 14, § 1, 1° within such places.

The controversy centers around the exemption of clerical exempt orders: whether a diocesan subject is juridically absent from his own territory by the mere fact of his presence within such a monastery, of the Dominicans for example. There are three positions taken by the canonists. The first position stresses the personal character of the privilege of exemption, and concludes that it cannot benefit diocesan subjects even when they are within the exempt places of regulars. The second position places emphasis upon the extension of the privilege to the houses and churches of regulars, and concludes that since the places are exempt, they are juridically outside of the surrounding territory, and that diocesan subjects who are within them are juridically

[22] Cf. *supra*, pp. 38, 67, 68.

[23] E.g., a prelacy or abbey *nullius*, presided over by a prelate or abbot, with a clergy and people living within the territory cut off from any diocese. Cf. Augustine, *A Commentary on Canon Law* (8 vols., St. Louis: Herder, 1931-1938), II (1936), 332—cited hereafter as Augustine, *Commentary*; Schaefer, *De Religiosis*, n. 419.

[24] Cf. Coronata, *Inst. Iuris Can.*, I, n. 621; Ramos, "De conditione saecularium in domibus religiosorum,"—*Commentarium pro Religiosis et Missionariis*, VI (1925), 29—hereafter this periodical will be cited as *CpR;* Schaefer, *De Deligiosis*, n. 419.

absent. The third position attempts a practical solution of the controversy in favor of the extension of the privilege of exemption to diocesan subjects by virtue of a doubt of law according to canon 15.

The majority of canonists since the Code have adopted the first position, namely that diocesan subjects are not juridically absent from their own territory by the mere fact that they happen to be within the territory of exempt religious, and consequently that they are as much bound by diocesan laws when they are within such places as they are outside of them.[25] They base this position upon their interpretation of the privilege of exemption of the churches and houses of regulars as a secondary privilege which exists only by virtue of the personal exemption enjoyed by the exempt regulars. In support of this position, canon 615 states that regulars are exempt from the jurisdiction of the ordinary of the place, except for cases expressed in the law. In order to give practical force to this exemption, the canon adds

[25] Cf. Chelodi-Bertagnoli, *Ius de Personis,* nn. 198, 281; Augustine, *Commentary,* III (1938), 337; Wernz-Vidal, *Ius Canonicum,* II (2.ed., 1937), n. 367; Blat, *Commentarium Textus Codicis Iuris Canonici* (6 vols., Romae: Ex Typographia Pontificia in Instituto Pii IX, 1921-1938), II (2.ed., 1921), n. 170—hereafter cited as Blat, *Commentarium Iuris Can.;* Creusen, *Religieux et Religieuse d'apres le Droit Ecclésiastique* (3.ed., Bruxelles: Dewit, 1924), n. 255; Vermeersch-Creusen, *Epitome Iuris Canonici* (3 vols., Mechliniae-Romae: H. Dessain, 1934-1937), I (n.ed., 1937), n. 717; De Meester, *Juris Canonici et Juris Canonico-civilis Compendium* (nova ed., 3 vols. in 4, Brugis: sumptibus et Typis Societatis Sancti Augustini, 1921-1928), I, n. 356—cited hereafter as *Juris Can. Compendium;* Prümmer, *Manuale Iuris Canonici* (4. et 5.ed., Friburgi Brisgoviae: Herder, 1927), n. 239; Cocchi, *Commentarium in Codicem,* IV (3.ed., 1932), n. 112; Fanfani, *De Iure Religiosorum ad Norman Codicis Iuris Canonici* (2.ed., Taurini-Romae: Marietti, 1925), n. 356—cited hereafter as *De Iure Religiosorum;* Claeys Bouuaert-Simenon, *Manuale Iuris Can.,* n. 164; Michiels, *Normae Generales,* I, 300, nota 2; Beste, *Introd. in Codicem,* p. 71; Maroto, *Inst. Iuris Can.,* n. 701; Toso, *Comm. Minora,* II, 166, 167; Van Hove, *De Legibus,* n. 211; Ojetti, *Commentarium in Codicem Iuris Canonici* (4 vols., Romae: Apud Aedes Universitatis Gregorianae, 1927-1931), I (1921), 119-123—cited hereafter as Ojetti, *Commentarium in Cod.;* Cappello, in his work *De Censuris Iuxta Codicem Iuris Canonici,* seems to incline towards the second position, but in the 1938 edition of his *Summa Iuris Canonici,* he absolutely adopts the position of the majority of commentators—cf. *De Censuris Iuxta Codicem Iuris Canonici* (3.ed., Augustae Taurinorum: Marietti, 1933), n. 9—hereafter cited as Cappello, *De Censuris; Summa Iuris Canonici* (3.ed., 3 vols., Romae: Apud Aedes Universitatis Gregorianae, 1936-1939), I (1938), n. 82.

"with their houses and churches."[26] The preposition "with" along with the relative pronoun "their" indicates clearly that the exemption of the houses and churches is not primary and absolute, but only relative to and by virtue of the exemption of the religious themselves. Therefore it should benefit only the religious, and not diocesan subjects who happen to be present within these places.[27]

Besides this argument from the text of the law, the proponents of this first position point to the difference between local ordinaries and ordinaries without territory as an argument in their favor.[28] This distinction is based mainly upon a difference in jurisdiction. The jurisdiction of an ordinary of the place arises from a territorial title, and is exercised mainly and primarily for those in and of his territory. The jurisdiction of an ordinary without territory, in contrast to a local ordinary, arises from a personal title, and is primarily exercised over those under him because of a personal subjection. Therefore the exemption of a regular is in itself personal, to contribute to his complete and personal subjection to his religious superior. When this primary reason for subjection to the religious superior is not present, then no exemption from the local ordinary can be claimed. Mere presence in the exempt places of exempt religious does not effect the personal relationship of subject to religious superior. Therefore, diocesan subjects cannot claim the favor of the exemption of religious when they are merely temporarily within their exempt places.[29]

[26] "Regulares . . . cum eorum domibus et ecclesiis . . . ab Ordinarii loci iurisdictione exempti sunt . . . "—canon 615.

[27] "Sed quia valde imminuta existeret talis exemptio regularium si et loca subiiciuntur Ordinario loci, additur subordinato nempe modo 'cum eorum domibus et ecclesiis', qua particula relativa 'cum' quae societatem, coniunctionem, communitatem significat et pronomen 'eorum' satis exprimitur domus et ecclesias non absolute et primario sed in relatione ad personas esse exemptas ob illud principium respectu ecclesiarum: exemptis ecclesiae clericis ecclesia censetur exampta."—Ramos, "De conditione saecularium in domibus religiosorum,"—*CpR*, VI (1925), 82. Cf. Vermeersch, "De locis in quibus Episcopi indulgentias concedere possunt,"—*Periodica de Re Canonica et Morali Utili Praesertim Religiosis et Missionariis,* XIX (1939), 25*, 26*—this periodical is hereafter cited as *Periodica.*

[28] Cf. canon 198, § 2.

[29] Cf. Wernz-Vidal, *Ius Canonicum,* II, n. 367; Maroto, *Inst. Iuris Can.*, n. 701; Toso, *Comm. Minora,* II, 166, 167; Blat, *Commentarium Iuris Can.*, II, n. 170; Ramos, "De conditione saecularium in domibus religiosorum,"—*CpR*, VI (1925), 83.

Those who hold the second position, namely that the churches and houses of regulars are juridically outside of the diocesan territory, base their position on a statement of Leo XIII that the churches of regulars are as though outside of the territory of the surrounding diocese.[80] This argument, however, is answered by the defenders of the first position by the observation that regardless of the true meaning of this text, the privilege of exemption has been restricted since the time of Leo XIII. For example, the ordinary of the place has jurisdiction over many things within the places of exempt regulars, particularly concerning the care of diocesan faithful who seek instruction and the administration of the sacraments from religious in their houses and churches.[81] Especially significant is the fact that the diocesan tribunal still retains competence over diocesan subjects even though they commit a delict within the territory of exempt places, or if they engage in a controversy therein.[82] Thus if the object of the litigation were located within the exempt place, the diocesan tribunal would still be competent according to canon 1579, § 3.[83] But judicial power is territorially circumscribed and cannot be exercised outside of the territory.[84] Therefore it follows that the exempt places of regulars are not of themselves outside of the territory of the surrounding diocese, nor are diocesan subjects present within them juridically absent from their own diocese.

These arguments are answered by the proponents of the second position favoring the exemption of diocesan subjects within the exempt places of regulars by the claim that the examples cited represent particular exceptions. It is argued that if the exemption of the churches and houses of regulars did not of itself extend to all within these

[80] "Sed quod eorum domus habitae fuerint iuris fictione quasi territorii ab ipsis dioecesibus avulsa,"—Leo XIII, const. "*Romanos pontifices,*" 8 maii 1881, § 7—*Fontes*, n. 582.

[81] Cf. canons 792; 783; 831, §3; 1338, § 2; 1261, § 2; 874; 1293; 1343, § 1; 1345; 1550; 2269, § 2.

[82] Cf. canon 1579, § 3.

[83] Cf. canons 1564; 1565; 1566; 1568.

[84] Cf. canon 201, § 2; Lega *Praelectiones in Textum Iuris Canonici—De Iudiciis Ecclesiasticis* (Vol. I, *De Iudiciis Ecclesiasticis Civilibus*, 2.ed., Romae, 1905), n. 334—hereafter this volume is cited as *De Iudiciis;* Ramos, "De conditione saecularium in domibus religiosorum,"—*CpR*, VI (1925), 84.

places, there would be no need for stating these exceptions in the law. The exception only strengthens the rule for cases not excepted.[35]

Further, the argument of extrinsic authority is invoked in favor of the second position, that the exempt places of regulars are juridically outside of the surrounding territory. They say that the limitations on the pre-Code exemption can be admitted. However, the interpretations of the accepted authors before the Code are to be followed whenever it is certain or solidly probable that the Code has retained the former law.[36] According to such authorities as Laymann, St. Alphonsus, and D'Annibale, a diocesan subject was considered juridically absent, before the Code, when he was present within the houses or churches of regulars, and consequently exempt from the particular laws of his own territory.[37] Nor are there lacking advocates for this position since the Code.[38] The Code, therefore, has not certainly departed from the pre-Code law, and as before the Code, so now, diocesan subjects are to be considered juridically outside the diocese when they are within the houses and churches of exempt religious.

The proponents of the first position, however, can appeal to an equally strong pre-Code authority against the juridical absence of diocesan subjects within the places of exempt religious.[39] Moreover, this position is by far the common opinion of the commentators on the Code. Therefore the appeal to the pre-Code law is not a conclusive argument in favor of the exemption of diocesan subjects within the places of exempt religious.

As a result of the existing controversy even since the Code, certain authors[40] adopt a third position, and consider that canon 615 is doubt-

[35] Cf. Coronata, *Inst. Iuris Can.*, I, n. 621, nota 4.

[36] Cf. canon 6, 3°, 4°.

[37] Cf. *supra*, pp. 38, 68.

[38] Cf. Coronata, *Inst. Iuris Can.*, I, n. 621; Génicot-Salsmans, *Institutiones Theologiae Moralis* (2 vols., Bruxellis: Alb. De Wit, 1927), I, n. 114; Noval, *Commentarium Codicis Iuris Canonici, Liber IV, De Processibus, Pars* I, *De Iudiciis* (Augustae Taurinorum: Marietti, 1920), n. 323—hereafter cited as *De Iudiciis;* Noldin-Schmitt, *De Principiis Theologiae Moralis* (26.ed., Oeniponte: Typis et Sumptibus Fel. Rauch, 1939), n. 152, nota 2—hereafter cited as Noldin-Schmitt, *De Principiis.*

[39] Cf. *supra*, pp. 38, 67, 68.

[40] Cf. Schaefer, *De Religiosis*, n. 424; Vermeersch, *Theologia Moralis*, I, n. 261.

ful in its extension to diocesan subjects who are within the places of exempt regulars. Because of this doubt of law, they conclude according to canon 15 that diocesan subjects may consider themselves juridically absent from their own territory and normally exempt from its particular laws when they are in the places of exempt regulars.

This practical conclusion, however, cannot be sustained. The doubt in question pertains to the interpretation of canon 615. Canon 615 states the privilege of exemption which obliges the ordinary of the place to refrain from exercising his jurisdiction over those who enjoy this privilege. According to canon 15, a doubtful law does not bind. Therefore in considering canon 615 doubtful in regard to diocesan subjects within the places of exempt regulars, it follows that the ordinary is not bound by this canon to refrain from normally exercising his jurisdiction in their regard while they are within the places of exempt regulars.

This solution of the doubt claimed to be in canon 615 in favor of the power of the ordinary of the place is in complete harmony with the principles of episcopal jurisdiction. Resident diocesan subjects come under the full jurisdiction of the diocesan ordinary. The local ordinary, as the Sacred Congregation of Bishops and Regulars so clearly pointed out,[41] has in his favor an intention founded in law, whereby his authority over his subjects remains in full force until an alleged exemption is proven by *certain* arguments.[42] The arguments advanced against the extension of the privilege of exemption to diocesan subjects who are within the houses or places of exempt regulars are not

[41] "Quemlibet ordinarium plena ex iure gaudere spirituali iurisdictione super omnes personas morantes intra fines Dioecesis a Romano Pontifice sibi concreditae. Ideoque huiusmodi iurisdictionem Antistitis cuiuslibet habentis fundatam in iure intentionem et generalem regulam in sui favorem, integram permanere donec allegans limitationem aut exceptionem *per lucidis probaverit argumentis*. . . . In dubio an exemptio exstet, regulae generali semper inhaerendum esse, *donec exceptio probetur eo qui exemptionem allegat*."—S. C. Ep. et Reg., 23 ian. 1880—ASS, X (1880), 30. (Italics inserted.)

[42] Cf. Ryan, *Principles of Episcopal Jurisdiction* (The Catholic University of America Canon Law Studies, n. 120, Washington, D. C.: The Catholic University of America Press, 1939), p. 101—cited hereafter as Ryan, *Episcopal Jurisdiction;* Bachofen, *Compendium Jurium Religiosorum* (Neo-Eboraci, Cincinnati, Chicagiae, 1903), p. 231.

only more intrinsically probable, but enjoy the extrinsic probability of the common opinion since the Code, and the more common opinion before the Code. Consequently diocesan subjects cannot certainly demonstrate their exemption from diocesan laws while they are within the exempt places of regulars. Until an authentic interpretation should declare otherwise, the exempt places of regulars cannot in practice be considered juridically outside of the surrounding diocese, and subjects from the surrounding diocese are bound to observe the particular laws of their own territory while they are within such places.

§ 2. *Juridical Absence Before Time of Departure*

Outside of the territory, the absent subject normally has the right to disregard the particular laws of his own territory. Does this right ever release him from the obligation of such particular laws while he is still within the territory, but about to depart before the time specified in the law for the fulfillment of the obligation? This question is chiefly a problem for moral theology. A brief resumé of the doctrine will suffice to indicate the juridical implications in the problem.

Laws may be divided into those with a positive obligation and those with a negative obligation. Negative obligations bind at all times (*semper et pro semper*). Therefore, the subject of a law is obliged to comply with its negative obligations even until the time he departs from the territory.[43] However, some negative obligations are accidentally indivisible. Thus the obligation of fasting is indivisible: it can only be fulfilled by continuous observance during the whole time specified in the law. Before this time has expired, the subject is released from the obligation by departing from the territory where the law is in force. But to use this right of exemption from the law, the absent subject is then unable to complete the obligation of fasting. Therefore, since the obligation does not admit of division, and since the subject cannot enjoy his right of exemption and observe the whole obligation, moralists hold that he is not bound to observe a negative indivisible obligation at all, when he leaves the territory before the time specified in the law for the fulfillment of the law.[44]

[43] This, for instance, is the case in regard to the law of abstinence.

[44] Cf. Merkelbach, *Summa Theologiae Moralis ad Mentem D. Thomae et Normam Iuris Novi* (3 vols., Parisiis: Typis Desclée de Brouwer et Soc., 1935), I, n. 359—

A positive obligation does not bind unceasingly (*semper sed non pro semper*) during the time alloted for its fulfillment. A subject is not bound to fulfill a positive obligation until the last possible moment within the time allowed for compliance with the obligation. Hence, according to some theologians, a subject is excused from the positive obligations of particular laws when he departs from the territory before the last possible moment in which to fulfill the obligation.[45] Others, however, hold the subject excused only when he departs before the last *opportunity* has been given to observe the law. For example, in a parish where the last Mass is said at 10:30 A.M. on a certain Holy Day, the subject would have to depart from the territory before 10:30 A.M. before he could be excused from the obligation of hearing Mass.[46]

§ 3. *Juridical Absence with Fraudulent Intention to Evade the Law*

Both canonists and theologians before the Code discussed the effect of the fraudulent intention to evade the law upon the juridical absence of the subject from his own territory. The express purpose to evade the law was considered fraudulent, and the subject departing with this intention was still held bound by the law he sought to evade: he was not juridically absent.[47] However, before the publication of the Code the concept of fraud in this regard became more precisely determined as existing only when the law itself forbade departure with

cited hereafter as *Summa Theol. Moralis*; Noldin-Schmitt, *De Principiis*, n. 152; Vermeersch, *Theologia Moralis*, I, n. 287; Van Hove, *De Legibus*, n. 212; Leroux, "Le sujet des lois ecclésiastiques,"—*REL*, XVI (1924-1925), 341.

[45] These authors, for example, would not require a subject to hear Mass on a Holy Day, if he left the territory where the law was in force before noon, regardless of the time of the last Mass. Cf. Ballerini-Palmieri, *Opus Theologicum Morale in Busembaum Medullam*, I, n. 189; Vermeersch, *Theologia Moralis*, I, n. 287; Sanchez, *De Matrimonio*, III, Disp. XVIII, n. 21; Laymann, *Theologia Moralis*, I, Tr. IV, c. XI, n. 6.

[46] Cf. Suarez, *De Virtute Religionis*, II, Tr. II, c. XIV, nn. 21-25; De Ligorio, *Theologia Moralis*, Lib. I, Tr. II, 157; Lehmkuhl, *Theologia Moralis*, I, n. 142; Noldin-Schmitt, *De Principiis*, n. 152; Merkelbach, *Summa Theol. Moralis*, I, n. 359; Leroux, "Le sujet des lois ecclésiastiques,"—*REL*, XVI (1924-1925), 341.

[47] Cf. *supra*, p. 69.

such an intention.[48] Examples of these laws were to be found in the *Tametsi* decree on the canonical form of marriage and in the *Lex Clementina* regarding reserved cases.[49] Both of these laws have been abrogated by the Code,[50] and nowhere in the Code is there to be found an example of a law forbidding a subject to leave the territory of the law with the express purpose to evade its obligation.[51] Nor does canon 14, § 1, 1° distinguish the intentions which prompt a subject to be absent from his own territory. The question of fraudulent intention does not limit the juridical absence of the subject of particular laws according to the present legislation of the Code. However, except in those cases where the Code concedes the subject the right to leave the territory to evade the law, a particular legislator could specifically forbid his subjects to depart from the territory to evade a particular law. The subject thus violating such a law would have a fraudulent intention, and would thereby be bound by the law even though physically absent from his territory.[52]

Article III. The Obligation of the Absent Subject to Observe the Laws of His Own Territory

Canon 14, § 1, 1° states that the absent subject is not bound by the laws of his own territory, unless they are personal or unless their transgression should cause harm in his own territory. Two sources of the obligation of the absent subject are hereby indicated: the will of the legislator and the content of the law.

§ 1. *The Will of the Legislator as Source of the Obligation of the Absent Subject*

The legislator who enacts particular laws may be either the universal legislator or a particular legislator with authority only over a definite territory.

[48] Cf. *supra*, p. 69.

[49] Cf. *supra*, pp. 45, 46.

[50] Cf. canons 1099 and 900, 3°.

[51] Cf. Deschepper, "De obligatione peregrinorum et vagorum,"—*Coll. Brug.*, XXIV (1924), 158; Onclin, *De Legis Indole*, p. 357. Jone, *Kanonischen Rechtes*, I, 32.

[52] Cf. Van Hove, *De Legibus*, n. 210.

When the universal legislator enacts a particular law, he can, if he wills it, extend the obligation of that particular law to include those subjects of the territory who are actually absent from it.[53] For the jurisdiction of the universal legislator extends directly and immediately to each member of the Church.[54] The only title required for subjection to the Holy See is membership in the Catholic Church acquired by the reception of baptism.[55] Therefore the subject of a particular territory remains as completely subject to the universal legislator while he is absent from his proper particular territory as he is while within it. The universal legislator, then, can enact a particular law which binds the subject while he is absent from his own territory. The primary source of the extra-territorial obligation of particular laws enacted by the universal legislator is the will of the legislator.

Particular laws enacted by particular legislators, however, could not bind the absent subject according to the pre-Code doctrine.[56] This conclusion was based chiefly upon the restriction of the jurisdiction of particular legislators to their own territories. The operative competence of particular legislators, however, is not actually determined by divine law.[57] The hierarchical organization of the Church provides for one supreme legislative authority for the whole Church, to which particular legislators are subordinated, and from which they receive the functional limits of their jurisdiction.[58] The Supreme Pontiff extends or restricts their legislative jurisdiction as regards both persons

[53] Cf. Chelodi-Bertagnoli, *Ius De Personis*, n. 63; Claeys Bouuaert-Simenon, *Manuale Iuris Can.*, I, 88; Deschepper, "De obligatione peregrinorum et vagorum,"—*Coll. Brug.*, XXIV (1924), 154.

[54] Canon 218, § 2. Cf. Concilium Vaticanum, Sess IV, c. 3—Denzinger-Bannwart, *Enchiridion Symbolorum Definitionum et Declarationum de Rebus Fidei et Morum* (16.et 17.ed., Friburgi Brisgoviae: Herder, 1928), n. 1831; Ryan, *Episcopal Jurisdiction*, pp. 64-67; Cavagnis, *Institutiones Iuris Publici Ecclesiastici* (4.ed., 3 vols., Romae, 1906), II, n. 187—cited hereafter as Cavagnis, *Inst. Iuris Pub. Eccl.*

[55] Cf. canon 87; Wernz-Vidal, *Ius Canonicum*, I, p. 197, nota 99.

[56] Cf. *supra*, p. 65.

[57] Cf. Ryan, *Episcopal Jurisdiction*, p. 87.

[58] Cf. canon 329, § 1. The *functional* limits of the jurisdiction of particular legislators are spoken of here to distinguish these limits from the potential capacity of episcopal jurisdiction. This latter is determined from a consideration of the episcopal office of governing under the authority of the Supreme Pontiff. The actual power is not necessarily equal to its potentiality. The actual power is determined by a positive

and territory.[59] The disposition established by Boniface VIII in the decretal *Ut animarum*[60] was a practical expression of the actual restriction of the jurisdiction of the particular legislator over his subjects to the time when the latter were within his territory. The Code has implicitly revoked this restriction in canons 8, § 2[61] and 201, § 3[62]. Canon 14, § 1, 1° expressly extends the power of the particular legislator to all of his subjects, whether they are within his territory or absent from it.[63] Thus the positive disposition of the Code has established that par-

juridical act actualizing the native but subordinate potentiality of episcopal jurisdiction. Cf. Ryan, *Episcopal Jurisdiction,* pp. 57 and 87.

[59] "Though the bishop's *potential* capability may be determined by its fundamental relationship to the primatial jurisdiction of the Roman Pontiff, its *actual* capacity within those natural bonds was left by Christ to be more or less determined by the supreme authority of the Pope as times and circumstances, either universal or local, demand."—Ryan, *Episcopal Jurisdiction,* p. 87. Cf. also: "At talis [episcoporum] potestas iure divino determinata non est quoad *personas* tales vel tale *territorium,* nec etiam nisi *generatim* circa actus et materias: R. Pontifex eam amplificare aut restringere potest, dummodo maneat potestas *substantialiter* perfecta etiam in foro externo."—Rivet, *Institutiones Iuris Ecclesiastici Privati* (3 vols., Romae, 1916), I, 371. Cf. Cavagnis, *Inst. Iuris Pub. Eccl.,* II, n. 51; Bachofen, *Summa Juris Ecclesiastici Publici* (Romae, 1910), n. 18; Ottaviani, *Institutiones Iuris Publici Ecclesiastici* (2.ed., 2 vols., [Civitas Vaticana]: Typis Polyglottis Vaticanis, 1935), I, n. 219—cited hereafter as Ottaviani, *Inst. Iuris Pub. Eccl.*

[60] C. 2, *de constitutionibus,* I, 2, in VI°.

[61] "Lex non praesumitur personalis, sed territorialis, *nisi aliud constet.*"—canon 8, § 2 (Italics inserted). Cf. Deschepper, "De obligatione peregrinorum et vagorum," —*Coll. Brug.,* XXIV (1924), 154; Onclin, *De Legis Indole,* p. 325; Van Hove, *De Legibus,* n. 118; Cicognani, *Ius Canonicum,* II, 19, 80; Coronata, *Inst. Iuris Can.,* I, n. 3; Claeys Bouuaert-Simenon, *Manuale Iuris Can.* I, 88.

[62] "Nisi aliud ex rerum natura aut ex iure constet, *potestatem voluntariam seu non-iudicialem* quis exercere potest . . . *in subditum e territorio absentem.*"—canon 201, § 3 (Italics inserted). By the explanation of voluntary jurisdiction as non-judicial jurisdiction in this canon, the Code signifies its intention to assimilate legislative power into the category of voluntary jurisdiction, even though it may not be voluntary jurisdiction in the proper sense of the word. Therefore the objection that Chelodi-Bertagnolli present, namely that legislative jurisdiction is not voluntary jurisdiction, is of no value. Cf. Chelodi-Bertagnolli, *Ius De Personis,* p. 107, nota 3, and n. 125. Cf. on the contrary Opetti, *Commentarium in Cod.,* I, 82; Maroto, *Inst. Iuris Can.,* I, n. 724; Michiels, *Normae Generales,* I, 311; Deschepper, "De indole personali legum episcopalium,—*Coll. Brug.,* XXIII (1923), 220, 221.

[63] "Peregrini non adstringuntur legibus particularibus sui territorii quamdiu ab eo absunt, *nisi . . . leges sint personales.*"—canon 14, § 1, 1° (Italics inserted).

ticular legislators may endow their laws with extra-territorial obligatory force, binding their subjects who are absent from the territory. The primary source of the obligation of the absent subject to observe the particular laws of his own territory is, therefore, the will of the legislator expressed in the law.

§ 2. *The Content of the Law as Source of the Obligation of the Absent Subject*

The Code recognizes another source of the extra-territorial obligation of particular laws, namely, the content of the law. Certain particular laws are enacted to safeguard the good of the territory in a special way. Thus particular laws may regard obligations to be performed within the territory. Others, for example, may be enacted to safeguard rights or goods pertaining to the territory. Such laws may be designated as materially territorial, because the matter which they regulate, or their content, is specifically in and of the territory. To violate such laws could cause harm in the territory, whether the violation were committed outside the territory or not. To prevent harm to the special good of the territory in this instance, the Code has established that these laws by their very content bind subjects of the territory even when these subjects are absent from the territory.[64]

Article IV. The Absent Subject Is Not Generally Bound By the Laws of His Own Territory

That it is within the power of the legislator to endow all or most[65] of his laws with extra-territorial obligatory force follows from what has been stated. In fact, the second provisional draft of the Code in

[64] "Peregrini non adstringuntur legibus sui territorii quandiu ab eo absunt, nisi . . . earum transgressio in proprio territorio noceat . . . "—canon 14, § 1, 1°. Cf. Deschepper, "De obligatione peregrinorum et vagorum,"—*Coll. Brug.*, XXIV (1924), 154; Van Hove, *De Legibus*, n. 209.

[65] Certain extrinsic limits on the power of the legislator to enact extra-territorial laws appear from the consideration of certain necessary obligations of the absent subject to observe the laws of the territory where he is, for example, laws which safeguard the public order of the territory where he is. Such obligations have a priority over extra-territorial obligations that might be urged upon the absent subject, and thus limit the power of the legislator to make personal laws in the same matter. These limitations will be treated in the next chapter.

1914 had just such a discipline, namely that particular laws were generally personal, and in doubt were to be presumed personal.[66] However, the Code finally adopted the position that the absent subject is not generally bound by the laws of his own territory. The extra-territorial obligation of law is restricted to the exceptional case, when either the the non-observance of the law would bring harm upon the territory, or when the legislator considers it necessary to make a personal law.[67] By comparison of the first number of canon 14, § 1 with the second paragraph of canon 8[68] it follows that the presumption in uncertain cases is to be maintained in favor of the freedom of the absent subject from the obligation of the particular laws of his own territory. The general wording of canon 8, § 2 indicates that it applies to all laws, including particular laws. Furthermore, the practical importance of a presumption favoring the territorial limitation of the obligation is found principally in reference to particular laws. Universal laws are of themselves territorially unlimited and bind their subjects everywhere, regardless of whether they are personal or territorial.[69] The original intention of the authors of the Code to annex this paragraph to the canon regulating the obligation of the traveler reveals the mind of the Code to apply this presumption to the territoriality of particular laws.[70] Wherefore, the commentators on the Code have been in agreement in maintaining that particular laws are to be presumed territorial when doubt arises concerning their extra-territorial force.[71] From

[66] Cf. *supra*, p. 76.

[67] Canon 14, § 1, 1°.

[68] "Lex non praesumitur personalis, sed territorialis, nisi aliud constet."—canon 8, § 2.

[69] Cf. Van Hove, *De Legibus*, n. 121; Cocchi, *Commentarium in Cod.*, I, n. 99; Berutti, *Inst. Iuris Can.*, I, n. 55; Simenon, "Territorialitas legum,"—*REL*, XXI (1929-1930), 184.

[70] Cf. *supra*, p. 75.

[71] Cf. Michiels, *Normae Generales*, I, 310; Claeys Bouuaert-Simenon, *Manuale Iuris Can.*, I, 89; Ayrinhac, *General Legislation in the New Code of Canon Law* (London, New York, Toronto: Longmans Green and Co., 1933), n. 94—hereafter cited as *General Legislation*; Onclin, *De Legis Indole*, p. 328; Cicognani, *Ius Canonicum*, II, 79; Van Hove, *De Legibus*, nn. 121, 122; Cocchi, *Commentarium in Cod.*, I, n. 98; Deschepper, "De obligatione peregrinorum et vagorum,"—*Coll. Brug.*, XXIV (1924), 154; Leroux, "Le sujet des lois ecclésiastiques,"—*REL*, XVI (1924-1925), 335.

the presumption established in canon 8, § 2 and applied to canon 14, § 1, 1°, follows the necessity of clearly indicating the extra-territorial force of particular laws before the absent subject can be held bound to obey them.

The positive disposition of the Code in canon 14, § 1, 1°, that the absent subject is not bound by the particular laws of his own territory unless in evident and exceptional cases, is more in harmony with the pre-Code law and its interpretation than the opposite disposition of a general rule that particular laws should be personal. The pre-Code law held as a principle that the absent subject was not bound by the laws of his own territory. When extra-territorial laws were found necessary to protect the good of the territory, these pre-Code authorities resorted to the fiction of moral presence in the territory to keep intact their principle of territoriality.[72]

Moreover, to limit the extra-territorial obligation of particular laws to exceptional cases, as it is limited by the Code, is the more practical discipline to adopt. The normal circumstances are provided for by the universal law of the Code. Particular laws are enacted to apply these general norms of the Code to the particular circumstances of the territory,[73] or to establish other norms, not contrary to the Code, because of the peculiar conditions of the place.[74] They are designed chiefly to counteract or take advantage of the geographic, climatic, or cultural influences of the locality and to guard against the special dangers that arise therefrom. But the absent subject is withdrawn from the influence of these particular circumstances. Therefore he is not subject to the particular dangers which motivated the legislator to enact the law, nor can he, in his absence, aid or hinder the attainment of the special purpose desired by the law in most cases. Generally, therefore, there

[72] Cf. *supra*, p. 67.

[73] Here it may be noted that numerous statutes of diocesan synods only reaffirm or emphasize obligations already existing in universal law. Such obligations bind outside the territory by virtue of the fact that they exist in universal law. And to the extent that they already exist in universal law, they do not enter into the present discussion. Cf. Leroux, "Le sujet des lois ecclésiastiques,"—*REL*, XVI (1924-1925), 336.

[74] Cf. Ryan, *Episcopal Jurisdiction*, pp. 133-136.

is no practical reason to burden the absent subject with the obligations of the laws of his own territory.[75]

With good reasons, therefore, the Code has established the general rule that the absent subject is not bound by the particular laws of his own territory. Extra-territorial obligations are to be the exception. Such obligations must be clearly indicated either by the will of the legislator clearly expressed in the law, or by the content of the law *evidently* requiring the law to be observed outside the territory to prevent harm in the territory. Doubtful cases are to be solved by the presumption in favor of the freedom of the absent subject from the obligation of the particular laws of his own territory.

[75] Cf. Michiels, *Normae Generales*, I, 307, 308; Van Hove, *De Legibus*, n. 126; Onclin, *De Legis Indole*, p. 328; Berutti, *Inst. Iuris Can.*, I, n. 55; Maroto, *Inst. Iuris Can.*, I, n. 183; Leroux, "Le sujet des lois ecclésiastiques,"—*REL*, XVI (1924-1925), 336; Simenon, "Territorialitas legum,"—*REL*, XXI (1929-1930), 184; Deschepper, "De obligatione peregrinorum et vagorum,"—*Coll. Brug.*, XXVI (1924), 154.

Chapter VI

OBLIGATIONS OF THE ABSENT SUBJECT TO OBSERVE THE PARTICULAR LAWS OF HIS OWN TERRITORY

The source of the obligation of the absent subject to observe the particular laws of his own territory is, as has been demonstrated, either the content of the law or the positive and clearly indicated will of the legislator. This chapter presents the specific interpretation of these exceptional obligations of the absent subject.

Article I. Extra-Territorial Obligation By Virtue of the Content of the Law

The Code indicates as the first class of particular laws binding the absent subject those laws whose transgression causes harm in the proper territory of the subject.[1] Along with this class of laws may be included those laws which are personal by their very nature because they directly affect the juridical status of persons.[2]

§ 1. *Meaning of the term: "Cause Harm in the Territory"* (in proprio territorio noceat)

In order to preserve intact the principle of territoriality of laws, the pre-Code authors resorted to the fiction of moral presence to explain the obligation of the absent subject to observe particular laws when their transgression would affect his proper territory.[3] This fiction was often expressed by the formula that the person, the act, and the object of the act had to be simultaneously entirely outside of the territory before the subject would be released from the obligation of the particular law.

Since the Code, many authors have continued to resort to this same fiction in explaining the extra-territorial obligation of certain parti-

[1] "Peregrini non adstringuntur legibus particularibus sui territorii . . . nisi earum transgressio in proprio territorio noceat."—canon 14, § 1, 1°.

[2] "Peregrini non adstringuntur legibus particularibus sui territorii . . . nisi . . . leges sint personales."—canon 14, § 1, 1°.

[3] Cf. *supra*, p. 67.

cular laws.[4] A fiction of the law is a disposition of the law which, for a just reason, posits as a fact something which is possible but really non-existent.[5] Since the Code recognizes the existence of particular personal or extra-territorial laws, there is no just reason to resort to a fiction of the law to explain these laws. When the transgression of the law by an absent subject would bring harm upon the territory, such a law is extra-territorial by reason of its content.[6]

The phrase "laws the violation of which causes harm in the territory" does not refer to the violation of every law. Although every violation of a law may somehow cause harm in the territory because the law is enacted for the good of the territory, this phrase refers to the special harm that is caused in the territory by the violation of the law by an absent subject.[7] Nor, on the contrary, is this phrase restricted to harm done to the social or public good of the territory, as in the violation of those laws which safeguard public order.[8] Rather, the harm done in the territory by the violation of such laws can be either spiritual or material, public or private, common or individual.[9] The Code merely requires that harm be done *in* the territory. The force of the preposition *in,* in the terminology of the Code, is to include any injury done in the territory by the violation of a law, and not just injury to the public or social good, that is harm done *to* the territory.

[4] Cf. Coronata, *Inst. Iuris Can.*, I, n. 15; Berutti, *Inst. Iuris Can.*, I, n. 61; Wernz-Vidal, *Ius Canonicum,* I, n. 156; Blat, *Commentarium Iuris Can.*, I, n. 71; Cappello, *Summa Iuris Canonici*, I, n. 79; Cocchi, *Commentarium in Cod.*, I, n. 56; Chelodi-Bertagnolli, *Ius De Personis,* n. 65; Sole, Iacobus, *De Delictis et Poenis* (Romae-[R]Atisbonae-Coloniae Agrippinae-Neo-Eboraci-Cincinnati: Pustet, 1920), n. 106; Cerato, *Censurae Vigentes Ipso Facto a Codice Iuris Canonici Excerptae* (2.ed., Patavii: Typis Seminarii, 1921), p. 19—hereafter cited as Cerato, *Censurae Vigentes*; Ojetti,*Commentarium in Cod.*, I, 114; Simenon, "Territorialitas legum,"—*REL*, XXI (1929-1930), 187.

[5] Cf. Van Hove, *De Legibus*, n. 336.

[6] Cf. Van Hove, *De Legibus*, n. 209; Toso, *Comm. Minora*, I. 41; Michiels, *Normae Generales*, I, 312; Vermeersch-Creusen, *Epitome Iuris Canonici,* I, n. 90; Maroto, *Iinst. Iuris Can.*, I, n. 201; Cicognani, *Ius Canonicum*, II, 103; Deschepper, "De obligatione peregrinorum et vagorum,"—*Coll. Brug.*, XXIV (1924), 154.

[7] Cf. Ojetti, *Commentarium in Cod.*, I, 114.

[8] Cf. *infra*, pp. 139-141.

[9] Cf. Berutti, *Inst. Iuris Can.*, I, n. 61.

The terminology of the Code, used to indicate the laws which are by their content personal, has been taken from the writings of some of the pre-Code authors.[10] Those same laws are referred to in the Code as extra-territorial which the pre-Code authors maintained were obligatory on the physically absent subject because of moral presence in the territory.[11] Therefore, although they alleged a different reason for their position, the explanations offered by the pre-Code authorities for the term "cause harm in the territory" are the norms for interpreting this phrase in canon 14, § 1 1°. The pre-Code authors used various formulae to express this concept. An examination of these formulae in themselves and as applied to the laws they indicate will bring out the full meaning of the term "cause harm in the territory."

§ 2. *Violation of Affirmative Laws Which Causes Harm in the Territory*

Pre-Code authors commonly taught that the violation of affirmative laws requiring an act to be placed within the territory caused harm in the territory.[12] The effect of an act of omission takes place in that place where the act should have been placed. This same concept was expressed by the pre-Code authors in the formulae which required not only the subject, but also the act and the object to be entirely outside the territory before the absent subject would be released from the obligation of the laws of his territory.

The classical example of such an affirmative law is the law of residence.[13] The law of residence requires that the subject "should not only

[10] Note that the Code uses the phrase *in proprio territorio noceat*; many pre-Code writers used the phrase *proprio territorio noceat*. The absence of the preposition *in* limited the extension of this phrase to social harm. The force of the preposition *in* is to include other expressions used by pre-Code authors to express moral presence in the territory.

[11] Cf. Van Hove, *De Legibus*, nn. 116, 209; Onclin, *De Legis Indole*, p. 357; Ojetti, *Commentarium in Cod.*, I, 114; *supra*, p. 67.

[12] Cf. *supra*, p. 67.

[13] Cf. canons 143; 144; 188, 8°; 338; 354; 418; 419, § 1; 448, § 2; 465; 471, § 4; 474; 476, § 5; 2168-2175; 2381; Prümmer, *Manuale Theologiae Moralis* (8.ed., 3 vols., Friburgi Brisgoviae: Herder, 1935-1936), I, n. 194—cited hereafter as Prümmer, *Theologia Moralis*; Bouquillon, *Theologia Moralis*, n. 147; Bucceroni, *Institutiones Theologiae Moralis* (3.ed., 2 vols., Romae, 1898), I, n. 199—cited hereafter

always be morally present within the territory to which he is appointed, but he should carry out the duties his appointment entails."[14] The reason for laws of residence is the service of the territory for which the cleric is ordained or appointed. The law is violated as much by neglect to provide for the proper discharge of the cleric's duties during his absence as by failure to return within the appointed time.[15] These laws are enacted, therefore, to guard against the harm caused by neglect of duty and of the care of souls. Acts or omissions violating the law of residence do harm in the territory. Particular legislators are empowered to make particular laws determining the universal laws of the Code in this matter.[16] Such particular laws are then extra-territorial in virtue of their content.

From the explanation of the laws of residence, it follows that all laws determining specific obligations to be performed in the territory have extra-territorial force. Such laws may be particular applications of the universal law establishing the pastor's obligation of preaching,[17] of giving catechetical instructions at specified times,[18] of keeping parish registers and account books, as well as making periodical reports concerning them.[19] A beneficiary is personally bound by the obligations attached to his benefice, even though the source of those obligations is particular law.[20] Even legitimate absence does not exempt those who hold an office in the territory from the personal responsibility for the obligations attached to that office and specifically determined by particular laws.

as Bucceroni, *Inst. Theol. Moralis;* Van Hove, *De Legibus,* n. 209; Coronata, *Inst. Iuris Can.,* I, n. 15; Jone, *Kanonischen Rechtes,* I, 33; Vermeersch-Creusen, *Epitome Iuris Canonici,* I, n. 90; Ayrinhac, *General Legislation,* n. 103; Cicognani, *Ius Canonicum,* II, 103; Beste, *Introd. in Codicem,* p. 63; Toso, *Comm. Minora,* I, 103; Chelodi-Bertagnolli, *Ius de Personis,* n. 65; Maroto, *Inst. Iuris Can.,* I, n. 201; Teodori, "Peregrini quoad leges servandas,"—*Consult. Iuris Can.,* I (1934), 18.

[14] Reilly, *Residence of Pastors* (The Catholic University of America Canon Law Studies, n. 97, Washington, D. C.: The Catholic University of America, 1935), p. 3—cited hereafter as *Residence of Pastors.*

[15] Cf. canon 1344 Reilly, *Residence of Pastors,* pp. 32, 33.

[16] Cf. canon 143.

[17] Cf. canons 1344; 1346.

[18] Cf. canon 1336.

[19] Cf. canons 1523; 1525.

[20] Cf. canons 1475; 1476; 1478.

Other particular laws may require the subject to be present in the territory at a definite time for a specific purpose. Such laws are by their very content extra-territorial. Authors commonly illustrate such laws by the example of a law requiring priests to attend a synod.[21] Particular laws specifying the time and place of junior clergy examinations[22] and of clerical conferences[23] are illustrations of more frequent occurrence. Absence from the territory, even when it is legitimate, does not absolve the subject from the obligation of these particular laws, because they are affirmative laws prescribing an act to be placed within the territory. The violation of these laws is an act which produces its harmful effect within the territory.

§ 3. *Violations of Laws Regarding a Thing Situated Within the Territory* (ratione rei sitae)

The pre-Code writers required that not only the person and the act, but also the object of the act be outside of the territory before the physically absent subject would be released from the obligation of the laws of his own territory. Or, conversely, they held that the subject remained bound by the laws of his own territory by reason of the thing which remained therein (*ratione rei sitae*). This same reason for subjection of the absent subject to the particular laws of his own territory is commonly found among the authors on Private International Law.[24] Since particular laws regarding objects in the territory are enacted to protect those objects, the violation of these laws does harm in the territory.[25] Moralists cite as an example of this kind of law a

[21] Cf. Van Hove, *De Legibus*, n. 209; Cicognani, *Ius Canonicum*, II, 103; Maroto, *Inst. Iuris Can.*, I, n. 201; Onclin, *De Legis Indole* p. 357; Jone, *Kanonischen Rechtes*, I, 33.

[22] Cf. canon 130, § 1.

[23] Cf. canon 131.

[24] Cf. Pillet, *Traité Pratique de Droit International Privé* (2 vols., Grenoble: Joseph Allier—Paris: Recueil de Sirey, 1923), I, nn. 342, 343, 348 *bis*—hereafter this work will be cited as *Traité de Droit Int. Privé*; Surville, *Cours Elémentaire de Droit International Privé* (7.ed., Paris: Rosseau & Cie., 1925), nn. 165-170—cited hereafter as *Cours de Droit Int. Privé.*

[25] Note that these laws are enacted in view of a general danger. The individual case may be presented where the non-observance of such laws might not harm the object in the territory. Nevertheless the law would still bind in this case by virtue of canon 21.

law regulating the sale of a piece of immovable property located within the territory. Although the subject was outside of his territory when he made the sale, the laws of his territory would govern the transaction.[26] Because they regard objects located within the territory, the particular laws governing the alienation or the renting of Church property located in his own territory,[27] and the particular laws establishing conditions required for the validity or licitness of acts beyond the ordinary limits of the administration of goods in the territory[28] bind the absent subject. Other examples of these laws may be found regulating the obligation of the beneficiary or patron to repair the property of the benefice.[29] Particular laws may establish the means to keep churches in repair,[30] or to support the Church and its ministers, such as laws regarding tithes, pew rents, and the like.[31] Particular laws regulating this matter, when they have application to an absent subject,[32] bind him because the object is situated within the territory.

Laws which safeguard the rights of persons in the territory are laws whose object is within the territory equally as much as those laws which regard a material object within the territory. The violation of a law which protects the right of a person in the territory does harm in the territory. Examples of these laws are frequently found in the legislation on the sacraments. While safeguarding the rights of the faithful to receive the sacraments at any time and in any place when

[26] Cf. Bucceroni, *Inst. Theol. Moralis,* I, n. 199; cf. canon 1529.

[27] Cf. canons 1479; 1530-1533; 1535; 1537-1543.

[28] Cf. canon 1527, § 1.

[29] Cf. canons 1477; 1469.

[30] Cf. canon 1186.

[31] Cf. canons 463, § 1; 1234 et 1236; 1502; 2349; Coronata, *Inst. Iuris Can.*, I, n. 482; Augustine, *Commentary,* I, 90, 91; S.C.C., decr., 11 dec. 1920—*ASS*, XIII (1921), 350. Note that the means of support enacted by these laws do not include the free will offerings obtained, for example, through collections. Cf. Coronata, *l.c.*; Vermeersch-Creusen, *Epitome Iuris Canonici,* I, n. 459; Augustine, *Commentary,* II (6.ed., 1936), 451; Fanfani, *De Iure Parochorum ad Normam Codicis Iuris Canonici* (2.ed., Taurini-Romae: Marietti, 1936), nn. 190, 191—cited hereafter as *De Iure Parochorum.*

[32] E.g., a law regulating pew rent, or the parochial portion due to the proper parish as often as a deceased person could have been conveniently buried from his own parish—canon 1236.

they reasonably seek them,[33] the Code establishes certain rights for the pastor in their administration.[34] Parochial subjects have a correlative obligation to seek the administration of the sacraments from their proper pastors, unless a just cause should excuse them.[35] The injury done to a pastor by the violation of this obligation on the part of the subjects may affect, not only his right to a means of support, but also the efficiency of his ministry. By avoiding the ministrations of their proper pastor, parochial subjects may render the vigilance and care of their proper pastor more difficult. The Code, therefore, indicates that the universal law may be applied to the exigencies of local conditions by particular laws regarding the administration of certain sacraments. Such particular laws are, to the extent of their obligation, extra-territorial. To facilitate the obligations of the pastor in regard to solemn baptism[36] the pastor has the right to confer solemn Baptism on his proper subjects. A particular law legitimately specifying the extent of this right in the concrete circumstances or correcting an abuse in this matter would be extra-territorial by its very content. Its violation would hinder the fulfillment of parochial duties and harm parochial rights.[37] Although the pre-Code legislation requiring the Paschal Communion to be received in each person's parish[38] has been abrogated, the Code desires that the same discipline be encouraged and that pastors be notified when their subjects receive their Easter Communion out-

[33] Cf. *infra,* p. 114.

[34] Cf. canons 462, 463, § 1.

[35] Cf. Chelodi-Bertagnolli, *Ius de Personis,* n. 226; Vermeersch-Creusen, *Epitome Iuris Canonici,* I, n. 548; Eichmann, *Lehrbuch des Kirchenrechts auf Grund des Codex Iuris Canonici* (4.ed., 2 vols., Paderborn: Verlag Ferdinand Schöningh, 1934), I, 299—cited as *Kirchenrechts;* Ferry, *Stole Fees* (The Catholic University of America Canon Law Studies, n. 59, Washington, D. C.: The Catholic University of America, 1930), pp. 47, 48—cited as *Stole Fees;* Cance, *Code de Droit Canonique,* I, n. 404.

[36] Cf. canons 766; 767; 777.

[37] Cf. Vermeersch-Creusen, *Epitome Iuris Canonici,* II (5.ed., 1934), n. 52; Ferry, *Stole Fees,* pp. 55, 64.

[38] Cf. Sanchez, *De Matr.,* III, c. XXIII, n. 12; Wernz, *Ius Decretalium,* III, n. 743; Vindex, "Domicilium et quasi-domicilium eorumque effectus in Codice Iuris Canonici,"—*Jus Pont.,* VI (1926), 118; IV Lateran Council (1513), c. 21—Mansi, XXII, 1007.

side of the parish.[39] A particular law enforcing this latter desire of the Code would be personal in virtue of its content. The Code gives ordinaries the right to restrain their subjects from licit reception of the Sacrament of Confirmation outside of their diocese.[40] If such a restriction were expressed in a particular law by the ordinary, it would bind outside the territory by that very fact. The laws of the proper bishop for Sacred Orders[41] evidently bind his subjects regarding the qualities and conditions for the reception of Sacred Orders, even when these subjects receive the Sacrament of Orders outside of the territory.

Although the ordinary cannot make a particular law restricting the licit or valid reception of Matrimony which would amount to a new impediment,[42] he is permitted to provide for the pre-nuptial examination of the freedom of his subjects to marry.[43] Such provisions expressed in particular laws bind the absent subject until they are dispensed from by the proper ordinary of one of the parties.[44]

§ 4. *Violations of Laws Enacted to Prevent Special Harm to the Territory*

The laws in the foregoing considerations are personal or extra-territorial because they concern objects or rights situated within the territory. A violation of such laws causes injury in the territory. Pre-Code authors also considered as extra-territorial those laws which were enacted with the specific end in view to prevent special harm to the territory, that is, public or social harm.[45] Such harm could easily arise from the publication of books and articles to be disseminated in the

[39] Cf. canon 859, § 3; Vindex, "Domicilium et quasi-domicilium eorumque effectus in Codice Juris Canonici,"—*Jus Pont.*, VI (1926), 118.

[40] Cf. canon 738, § 1.

[41] Cf. canon 956.

[42] Cf. canon 1038, § 2.

[43] Cf. canon 1020, § 3; S.C. de Sacr. Instr. "*Sacrosanctum matrimonii*," 19 iun, 1941, n. 4—*AAS*, XXII (1941), 539.

[44] Cf. canon 1928; S.C. de Sacr. Instr., 19 iun, 1941—*AAS* (1941), 540.

[45] Note that, as has already been pointed out, this class of laws has a less extensive application than the term used in canon 14, § 1, 1°: "cause harm *in* the territory." To cause harm *to* the territory refers only to the social good of the territory, whereas to cause harm *in* the territory extends to all of the various classes of laws thus far.

territory. The danger of such an injury becomes accentuated when the author of the book or article is a cleric, because of the added authority his status gives him. Wherefore the Code entrusts proper ordinaries with vigilance over the public writings of clerics.[46] The particular laws enacted to exercise this vigilance are by their very content binding outside of the territory.[47] Aside from these cases, however, the laws of the ordinary regarding the approbation of books and articles do not, by their content alone, bind outside the territory.[48]

Besides the previous censorship of books, the Code enables ordinaries to protect their subjects from harmful reading by means of the prohibition of books.[49] Books may be prohibited not only because of the harm they may cause in the territory by undermining discipline and morality, but also because of the particular circumstances of the time and place. The reading of a forbidden book does not necessarily cause harm to the territory. Particular laws prohibiting books are not invariably personal because of their content alone. The legislator should clearly indicate when he wishes to make such a law binding on his subjects outside of their territory.

Finally, the question arises concerning the extra-territorial force of penal laws. Penalties are sanctions of the law. As such they are accessories to the principal, and as accessories, they follow the nature of the principal, the law. Subjection to the penalty depends upon subjection to the law. The general principle then can be established that a penal law is extra-territorial only when the law is extra-territorial of itself, independently of the penal sanction.[50] However, the precise question involved is whether the presence of

[46] Cf. canon 1386, § 1.

[47] Cf. Claeys Bouuart-Simenon, *Manuale Iuris Can.*, I, n. 919, nota 2.

[48] Note that canon 1386, § 2 speaks of the permission of the ordinary *of the place* required to publish articles in journals or periodicals which habitually attack faith or morals. Canon 1385, § 2 gives the author the right to seek approbation from his own ordinary, the ordinary of the place of printing, or of the place of the publication of his work.

[49] Cf. canon 1395, § 1.

[50] Cf. 2226, § 1; Chelodi, *Ius Poenale et Ordo Procedendi in Iudiciis Criminalibus Iuxta Codicem Iuris Canonici* (4.ed., recognita et aucta a Vigilio Dalpiaz, Tridenti: Libraria Moderna Editrice A. Ardesi, 1935), n. 26—cited as *Ius Poenale.*

a penal sanction is indicative of laws enacted to prevent special harm done to the territory. Indeed the intrinsic purpose of penalties is the reparation of the social order.[51] However, the essential difference between the ecclesiastical society and the civil society consists in the difference of objectives. The Church seeks as its ultimate and proper objective the sanctification of each of the faithful,[52] while the State seeks only the common temporal good of its citizens.[53] Since the sanctification of the faithful is the specifying and essential objective of the Church, the correction of the delinquent is an intrinsic objective in the penal system of the Church, so that it is intended directly and primarily in many of the penalties of the Church.[54] Not every penal law, therefore, is indicative of a law enacted to prevent special harm to the territory. The transgression of a penal law does not necessarily result in harm in the proper ter-

[51] Cf. canons 1552; 1554; 2215; Chelodi, *Ius Poenale*, n. 18; Vermeersch-Creusen, *Epitome Iuris Canonici*, III (5.ed., 1936), n. 403; Hollweck, *Die kirchlichen Strafgetze* (Mainz, 1899), n. 20; Roberti, *De Delictis et Poenis* (2.ed., vol. I, Pars. I, Romae: Apud Custodiam Librariam Pontificii Utriusque Iuris, [1939]), n. 223; Hinschius, *Das Kirchenrecht der Katholiken und Protestanten in Deutschland* (6 vols., Berlin, 1869-1897), IV (1888), 747, 748—cited hereafter as *Kirchenrecht*; Wernz, *Ius Decretalium*, VI, n. 73; Cappello, *Summa Iuris Publici Ecclesiastici* (3. ed., Romae: Apud Aedes Universitatis Gregorianae, 1932), n. 91—cited as *Summa Iuris Pub. Eccl.*; Ottaviani, *Inst. Iur's Pub. Eccl.*, I, nn. 64, 171; Cavagnis, *Inst. Iuris Pub. Eccl.*, I, nn. 299-303.

[52] Cf. Cavagnis, *Inst. Iuris Pub. Eccl.*, I, n. 301; Ottaviani, *Inst. Iuris Pub. Eccl.*, I, nn. 88-90; II, n. 303.

[53] Cf. Ottaviani, *Inst. Iuris Pub. Eccl.*, II, nn. 250, 303.

[54] Cf. Ottaviani, *Inst. Iuris Pub. Eccl.*, I, n. 171; Lega, *Praelectiones in Textum Iuris Canonici—De Delictis et Poenis* (Romae, 1910), nn. 9, 11—cited hereafter as *De Delictis*; Hollweck, *Die kirchlichen Strafgesetze*, n. 21, p. 81, nota 1; Vermeersch-Creusen, *Epitome Iuris Canonici*, III, n. 404; Sole, *De Delictis et Poenis*, n. 106; Cerato, *Censurae Vigentes*, p. 3; Van Hove, "Leges quae ordini publico consulunt,"—*ETL*, I (1924), 164, 165. Others hold that the correction of the delinquent is merely extrinsic and secondary in the penal system of the Church; that the reparation of the social order is the only intrinsic purpose of penal laws in the Church—cf. Wernz, *Ius Decretalium*, VI, n. 73; Chelodi, *Ius Poenale*, n. 18; Coronata, *Inst. Iuris Can.*, IV, n. 1688; Roberti, *De Delictis et Poenis*, n. 223. However, this view fails to give proper consideration to the specific and intrinsic purpose of the Church, namely the sanctification of souls. It logically leads to the conclusion that the absent subject is bound by all of the penal laws of his own territory. Cf. Roberti, *De Delictis et Poenis*, n. 60.

ritory. The absent subject, therefore, is bound by virtue of the content of the penal law only when the law considered in itself and independently of its penal character is extra-territorial.[55]

§ 5. *Laws Regarding the Legal Status of Persons*

Incapacitating laws and laws regarding the juridical status of persons have been considered personal by authorities on Private International Law since the time of Bartolus.[56] Pre-Code canonists and moralists were divided on the question of the obligation of the physically absent subject to observe these laws. However, incapacitating laws and laws regarding the juridical status of persons directly affect the juridical person of the subject. As such they are laws which are personal by their very content and nature.[57] The Code, by a positive disposition of the law grants extra-territorial force to all personal laws.[58] Since the Code, therefore, particular laws regarding legal capacity or incapacity and laws directly affecting the juridical status of persons are to be considered extra-territorial.[59] Thus, for example, if a particular law should be enacted by the Holy See establishing a particular matrimonial impediment,[60] such a law would bind its subjects outside of the territory.

[55] Cf. Cappello, *De Censuris*, n. 19; Vermeersch-Creusen, *Epitome Iuris Canonici*, III, n. 416; Sole, *De Delictis et Poenis*, n. 104; Cerato, *Censurae Vigentes*, p. 19; Chelodi, *Ius Poenale*, n. 26; Crnica, *Modificationes in Tractatu de Censuris per Codicem Iuris Canonici Introductae* (S. Mauritii Agaunensis, 1919), p. 22. Note that only penal *laws* are treated here. Precepts given to individuals bind everywhere according to canon 24. Likewise penalties which have been inflicted and neither dispensed from nor absolved bind their subjects wherever they are.—Canon 2226, § 4. Reservations, on the contrary, do not bind outside of the territory of the one reserving, except in the case of censures *inflicted ab homine*—canons 900, 3°; 2217, § 1; 2236; 2245; § 2; cf. *infra*, pp. 121-126.

[56] Cf. Pillet, *Traité de Droit Int. Privé*, I, nn. 229-237; Surville, *Cours de Droit Int. Privé*, n. 140; *supra*, p. 40.

[57] Cf. Van Hove, *De Legibus*, n. 156; Wernz-Vidal, *Ius Canonicum*, I, n. 162; Ojetti, *Commentarium in Cod.*, I, 115.

[58] "Peregrini non adstringuntur legibus sui territorii . . . *nisi leges sint personales.*" —canon 14, § 1, 1°.

[59] Cf. Beste, *Introductio in Cod.*, p. 63; Ayrinhac, *General Legislation*, p. 111; Ojetti, *Commentarium in Cod.*, I, 115; Vermeersch-Creusen, *Epitome Iuris Canonici*, I, n. 90; Cance, *Code De Droit Canonique*, I, n. 38; Maroto, *Inst. Iuris Can.*, I, n. 183; Onclin, *De Legis Indole*, p. 355; Michiels, *Normae Generales*, I, 311.

[60] Cf. canon 1038.

Here it may be noted that the Code gives sanction to the matrimonial impediment of legal relationship according to Civil Law.[61] Thus this impediment has the nature of a particular ecclesiastical law where it exists as a secular law. But in giving canonical sanction to the Civil Law impediment of legal relationship, the Code does not intend to give this impediment greater extension than it has in Civil Law.[62] Therefore the difference between Anglo-American and European Continental law has singular importance in Canon Law. Anglo-American Law follows the principle of strict territoriality of law. Thus the impediment of legal relationship would not bind the traveler who wished to contract marriage outside of his own territory and in a territory where it was not in force.[63] In Continental Law and in South American Law, the principle of personality of law is in force regarding the impediments to marriage. Thus a European or South American bound by the impediment of legal relationship according to the laws of his own country remains bound by that impediment wherever he goes.[64] It is therefore important, in

[61] Cf. canons 1059, 1080.

[62] "Qui *lege civili* inhabiles ad nuptias inter se ineundas habentur . . . nequeunt vi iuris canonici matrimonium inter se valide contrahere."—canon 1080.

[63] "**Le droit du mariage en Angleterre.** Il n'en est pas de même en Angleterre et dans les États-Unis d'Amérique. Ces pays sont surtout attachés en cette matière à la loi du domicile; encore faut-il observer que, primitivement, la jurisprudence anglaise ne distinguait pas entre la capacité et la forme en matière de mariage, soumettant l'une et l'autre à la loi du lieu dans lequel l'union etait célébrée; . . ."

"Dans les États-Unis d'Amérique, la jurisprudence . . . s'attache surtout en matière de capacité matrimoniale, à faire prévaloir l'autorité de la loi du lieu oü le mariage est célébré . . . "—Pillet, *Traité de Droit Int. Privé,* I, n. 261.

Sometimes, however, American Civil Law expresses itself as extra-territorial for those who leave the territory with the fraudulent intention to evade the law—cf. *infra,* p. 130, note 72.

[64] "Le mariage n'intéresse véritablement que l'État auquel appartiennent les époux et dont fera partie la famille qu'ils vont fonder; il n'intéresse en aucune façon l'État sur les terres duquel ceux-ci se trouvraient domiciliés s'ils appartenaient à une nationalité différente. Cette raison décisive a fait prévaloir sur le continent européen la loi de la nationalité qui est presque partout considérée comme étant celle qui doit fixer les conditions du mariage. Ainsi un mariage contracté à l'étranger entre beau-frère et belle-soeur français est nul s'il n'a pas été précedé par l'autorisation du Gouvernement français."

the pre-nuptial investigation of aliens from Continental Europe or South America, to examine into this impediment if it is at all suspected.

Article II. Extra-Territorial Obligation By Virtue of the Will of the Legislator

Thus far, only those laws have been considered which are extra-territorial by their very content: because the violation of the law causes harm in the territory, or because the law directly affects the juridical status of the subject. The Code indicates that the will of the legislator is a second source of the obligation of the absent subject to observe the particular laws of his own territory. This difference is to be noted between the two sources of extra-territorial obligations: when the obligation of the absent subject is imposed by the will of the legislator, that extra-territorial obligation must be clearly expressed in the law, or it cannot be urged upon the subject; when the extra-territorial obligation of the law is derived from its content, it is frequently sufficiently evident in the law itself that it binds outside of the territory.

Examples of personal obligations established by the will of the universal legislator can be easily found among laws regulating liturgy.[65] The universal legislator has established the liturgical calendar for the particular territory as a personal law to be followed by priests saying Mass in a private oratory outside of their territory.[66] Likewise the liturgical calendar of his own territory is to be followed as though a particular personal law by the absent subject in the recitation of the

Dans les divers États de l'Amérique du Sud, le caractère personnel et permanent des lois sur la capacité en matière de mariage est mieux respecté [qu'aux États Unis d'Amérique]. Ces États se rattachent de préférence à la loi du domicile, sauf quelques exceptions cependant."—Pillet, *o.c.*, nn. 260, 261.

[65] Cf. Maroto, *Inst. Iuris Can.*, I, n. 183; Claeys Bouuaert-Simenon, *Manuale Iuris Can.*, I, n. 154, p. 89, nota 1; Cocchi, *Commentarium in Cod.*, I, n. 99; Ojetti, *Commentarium in Cod.*, III (1930), 132, nota 24.

[66] S.R.C., decr. *Urbis et Orbis*, 9 iulii 1895, rata et confirmata, 9 dec. 1895—*Decreta Authentica Congregationis Sacrorum Rituum ex actis eiusdem collecta eiusque auctoritate promulgata* (6 vols, Romae, 1898-1927), n. 3862—Hereafter cited as *Decreta Authentica; Ruthenen.*, 22 maii 1896—*Decreta Authentica*, n. 3910. Cf. Moretti, *De Sacris Functionibus Episcopo Celebrante-Assistente-Absente* (4 vols., Taurini: Marietti, 1936-1939), I, n. 363—cited hereafter as *De Sacris Functionibus.*

breviary as often as he has a benefice in his territory,[67] or he is a pastor or his substitute,[68] a teacher or a student in a seminary,[69] a religious bound to recite the Office in choir,[70] or a residential bishop.[71]

The particular legislator, however, may not arbitrarily exercise his power of enacting extra-territorial laws. Canon 201, from which the legislative jurisdiction of the particular legislator over his absent subject is basically derived, indicates certain limits arising from the nature of the object or from law.[72] Although the particular legislator can certainly enact personal laws in some matters, and is certainly prevented by universal law from imposing personal obligations in other matters, the use of legislative jurisdiction over the absent subject is largely left to his prudent judgment.

§ 1. *Matters Wherein the Particular Legislator Certainly May Legitimately Enact Personal Laws*

As often as the circumstances render it advisable, the particular legislator can evidently enact particular personal laws in any of the matters treated in the previous article. In fact, the particular legislator cannot declare that those laws, which are personal by their content, are to be interpreted as exclusively territorial. The personality of these laws is derived from the universal law expressed in canon 14, § 1, 1°. To attempt to render them exclusively territorial is, therefore, against the Code.[73] Again it may be noted that whenever it is

[67] Cf. De Herdt, *Sacrae Liturgiae Praxis Iuxta Ritum Romanum* (8.ed., 3 vols., Lovanii, 1888-1889), II, 209, 228; Ojetti, *Commentarium in Cod.*, III, 132, nota 24.

[68] S.R.C., *Mechlinien.*, 7 dec., 1844—*Decreta Authentica,* n. 2872.

[69] S.R.C., *Adrien.*, 7 sept. 1850—*Decreta Authentica,* n. 2980.

[70] S.R.C., *Ordinis Minorum Capuccinorum,* 31 aug. 1839—*Decreta Authentica,* n. 2801; *Societatis Iesu,* 18 sept. 1877—*Decreta Authentica,* n. 3436.

[71] S.R.C., *Pro regulari promoto ad episcopatum,* 11 iunii 1605—*Decreta Authentica,* n. 181; *Valven et Sulmonen.*, 17 ian., 1880—*Decreta Authentica,* n. 2508. Outside of the cases enumerated, the absent subject is free to choose between the calendar of the place where he is and the calendar for his own territory, although he is counseled to follow the calendar of his own territory. Cf. S.R.C., *Marsorum,* 12 nov. 1831—*Decreta Authentica,* n. 2682.

[72] "Nisi aliud *ex rerum natura* aut *ex iure* constet, potestatem iurisdictionis voluntariam seu non-iudicialem quis exercere potest . . . in subditum e territorio absentem."—canon 201, § 3.

[73] Cf. Michiels, *Normae Generales,* I, 312.

not sufficiently clear that the law is extra-territorial from its content, the force of the law will be limited to the territory unless the legislator clearly indicates his intention to make it personal.

Several authors present, as examples of laws which the legislator may make personal, the obligations peculiar to the clerical state, such as prohibitions to participate in or frequent places of amusement, recreation, or pusuits dangerous to their own spiritual life, or liable to lessen the dignity and respect due to the clerical state, or to give scandal to the faithful.[74] The Code specifically mentions certain matters in which the ordinary can adapt the universal law to his subjects by means of personal particular laws. Thus, for instance, the ordinary can enact a personal law extending the time for the fulfillment of the paschal precept.[75] Or he can enact personal laws forbidding his subjects to read or possess certain dangerous books.[76] The exercise of the power to enact personal or extra-territorial laws in cases such as these is certainly legitimate.

§ 2. *Matters Wherein the Particular Legislator Cannot Legitimately Enact Personal Laws*

The power of the particular legislator to enact laws binding the absent subject, however, is certainly limited, not because of the defect of jurisdiction, as such, but by extrinsic sources.

The most evident limit placed upon the legitimate exercise of the power to enact particular personal laws arises from the necessary obligation of the absent subject to observe the laws which secure public order or determine the solemnities of acts in the place where he is visiting.[77]

Some authors infer from this that the particular legislator cannot

[74] Cf. canons 138; 139; 140; Maroto, *Inst. Iuris Can.*, I, nn. 183, 200; Ayrinhac, *General Legislation*, n. 94; Claeys Bouuaert-Simenon, *Manuale Iuris Can.*, I, n. 154; Beste, *Introd. in Codicem*, p. 63; Onclin, *De Legis Indole*, p. 357; Ojetti, *Comm. in Codicem*, I, 83; Leroux, "Le sujet des lois ecclésiastiques,"—*REL*, XVI (1924-1925), 336.

[75] Cf. canon 859, § 2; Onclin, *De Legis Indole*, p. 357.

[76] Cf. canon 1395; Maroto, *Inst. Iuris Can.*, I, n. 200; Schaefer, *De Religiosis*, n. 487; Ojetti, *Commentarium in Cod.*, I, p. 83.

[77] Cf. canon 14, § 1, 2°; Van Hove, *De Legibus*, nn. 126, 209; Michiels, *Normae Generales*, I, 312; Deschepper, "De obligationne peregrinorum et vagorum,"—*Collat. Brug.*, XXIV (1924), 154.

place a personal obligation on similar laws of his own territory.[78] Although absolutely territorial laws are not generally personal also, there is nothing in the nature of law, or in the Code, which excludes particular laws of such a mixed character. The *Tametsi* law[79] regarding the juridical form of marriage was both territorial and personal. It was territorial because it determined the solemnities of the juridical act of marriage. It was personal because of the positive will of the legislator. Nowhere in the Code is the particular legislator deprived of the right to enact a personal law which is also absolutely territorial.[80] In the case where the traveler is bound by a conflict of contrary obligations, the one imposed by a personal law of his own territory and the other arising from an absolutely territorial law of the place where he is visiting, the obligation of the absolutely territorial law prevails in virtue of the universal law expressed in canon 14, § 1, 2°.[81] On the other hand, the subject may be bound by two compatible obligations arising from different particular laws either because he has several proper territories, or because one obligation is derived from a personal law of his proper territory and the other arises from an absolutely territorial law of the place where he is. In this case, he is bound to observe both of the laws if they are prohibitive. If they are positive obligations, canonical equity would allow him to observe either one or the other according to his wish.[82]

The Legitimate exercise of the power of particular legislators to enact particular personal laws is limited by universal law in several matters. The most frequently occurring examples of these specific limits on extra-territorial jurisdiction are found in the legislation of the sacraments. Although, as has been explained, the particular legislator can safeguard parochial rights, he cannot insist upon the maintenance of these rights to the extinction of all of the right of the faithful to the reception of the sacrament outside of their proper territory. A law which insists upon the reception of Solemn Baptism from the proper pastor of the subject even at the grave inconvenience of

[78] Cf. Onclin, *De Legis Indole*, p. 329, nota 1.

[79] Cf. *supra*, p. 46.

[80] Cf. Van Hove, *De Legibus*, n. 123; Onclin, *De Legis Indole*, p. 320; Eichmann, *Kirchenrechts*, I, 55.

[81] Cf. Cicognani, *Ius Canonicum*, II, 78.

[82] Cf. Van Hove, *De Legibus*, n. 209.

the subject or delay in the administration of the sacrament is against the Code.[83] Nor can a personal law be enacted in view of reserving the right of admitting children to their first Holy Communion to their proper pastors. The judgment concerning the proper dispositions of the child to make first Holy Communion pertains to the parents and to the confessor.[84] Although the pre-Code law required the paschal precept to be fulfilled in the proper parish,[85] the Code concedes the right to the faithful to receive it elsewhere.[86] A personal law enacted by a particular legislator depriving his subjects of this right would therefore be against the Code. It is equally evident that a law requiring Viaticum or Extreme Unction to be received exclusively from the proper pastor of the infirm person would be against the Code.[87] No reservation of sins or censures by a particular legislator can be personal, and a particular law enacted by a particular legislator forbidding departure from the diocese to evade a reservation would be against the Code.[88]

The universal law places specific limits on the power of particular legislators to enact personal laws in other matters besides the sacraments. The amounts fixed by particular law to be offered for acts of voluntary jurisdiction, or on the occasion of the administration of the sacraments pertain only to that diocese or province for which they are determined.[89] Likewise the law or custom which determines the amount

[83] Cf. canon 738, § 2; Vindex, "Domicilium et quasi-domicilium eorumque effectus in Codice Juris Canonici,"—*Jus. Pont.*, VI (1926), 114.

[84] Cf. canon 854, § 4; Cappello, *Tractatus Canonico-Moralis De Sacramentis* (3 vols. in 6, Taurinorium Augustae: Marietti-Romae: Marietti-Apud Aedes Univ. Gregorianae, 1932-1939), I (3.ed., 1938), nn. 529, 534—cited hereafter as *De Sacramentis.*

[85] IV Lateran Council (1513), c. 21—Mansi, XXII, 1007; Wernz, *Ius Decretalium*, III, n. 743; Sanchez, *De Matr.*, III, c. XXIII, n. 12.

[86] Cf. canon 859, § 3.

[87] Cf. canons 864, 865, 866, § 3; 938, § 2.

[88] Cf. canons 900, 3°; 2247, § 2. Reserved cases directly affect the power of the confessor. Yet the limitation on the power of the confessor is restricted to the territory of the person reserving the case. Thus a pastor hearing the confessions of his subject outside of the diocese, or the priest hearing confessions during a sea voyage according to canon 883, § 1, can absolve from the sins and censures reserved by the particular laws of his own territory. Cf. *infra*, p. 124.

[89] Cf. canons 1507; 1909.

to be offered as a manual Mass stipend has no force outside of the territory.[90] Universal law directs the particular legislators to guard over the divine worship in their own territories,[91] thereby restricting the particular laws they enact in this matter to their own territories.

These examples illustrate the restriction placed by universal law in various instances upon the power of particular legislators to enact personal laws.

§ 3. *Matters Wherein the Particular Legislator May Enact Personal Laws in Exceptional Cases Only*

Although the particular legislator has the jurisdiction to enact personal laws, and although there may be no definite universal law or absolutely territorial law of another territory to limit the exercise of that power, the particular legislator must still take into account the utility of the personal law he may contemplate enacting. He must consider whether the personal law will attain the purpose desired, and whether it is necessary as a means to attain that purpose.

The mind of the universal legislator is clearly indicated in canons 8, § 2 and 14, § 1, 1°, namely, that personal laws should be the exception rather than the rule. A greater restriction is placed upon the freedom of the subject by personal laws than by territorial laws. On the other hand, as has been pointed out, the absent subject is generally neither subject to the influence of his home environment nor able to affect the common good of his proper territory. Therefore, before the legislator places the added restriction of a personal law upon his subjects, natural equity[92] should counsel him to consider well whether the

[90] Cf. canon 831. Since the Code, the law of the place where the stipend is *offered* determines the amount of the stipend. Cf. canon 830; Keller, *Mass Stipends* (The Catholic University of America Canon Law Studies, n. 27, Washington, D. C.: The Catholic University of America, 1925), pp. 87, 88.

[91] Cf. canon 1261, § 2.

[92] The term *natural equity* is used here because it is not a question of the *right* of the legislator to enact a personal law, but of the proper *exercise* of that power. The meaning of natural equity is aptly given by Van Hove: "Ut virtus specialis, aequitas est media inter iustitiam et caritatem, proximior tamen iustitiae, cuius est pars potentialis; hac homo inclinatur ad moderatum et humanum usum iuris sui; dicit in aequitatis studioso aliquam remissionem iuris, in eo cui aequitas prodest aliquem titulum imperfectum ad hanc postulandam vel expectandam."—*De Legibus*, n. 295.

exigencies of the common good of the territory demand such a legislation.[93]

Although, taking into account the limitations placed by universal and particular laws as just demonstrated, the final judgment concerning the justice and equity of the personal law is left to the conscience of the particular legislator, he must never exercise his powers arbitrarily and absolutely. Taking his inspiration from pontifical sources,[94] Ryan very aptly writes:

> However, even within the limits placed by positive ecclesiastical law upon the bishop's natural prerogatives, his authority is not absolute or arbitrary. It is intended for the maximum spiritual utility of those whom it governs, and is ordained in its use to the building up of the mystical body of Christ, not merely on the basis of legal uniformity or extremity and far less by force of official domination, but rather, and to a great extent, on the foundation of that paternal and pastoral care which alone can beget the trusting confidence and love of his spiritual children, one for another, of the flock for its shepherd, and unite them, as members of Christ's body, with the visible head of the Church.[95]

[93] The exceptional character of personal laws is variously emphasized by the canonists. Michiels states: "Dixi 'legitime declaravit', quia ex hoc quod legislatori inferiori potestas ferendi leges personales indubitanter competit, immerito concluderetur potestatem illam, ad usum quod attinet, esse sine ulla limitatione in proprio ejus arbitrio positam. Jam *in genere* enim retinendum est, quod nonnisi *exceptionaliter* hac sua potestate uti debeat; Codex enim, . . . in can. 8, § 2 . . . aperte innuit bono communi, quod mensuram potestatis legislativae determinat, regulariter provideri per leges mere territoriales."—*Normae Generales,* I, 312. Deschepper writes: "Sane non posset legislator inferior omnes suas leges particulares 'personales' dicere; exceptionaliter tantum uti potest hac potestate; mensura enim potestatis legislatoris est 'bonum commune.' Porro jus commune . . . in can. 8 . . . jam innuit plerumque bonum commune satis per leges territoriales intendi."—"De obligatione peregrinorum et vagorum,"—*Coll. Brug.,* XXIV (1924), 154. Van Hove gives the following succinct counsel: "Res [statuendi leges personales] committitur conscientiae legislatoris pro exigentia boni communis, de quo iudicium ferre ad ipsum pertinet."—*De Legibus,* n. 209.

[94] Cf. Leo XIII, ep. encycl. "*Cum multa,*" 8 dec. 1882, n. 4.—*Fontes,* n. 587; Benedict XIV, *De Synodo Diocesana,* Lib. II, c. VII, n. 6.

[95] *Episcopal Jurisdiction,* p. 97.

Chapter VII

THE STRANGER AND THE PARTICULAR LAWS OF HIS PLACE OF TEMPORARY RESIDENCE

Canon 14, § 1, 2°[1] states the principles governing the obligations of the stranger[2] to observe the particular laws of the territory of his temporary residence.

Article I. What Laws Are Included in Canon 14, § 1, 2°

Although this number of the first paragraph of canon 14 does not explicitly mention particular laws, it evidently refers only to particular laws. The text of this part of the canon concerns the "laws of the territory." This phrase, interpreted by canon 13, § 2,[3] refers to those laws enacted for a definite territory. The restriction of this number of canon 14 to particular laws follows from a consideration of the third number of the same canon. Canon 14, § 1, 3° states the discipline regarding universal laws in force in a particular territory. This reference in canon 14, § 1, 3° would be unnecessary if the previous paragraph had reference to universal laws as well as particular laws. As a consequence, canon 14, § 1, 2° refers to particular laws, and only to particular laws.

From this it follows that the laws of a purely personal community are, by their very nature, excluded from this number of canon 14. A personal community has no definite territory as such. On the other hand, all of the particular laws of a particular territory, whether they are enacted by the supreme legislator or by a particular legislator, are included in the scope of canon 14, § 1, 2°. This canon does not dis-

[1] "[Peregrini] Neque legibus territorii in quo versantur [tenentur], iis exceptis quae ordini publico consulunt, vel actuum sollemnia determinant;"—canon 14, § 1, 2°.

[2] By stranger is meant here the peregrin in the proper sense of the term, that is, he who has a domicile or quasi-domicile or both, but who at the moment is absent from the territory of both his domicile and quasi-domicile. Cf. *supra*, p. 2.

[3] "Legibus conditis pro peculiari territorio ii subiiciuntur pro quibus latae sint, quique ibidem domicilium vel quasi-domicilium habent et simul actu commorantur, firmo praescripto can. 14."—canon 13, § 2.

tinguish between those particular laws which come from the supreme authority in the Church and those which come from local authority. Moreover, since the same principles apply to custom as to law, unwritten laws are also included in canon 14, § 1, 2°.

Article II. General Rule of the Exemption of the Stranger from the Laws of His Place of Temporary Residence

Those particular laws which are enacted for a definite territory by the supreme legislator can bind the stranger in the territory or not according to the will of the supreme legislator. The jurisdiction of the Holy See extends directly and immediately to each of the faithful, as has been demonstrated. Territorial divisions do not affect the power of the universal legislator considered in itself. The general exemption of the stranger from those particular laws enacted by the universal legislator for the territory is derived simply from the will of the legislator expressed in canon 14, § 1, 2°.

The extension of the native power of the particular legislator to strangers within his territory was a matter of controversy before the Code. Suarez and his followers maintained that the particular legislator had complete jurisdiction over the strangers in his territory because his office was to provide for the good government of the territory, and therefore his jurisdiction affected all within the territory through a territorial medium.[4] Sanchez and his followers held that the complete jurisdiction of the particular local legislator extended directly only to those who were inhabitants of his territory by reason of domicile or quasi-domicile.[5] The latter position was almost unanimously supported in the XIX Century, and was adopted by the Code in the canon under present discussion. Since, however, it is within the power of the supreme legislator to extend or limit the actual operative competence of the particular legislator, the practical solution of the problem in canon 14, § 1, 2° cannot be construed as a doctrinal solution of the pre-Code controversy.[6]

[4] Cf. *supra*, pp. 49-53.

[5] Cf. *supra*, pp. 54-58.

[6] "Nihil enim obstat, quominus S. Sedis, si velit, peregrinos vel suis legibus particularibus pro peculiari territorio latis obliget, vel etiam, propter bonum commune in illo loco securius procurandum, legibus territorialibus Superioris localis subjiciat."

However, it is more in harmony with the juridical system of the Church. The particular government of the Church is, by Apostolic constitution at least,[7] practically accomplished through territorial divisions, particular churches.[8] Over these particular churches are placed local legislators, normally residential bishops.[9] Hence the basis of the legitimate exercise of particular legislative power is, regularly, the territory over which the particular legislator presides.[10]

The formal object of all ecclesiastical jurisdiction, however, and of legislative jurisdiction in particular, is a personal object, the government of subjects for the sanctification of their souls.[11] As Ryan states, whatever legislative jurisdiction embraces, it does so by reason of a personal reference to subjects.[12] Subjection to the authority in a society is derived from membership in that society by reason of some title. In a particular society, whose medium of jurisdiction is territorial, this membership is naturally derived from a local association or bond.[13] Since membership in a society implies a mutual activity of all of the members for a common objective,[14] the membership in the society is more complete as this local association is more stable.[15] There-

—Michiels, *Normae Generales*, I, 316. Cf. Deschepper, "De subjecto legis ecclesiasticae particularis,"—*Coll. Brug.*, XXIV (1924), 55.

[7] Authors hesitate to attribute territorial divisions of the Church immediately to divine ordinance. They say it is fundamentally of divine ordinance as the necessary complement of the organization of the Church. Cf. Ottaviani, *Inst. Iuris Pub. Eccl.*, I, n. 201; Cappello, *Summa Iuris Canonici*, I, n. 360; Ryan, *Episcopal Jurisdiction*, pp. 44, 45.

[8] Cf. canon 215.

[9] Cf. canon 329, § 1; Ryan, *Episcopal Jurisdiction*, p. 45.

[10] "Quare omnes qui cum territorio sunt aliqua stabili ratione colligati, sive ratione originis et domicilii, sive ratione tantum domicilii, obnoxios regulariter esse eidem episcopali auctoritati."—S.C.C., *"Iurisdictionis,"* 12 aug., 1871, II—*ASS*, VI (1870-1871), 587; Cf. canon 94, § 1; Ryan, *Episcopal Jurisdiction*, p. 100.

[11] Cf. Ottaviani, *Inst. Iuris Pub. Eccl.*, I, nn. 113,117; Tarquini, *Juris Ecclesiastici Publici Institutiones* (Romae, 1862), n. 15; Cavagnis, *Inst. Iuris Pub. Eccl.*, I, n. 35; Chelodi-Bertagnolli, *Ius de Personis*, n. 125.

[12] *Episcopal Jurisdiction*, p. 100.

[13] Cf. Wernz-Vidal, *Ius Canonicum*, I, n. 147, p. 199, nota 99; Ryan, *Episcopal Jurisdiction*, p. 100.

[14] Cf. Ottaviani, *Inst. Iuris Pub. Eccl.*, I, n. 17.

[15] Cf. Böckhn, *In Jus Canonicum*, I, Lib. I, Tit. II, n. 52; Laymann *Theologia Moralis*, I, Tr. IV, c. XI, n. 1; Ryan, *Episcopal Jurisdiction*, p. 100.

fore the ordinary and complete title of subjection to the local legislator is the stable residence by which a domicile or quasi-domicile is acquired.[16] The care of those who have a stable residence in the territory is the primary and principle purpose of the institution of a particular legislative authority in the Church.[17] Strangers, who have a stable residence elsewhere, remain essentially and virtually subject to the local legislator of the place of their stable residence.[18] Their association with the place where they are visiting is only accidental and exceptional. Therefore the ordinary title of jurisdiction over them belongs to the legislator of their place of stable residence, and not to the legislator in whose territory they are strangers.[19] Therefore the local legislator of the place where they temporarily are cannot ordinarily oblige them to observe his laws. They are only exceptionally subject to him, and his care for their spiritual welfare is limited.[20]

Article III. Exceptional Obligation to Observe the Laws of the Place of Temporary Residence

But this defect of the ordinary title of subjection to the local particular legislator does not exclude certain extraordinary titles of subjection. Since their presence and conduct may at times affect the welfare of the ordinary subjects of the particular territorial jurisdiction, they must be liable at such times to the control of the particular legislator of the territory.[21] In his function as guardian of the spiritual welfare and public good of all the ordinary and complete subjects of his particular territory, the local legislator requires all the power necessary to maintain that welfare unimpaired. Therefore there are certain

[16] Cf. canons 13, § 2; 94; Chelodi-Bertagnolli, *Ius de Personis*, n. 65; Vindex, "Domicilium et quasi-domicilium eorumque effectus in Codice Juris Canonici,"—*Jus Pont.*, VI (1926), 52.

[17] "They [who have a stable residence in the territory] are those for whose spiritual welfare the institution of the episcopate as a territorial authority was intended by Christ, and whom, as a result, diocesan divisions and organization in the Church naturally and primarily regard. They consequently are also the most completely subject to episcopal jurisdiction."—Ryan, *Episcopal Jurisdiction*, pp. 100, 101.

[18] Cf. *supra*, pp. 92-94.

[19] Cf. Deschepper, "De subjecto legis ecclesiasticae particularis,"—*Col. Brug.*, XXIV (1924), 56.

[20] Cf. canon 14, § 1, 1°.

[21] Cf. Ryan, *Episcopal Jurisdiction*, p. 104.

extraordinary and exceptional titles of subjection to the jurisdiction of the local legislator, namely, indirect subjection, the natural law, universal law, civil law and public order.

Since the jurisdiction of the local legislator over the stranger in his territory is exceptional and limited to extraordinary titles, the presumption in a doubtful case follows the rule and favors the freedom of the stranger. No particular law of the territory binds the stranger unless that obligation is evident from the law itself or from the authentic declaration of the legislator. Particular legislators should make it clearly understood when they intend to bind strangers by their laws.[22]

§ 1. *Indirect Subjection to the Laws of the Place of Temporary Residence*

Subjection to the laws of a territory may be indirectly communicated to strangers through a relationship into which they enter with the habitual subjects of the territory. The most apparent example of this is the indirect subjection of strangers to the particular reserved cases in the territory. This obligation is communicated to the stranger when he enters into the relationship of penitent to a confessor who has received his jurisdiction from the local ordinary and is exercising it within the latter's territory.[23] Certain authors,[24] writing since the Code, maintain that strangers are bound by the particular reservations of the place because, in virtue of canon 897,[25] these laws secure public order. This canon indicates the purpose of reservations, as disciplinary measures rather than penal measures.[26] It follows from canon 897 that

[22] Cf. Claeys Bouuaert-Simenon, *Manuale Iuris Can.*, I, n. 164; Beste, *Introductio in Cod.*, p. 72.

[23] Cf. canons 893; 2246; PCI, 24 nov. 1920—*AAS*, XII (1920), 575.

[24] Cf. Toso, Annotationes,"—*Jus Pont.*, III)1923), 7; Coronata, *Inst. Iuris Can.*, I, 15; Donovan, Joseph P., "Is the interpretation of canon 900 also dated?"—*The Homiletic and Pastoral Review*, XLII (1942), 436. This periodical is hereafter cited by the initials *HPR*.

[25] ". . . ipsa vero reservatio ne ultra in vigore maneat, quam necesse sit ad publicum aloquod inolitum vitium exstirpandum et collapsam forte christianam disciplinam instaurandam."—Canon 897.

[26] Cf. Darmanin, "De reservatione peccatorum iure Codicis Piano-Benedictino,"—*Angelicum*, V (1928), 224; Dargin, *Reserved Cases According to the Code of Canon*

reserved cases are enacted on account of the public good. However, as will be pointed out, the public good is not the same as the public order. The reservation of a case is not an invariable sign of a law enacted to secure public order.

Rather, as Van Hove[27] states, strangers are subject to local reservations because of the limitation on the power of the confessor.[28] The reservation of a case, according to canon 893, §§ 1 and 2, means the submitting of a sin to the judgment of a competent superior for absolution with the consequent restriction upon the power of a subordinate confessor to absolve that sin.[29] The Pontifical Commission for the Authentic Interpretation of the Canons of the Code was asked whether strangers are subject to the reservations of the place where they are *according to the prescriptions of canon* 893, § 1 and § 2. The Commission responded in the affirmative.[30] The direct reference to canon 893, §§ 1 and 2 and the unqualified affirmative response of the Code Commission authentically indicate that the *one reason* for the

Law (The Catholic University of America Canon Law Studies, n. 20, Washington, D. C.: The Catholic University of America, 1924), p. 11. Cited hereafter as Dargin, *Reserved Cases.*

[27] "La réponse de la Commission d'Interpretation du Code, du 26 novembre, 1920, soumet les étrangers aux cas réservés (canon 893) . . . uniquement parce qu'en vertu de la réserve le confesseur n'a pas le pouvoir d'absoudre des cas réservés."—"Leges quae ordini publico consulunt,"—*ETL*, I (1924), 159. Cf. also, Van Hove, *De Legibus*, n. 220; Michiels, *Normae Generales*, I, 319, nota 3; Claeys Bouuaert-Simenon, *Manuale Iuris Can.*, I, n. 164; Cappello, *De Sacramentis*, I, Pars II (3 ed., 1938), n. 527; Torrubiano Ripoli, *Novísimas Instituciones de Derecho Canónico* (2.ed., 2 vols., Madrid: Otero-Portela, 1934), I, n. 102—cited hereafter as *De Derecho Canónico;* Dargin, *Reserved Cases*, pp. 35, 75; Vermeersch, "Annotationes,"—*Periodica*, X (1922), 255, 256; Sartori, *Enchiridion Canonicum seu Sanctae Sedis Responsiones post editum Codicem J. C. datae* (Vicetiae: Ex Typographica Commerciali, 1938), pp. 20, 21; Leroux, "Le sujet des lois ecclésiastiques,"—*REL*, XVI (1924-1925), 339; Deschepper, "De obligatione peregrinorum et vagorum,"—*Coll. Brug.*, XXIV (1924), 156; Simenon, "Territorialitas legum,"—*REL*, XXI (1929-1930), 186.

[28] Cf. canons 881; 893, 894.

[29] Cf. canon 893, §§ 1, 2; Dargin, *Reserved Cases*, p. 4; Darmanin, "De reservatione peccatorum iure Codicis Piano-Benedictino,"—*Angelicum*, V (1928), 69.

[30] "Utrum, *ad normam canonis 893*, §§ *1 et 2*, peregrinus teneatur reservationibus loci in quo degit."

"R. Affirmative."—PCI, 24 nov. 1920—*AAS*, XII (1920), 575 (Italics inserted).

subjection of the stranger to local reservations is the restriction upon the faculty of the subordinate confessor as stated in that canon.

A difference between the manner of expression in the Code and in the pre-Code instruction of the Holy Office,[81] issued July 16, 1916, has been urged as a demonstration that a penitent is not bound by the reservations of the place where he is a stranger when he has committed the sin elsewhere.[82] The instruction of 1916 states that penitents can be absolved from sins reserved in one diocese when they are in another diocese where the sins are not reserved.[83] Since canon 900, 3°[84] does not repeat the clause "where the sins are not reserved," it is argued that this canon gives the confessor faculties to absolve strangers from sins reserved in the diocese, but which the visiting penitent did not commit in the diocese. This argumentation overlooks the difference in the entire expression of the Instruction of 1916 and of canon 900, 3°. The instruction speaks of penitents seeking absolution in another diocese. Without the restriction placed by the clause "where the sins are not reserved," it clearly follows that when penitents go out of the diocese where they committed a reserved sin, they could be absolved from it regardless of the particular reservations in force in that other diocese. But the clause "where the sins are not reserved" is entirely unnecessary in reference to canon 900, 3°. This canon states that every reservation is without force outside of the territory of a superior making the reservation. The entire grammatical construction of the main clause of canon 900, 3° is entirely different from the construction of the same law in the instruction of 1916. Therefore to use a verbal difference in the two laws as the basis of an argument is liable tc result in misinterpretation. According to canon 900, 3°, as Dargin states clearly,[85] a stranger in a diocese where a sin is reserved is not outside of the territory of a superior reserving the sin. To add the clause "where the

[81] S.C.S.Off., instr., 16 iul. 1916—*AAS*, VIII (1916), 315.

[82] Cf. Donovan, "Is the interpretation of canon 900 also dated?"—*HPR*, XLII (1942), 435, 436.

[83] "Postremo, a peccatis in aliqua dioecesi reservatis absolvi possunt poenitentes in alia dioecesi, ubi reservata non sunt . . . "—S.C.S.Off. instr., 16 iul. 1916, n. 7,—*AAS*, VIII (1916), 315.

[84] "Quaevis reservatio omni vi caret: . . . Extra territorium reservantis . . . "—canon 900, 3°.

[85] *Reserved Cases*, p. 36.

sins are not reserved" would be useless repetition in canon 900, 3°. From the omission of this clause, therefore, it cannot be argued that the Code has changed the instruction of the Holy Office, issued in 1916.

There are then two principles to bear in mind regarding the indirect subjection of strangers to the reservations of the place where they are. Strangers are absolved by virtue of jurisdiction derived from the ordinary of the place where the confessions are heard. The reservation directly affects this jurisdiction of the confessor, and only indirectly affects the penitent. Thus, if a pastor from another diocese should hear the confession of his subject in a diocese where a particular reservation was in force, he could absolve his subject from that sin or censure which was reserved in the place where the confession was heard.[86] Similarly, a confessor hearing confessions during an ocean voyage is not limited by the reservations of the port or of the place from which he has received his jurisdiction, when he has not received his jurisdiction from the ordinary of the port.[87]

Finally, it should be observed that canon 893, §§ 1 and 2 refers to sins reserved by reason of themselves, as well as to sins reserved by reason of censures. As a consequence, the interpretation of the Code Commission applies to reserved censures as well as to reserved sins. Strangers are subject to the reserved censures of the place where they are because of the limitation on the jurisdiction of the subordinate confessors who have received their jurisdiction from the ordinary of the place.[88]

A similar indirect subjection of the stranger is exemplified in the inflicting of a local interdict.[89] A local interdict affects the place directly, and, for that reason, indirectly extends to everyone in the

[86] Cf. canons 873, § 1 et 881, § 2.

[87] Cf. canon 883, § 2; PCI, 20 maii 1923—*AAS*, XXVI (1924), 114; Van Hove, *De Legibus*, n. 220.

[88] Cf. Dargin, *Reserved Cases*, pp. 75, 76.

[89] Cf. canons 2268, 2; 2269, § 2; Roberti, *De Delictis et Poenis*, n. 351; Chelodi, *Ius Poenale*, n. 39; Cappello, *De Censuris*, n. 468; Van Hove, *De Legibus*, n. 220; Onclin, *De Legis Indole*, p. 338; Jone, *Kanonischen Rechtes*, I, 33; Deschepper, "De obligatione peregrinorum et vagorum,"—*Coll. Brug.*, XXIV (1924), 156; Leroux, "Le sujet des lois ecclésiastiques,"—*REL*, XIV (1924-1925), 338.

place. However, the inflicting of a local interdict is not so much a matter of a particular law as of a particular act imposed by the superior.[40]

§ 2. *Obligation Arising from the Natural Law*

The natural law provides that grave scandal should be avoided. Scandal is defined by St. Thomas as any immoral word or deed which offers the occasion of spiritual ruin.[41] Scandal is not to be understood, therefore, in the popular sense of the word as that which arouses wonderment, surprise, or even horror at the sins of another.[42] Rather it is that act or deed, immoral in itself, or because of the circumstances, which becomes the occasion of probably leading another into a sin which he would not otherwise commit.[43] Scandal is, of its nature, a grave sin against the virtue of charity.[44]

Therefore, when the stranger foresees that the non-observance of a particular law will be the occasion of the violation of the law by those habitually subject to it, he is bound exceptionally to observe it himself. An example of such an occasion can easily arise in the matter of fast and abstinence or of the observance of a holy day.[45] Some authors consider that laws whose violation may cause scandal are laws which secure public order.[46] The obligation of avoiding scandal refers

[40] Cf. canon 2269, § 1; Van Hove, "Leges quae ordini publico consulunt,"—*ETL,* I (1924), 158, 159; Michiels, *Normae Generales,* I, 320.

[41] " . . . dictum vel factum minus rectum praebens occasionem ruinae [spiritualis]."—*Summa Theologica,* IIa IIae, Q. XLIII, A. I, c.

[42] Cf. Merkelbach, *Summa Theol. Moralis,* I, n. 957.

[43] Cf. St. Thomas Aquinas, *Summa Theologica,* IIa IIae, Q. XLII, A. I, ad 4; Merkelbach, *Summa Theol. Moralis,* I, n. 859; Tanquerey, *Theologia Moralis Fundamentalis* (9.ed., Parisiis-Tornaci-Romae: Desclée et Socii, 1931) n. 833; Marc-Gestermann-Raus, *Institutiones Morales Alphonsianae* (19.ed., 2 vols., Lugduni: Lutetiae Parisiorum, 1933), I, n. 505.

[44] Cf. Merkelbach, *Summa Theol. Moralis,* I, n. 959; Tanquerey, *Theologia Moralis Fundamentalis,* n. 835; Marc-Gestermann-Raus, *Institutiones Morales Alphonsianae,* I, n. 506.

[45] Cf. Kinane, " 'Peregrini' and the laws which take care of public order,"—*The Irish Ecclesiastical Record,* XLIII (1934), 122. Hereafter this periodical is cited by the initials *IER*.

[46] Cf. Michiels, *Normae Generales,* I, 320; Torrubiano Ripoli, *De Derecho Canónico,* I, n. 102; Jone, *Kanonischen Rechtes,* I, 33

directly to the spiritual good of individuals and of itself exists independently of a consideration of public order.[47] The obligation of avoiding scandal pertains to public order only when the word or deed tends directly and in every circumstance to lead others to sin.[48] In such a case, the avoiding of scandal is the express purpose of the law.[49] When scandal arises, as is very frequently the case, because of the peculiar circumstances or because of the condition of the persons influenced, the obligation to avoid it arises from the virtue of charity. This, however, does not minimize the obligation. The obligation to avoid scandal is sanctioned by the Code so that the local ordinary can punish those, not regularly bound by the particular law, when their non-observance caused exceptional scandal.[50]

§ 3. *Obligations Arising from Special Prescription of Universal Law*

Although canon 14, § 1, 2° states the norm for establishing exceptional legislative jurisdiction over strangers, there are several special prescriptions of the universal law which explicitly empower the particular legislator to enact laws binding upon the stranger.[51]

An evident example of this explicit legislative power over strangers by virtue of universal law is the right of the local ordinary to estab-

[47] Cf. Van Hove, *De Legibus*, n. 216, p. 222, nota 3; Onclin, *De Legis Indole*, p. 346; Kinane, " 'Peregrini' and the laws which take care of public order,"—*IER*, XLIII (1934), 122.

[48] Cf. Van Hove, *l.c.*

[49] Cf. Vermeersch, *Periodica*, XII (1927), (111)-(114).

[50] Cf. canon 2222, § 1; Van Hove, "Leges quae ordini publico consulunt,"—*ETL*, I (1924), 160, 161. Note, however, that the scandal which justifies the use of the extraordinary powers of canon 2222, § 1 must be exceptional and notably grave. Cf. Coronata, *Inst. Iuris Can.*, IV, n. 1695; Ayrinhac-Lydon, *Penal Legislation in the New Code of Canon Law* (Revised edition, New York: Benziger, 1936), p. 33—cited hereafter as *Penal Legislation;* Noval, "De ratione corrigendi ac puniendi sive in judicio sive extra jure Codicis J.C.,"—*Jus Pont.*, III (1923), 39; Esswein, *The Extrajudicial Coercive Power of Ecclesiastical Superiors* (The Catholic University of America Canon Law Studies, n. 127, Washington, D. C.: The Catholic University of America Press, 1941), n. 117—cited as *Extrajudicial Power*. Cf. also canon 144.

[51] Cf. Van Hove, *De Legibus*, n. 220; Onclin, *De Legis Indole*, p. 337; Van Hove, "Leges quae ordini publico consulunt,"—*ETL*, I (1924), 158.

lish norms regulating the permission of visiting priests to celebrate Mass in his territory.[52]

Canon 1251, § 1 states that the approved custom of the place is the norm to determine both the quantity and the quality of the food to be eaten at the morning and evening meals on a fast day.[53] Whether the custom to be followed is that of the place of permanent residence or that of the place where the stranger is visiting is not absolutely clear in the canon. Some authors, following the principles of canon 14, § 1, 2°, hold that the stranger is free to follow whichever of the two customs he wishes.[54] The declaration of the Sacred Congregation of the Consistory in 1916[55] relative to the clerical dress in Canada indirectly favors this interpretation. The law of fasting, however, has been reorganized by the Code.[56] The lack of a universal norm for the whole world regarding the manner of observing the law of fasting might be attributed to the varying needs of different places due to physical and climatic differences. According to a response of the Sacred Congregation of the Council, given on November 14, 1924,[57] pilgrims in Rome during the Holy Year were to observe the customs of Rome regarding the quality and the quantity of food to be eaten on a fast day, unless they enjoyed an indult permitting them to retain

[52] Cf. canons 804, § 3; 1303 §§ 2-4; S.C.C., litt. circ., 1 iul. 1926, n. 6—*AAS*, XVIII (1926), 312; Cappello, *De Sacramentis*, I, n. 737; Vermeersch-Creusen, *Epitome Iuris Canonici*, II, n. 76; Van Hove, *De Legibus* n. 220; Michiels, *Normae Generales*, I, 319; Jone, *Kanonischen Rechtes*, I, 33; Onclin, *De Legis Indole*, p. 337; Van Hove, "Leges Quae ordini publico consulunt,"—*ETL*, I (1924), 150; Deschepper, "De obligatione peregrinorum et vagorum,"—*Coll. Brug.*, XXIV (1924), 156; Leroux, "Territorialitas legum," *REL*, XVI (1924-1925), 338.

[53] " . . . sed non vetat aliquid cibi mane et vespere sumere, servata tamen circa ciborum quantitatem et qualitatem probata locorum consuetudine."—canon 1251, § 1.

[54] Cf. Creusen, "Casuistique de Carême,"—*NRT*, LI (1924), 157; Coronata, *De Locis et Temporibus Sacris* (Augustae Taurinorium: Marietti, 1922), n. 302.

[55] S.C. Consist. (ad archiep. Quebecen.), 13 mar. 1916, n. 3—*ASS*, VIII (1916), 150.

[56] Cf. Coronata, *De Locis et Temporibus Sacris*, n. 297; Vermeersch-Creusen, *Epitome Iuris Canonici*, II, n. 566.

[57] Cf. *Il Monitore Ecclesiastico*, XXXVII (1925), 106; *AKKR*, CV (1925), 660; Cicognani, *Ius Canonicum*, II, 106; Cicognani-O'Hara-Brennan, *Canon Law* (Second revised edition, Philadelphia: The Dolphin Press, 1935), p. 584.

the custom of their place of permanent residence. This indication of the change in the intention of the legislator of the Code furnishes proof that the accepted usages of the place where the meal is taken are the norms to determine the amount and the kind of food permitted on a fast day.[58]

Canon 3 generally excludes liturgical laws from the Code. Sometimes, however, the obligation of the stranger to observe local prescriptions arises from the positive disposition of universal liturgical laws.[59] Visiting priests, for instance, are to observe the particular laws of the place where they say Mass regarding certain prescribed collects in the Mass.[60] Likewise, they are obliged, by universal liturgical laws, to follow the liturgical calendar of the place where they are visiting as often as they celebrate Mass in a church, or a semi-public or public oratory.[61]

Finally, it may be observed that the universal law makes the accepted means of reckoning time generally obligatory upon strangers.[62]

§ 4. *Obligations Arising From Civil Law*

In several instances the Code has given canonical sanction to the Civil Law in force in the territory. As a result, the stranger is bound

[58] Cf. Vermeersch-Creusen, *Epitome Iuris Canonici*, II, n. 566; Van Hove, *De Legibus*, n. 220; Michiels, *Normae Generales*, I, 319; Onclin, *De Legis Indole*, p. 338; Vermeersch, *Theologia Moralis*, I, n. 287; Berutti, *Inst. Iuris Can.* I, 79, 80; Cicognani, *Ius Canonicum*, II, 106.

[59] Cf. Van Hove,*De Legibus*, n. 220; Onclin, *De Legis Indole*, p. 352; Leroux, "Le sujet des lois ecclésiastiques,"—*REL*, XVI (1924-1925), 338; Deschepper, "De obligatione peregrinorum et vagorum,"—*Coll. Brug.*, XXIV (1924), 156; Simenon, "Territorialitas legum,"—*REL*, XXI (1929-1930), 187.

[60] S.R.C., decr. gen., 3 apr. 1821—*Decreta Authentica*, n. 2613; dubium, 5 mar. 1898—*Decreta Authentica*, n. 3985; Felici, "De seminario in aliena dioecesi rusticanti,"—*Apollinaris*, XII (1939), 264; Teodori, "Peregrini quoad leges servandas," —*Consult. Iuris Can.*, I (1934), 18.

[61] S.R.C., decr. Urbis et Orbis, 9 iul. 1895, rata et confirmata, 9 dec. 1895—*Decreta Authentica*, n. 3862; Felici, "De seminario in aliena dioecesi rusticanti,"—*Apollinaris*, XII (1939), 264.

[62] Cf. canons 33, § 1; 1529; Dubé, *The General Principles for the Reckoning of Time in Canon Law* (The Catholic University of America Canon Law Studies, n. 144, Washington, D. C.: The Catholic University of America Press, 1941), pp. 116-121, 131-138.

in these instances by a canonical obligation to observe the Civil Law as it is in force in the territory.

Reserving for its own exclusive competence the substance of the marriage contract where at least one party is baptized, the Church recognizes the competence of the civil government over the merely civil effects of marriage.[63] The merely civil effects of marriage are those temporal and separable effects of the contract, such as rights of succession, which do not result necessarily, essentially and naturally from the matrimonial state.[64] In order to exercise this competence over the merely civil effects of marriage, the State has the right to enact laws regarding the registration of marriage in public records, and to establish definite limits of time within which such registration must take place.[65] And in general, the State may enact even antecedent conditions with which a marriage must comply to obtain the civil effects, provided these conditions do not prohibit the celebration of a marriage that is both valid and licit in the Church.[66] Consequently there is a real juridical obligation derived from Canon Law to observe those Civil Laws enacted within the competence of the State to provide for the civil effects of marriage.[67] Moreover, when the Church has extended special privileges to the State in this matter through a concordat, those civil requirements, such as a license to marry, the observance of an interval of time between the application for the license

[63] Cf. canon 1016; 1961; Leo XIII, ep. encycl. "*Arcanum,*" 19 febr. 1880—*Fontes*, III, n. 580.

[64] Cf. Alford, *Jus Civile Matrimoniale in Statibus Foederatis Americae Septentrionalis Cum Jure Canonico Comparatum* (Romae: Anonima Libraria Cattolica Italiana—New York: P. J. Kenedy & Sons, 1938), n. 11—cited hereafter as *Jus Mat. Comparatum;* Ottaviani, *Inst. Iuris Pub. Eccl.*, II, n. 336; Cappello, *De Sacramentis*, III, Pars I (4.ed., 1939), n. 71; Cavagnis, *Inst. Iuris Pub. Eccl.*, III, n. 203; Gasparri, *Tractatus Canonicus De Matrimonio* (ed. nova ad mentem Codicis I.C., 2 vols., [Civitate Vaticana]: Typis Polyglottis Vaticanis, 1932), I, n. 237—hereafter this edition of Gasparri will be cited by the abbreviated title of *De Matrimonio.*

[65] Cf. Alford, *Jus Mat. Comparatum*, n. 12; Gasparri, *De Matrimonio*, I, n. 239; Cappello, *De Sacramentis*, III, Pars I n. 71; Ottaviani, *Inst. Iuris Pub. Eccl.*, II, n. 337.

[66] Cf. Ottaviani, *Inst. Iuris Pub. Eccl.*, II, n. 337; Cavagnis, *Inst. Iuris Pub. Eccl.*, III, n. 203; Cappello, *De Sacramentis*, III, Pars I, n. 71.

[67] Cf. Gasparri, *De Matrimonio*, II, n. 1295; Cappello, *De Sacramentis*, III, Pars I, n. 74.

and the celebration of the marriage, the consent of the parents for minors, and the like, assume a special obligation for the members of the Church.[68] Where there is no concordat in effect, the civil requirements, which, although in themselves just,[69] exceed the civil competence, are *regularly* to be observed because of the virtue of charity to avert serious harm to the subjects of the Church.[70]

The principle generally in force in Civil Law is that the laws of the place of celebration, and not those of the place of domicile, govern the conditions required for the marriage. A marriage once validly contracted according to the laws of one state is generally recognized as such everywhere.[71] In the United States, this general principle admits of but few exceptions, even in the case where the parties contract a foreign marriage to evade a *general* prohibition to remarry within the state of their domicile.[72] Generally, then, the stranger has an obliga-

[68] Cf. S.C. de Sac., instr., "*Sacrosanctum matrimonii,*" 29 iunii 1941, n. 11—*AAS,* XXII (1941), 549.

[69] Cf. Moore, "Marriage and venereal disease,"—*American Ecclesiastical Review,* CIII (1940), 30, 31—hereafter this periodical will be cited by the initials *AER;* Donnelly, "Compulsory blood tests before marriage,"—*AER,* CI (1939), 18, 19.

[70] Cf. Cappello, *De Sacramentis,* III, Pars I, n. 74; Alford, *Jus Mat. Comparatum,* n. 12; Gasparri, *De Matrimonio,* II, n. 1295; Leo XIII, ep. encycl. "*Arcanum,*" 10 febr. 1880—*Fontes,* III, n. 580; S.C.S.Off., 12 ian. 1881—*Collect. S.C.P.F.,* II, n. 1545.

[71] Cf. Weiss, *Traité Théorique et Pratique de Droit International Privé,* Vol. III (12.ed., *Le Conflict des Lois,* Paris, 1912), 568—cited hereafter as *Traité de Droit Int. Privé,* III; Surville, *Cours de Droit Int. Privé,* n. 365; Pillet, *Traité de Droit Int. Privé,* I, nn. 255, 271. On July 12, 1902, the Union of the Hague was entered into by France, Germany, Austria-Hungary, Belgium, Spain, Italy, Luxembourg, Holland, Portugal, Sweden, and Switzerland. It is worthy of note here because it shows the universality of the principle that a marriage contracted validly in one state is held to be such everywhere. It is as follows: "[Le contrat de mariage est valable quant à la forme s'il a été conclu] soit conformément à la loi du pays ou il a été fait, soit conformément à la loi nationale de chacun des futurs époux au moment de la célébration du mariage, ou encore, s'il a été conclu au cours du mariage conformément à la loi de chacun des époux."—Cf. Surville, *Cours de Droit Int. Privé,* n. 365; Pillet, *Traité de Droit Int. Privé,* I, n. 272; Weiss, *Traité de Droit Int. Privé,* III, 569.

[72] "Except as stated in §§ 131 and 132, a marriage is valid everywhere if the requirements of the marriage law of the State where the contract of marriage takes place are complied with."—American Law Institute at Washington, D. C., May 11,

tion sanctioned in Canon Law, particular concordat, or the precept of charity, to observe the just civil statutes of the place where he is in regard to the celebration[73] of marriage.

The Code also gives full canonical sanction to the Civil Law in each particular territory concerning contracts and their execution, in as far as consonant with divine and Canon Law.[74] According to the principles of Civil Law, it is generally the law of the place where the instrument is drawn up that governs the formalities,[75] and of the place of performance[76] that governs the execution of the contract.[77] In the execution of a contract, then, the stranger is generally bound to observe the Civil Law of the place where he is as regards the manner,

1934, *Restatement of the Law of the Conflict of Laws* (St. Paul, Minn.: American Law Institute Publishers, 1934), § 121. This work, it should be noted, is not an expression of actual law, but a uniform plan proposed for adoption by all states. However it presents a composite picture of the average American Civil Law. Hereafter it will be cited as *Restatemnt of Conflict of Laws.* §§ 131 and 132 state that prohibitions to marry are not extra-territorial unless they forbid polygamy, incest, miscegenation, remarriage after a divorce within the time specified to make an appeal, or when the statute of the place of domicile makes the marriage void even though celebrated in another State.—*Restatement of Conflict of Laws,* §§ 131, 132. Besides these exceptions to the general principle that the law of the place of contract governs the conditions for marriage, authors add the exception of the particular prohibition to marry the paramour after a divorce. Cf. Beale, "Marriage and the domicile,"—44 *Harvard Law Review* (1930-1931), 513; Vernier-Frank, *American Family Laws* (5 vols, and 1938 Supplement, Stanford University, Cal.: Stanford University Press, 1931-1938), I, Sec. 32; "Developments in the law—Conflict of Laws,"—50 *Harvard Law Review* (1936-1937), 1190-1192; Alford, *Jus Mat. Comparatum,* nn. 399-407.

[73] Concerning the Civil Law regarding the legal *capacity* to marry, cf. *supra,* pp. 122-123.

[74] Canon 1529.

[75] The place of contracting is the place where the last act necessary to make a binding agreement takes place. Cf. "Developments in the law—Conflict of laws."—50 *Harvard Law Review* (1936-1937), 1160.

[76] Cf. "Developments in the law—Conflict of laws,"—50 *Harvard Law Review* (1936-1937), 1164.

[77] Authors allow exceptions to this general principle when they are expressly stated in the contract. Cf. Surville, *Traité de Droit Int. Privé,* nn. 246, 247; *Restatement of Conflict of Laws,* § 358; "Developments in the law—Conflict of laws," 50 *Harvard Law Review* (1936-1937), 1159, 1160.

the time, the persons by or for whom, the sufficiency, and the excuses for failure to perform the contractual obligation.[78]

Moreover, a strict obligation is placed upon testators to observe the formalities of Civil Law for the validity of wills when they make bequests to the Church.[79] This obligation is explicitly placed upon cardinals, residential bishops, and other beneficiaries to observe the civil formalities when they make a will or execute some legal instrument adequate to preserve the property of the Church.[80] The Civil Law of the place generally governs the requirements for the testament or other legal instrument, instead of the law of the domicile of the testator.[81]

Finally, the universal law of the Church recognizes Civil Law in regard to judicial compromises[82] in as far as compatible with divine and Canon Law.[83] Because of the canonical importance of Civil Law in these matters, the particular civil statutes bind strangers in the locality as regards both the formalities of these juridical acts and the execution of them.[84]

§ 5. *Obligation to Observe Laws Determining the Solemnities of Acts*

Following the principle that the "law of the place governs the act" (*locus regit actum*), canonists since the XIII Century have regarded the stranger as subject to those laws which determine the solemnities required to give an act juridical effects and to facilitate its proof at a later date. The Code has adopted this doctrine in canon 14, § 1, 2°.[85]

Therefore, the primary basis for the subjection of strangers to the particular laws of the place regarding the solemnities of acts is the

[78] Cf. *Restatement of Conflict of Laws*, § 358.

[79] Cf. canon 1513, § 2; Hannan, *The Canon Law of Wills* (Philadelphia: The Dolphin Press, 1935), nn. 469-472.

[80] Cf. canon 1301, § 1; Hannan, *The Canon Law of Wills*, nn. 317-330.

[81] Cf. Surville, *Cours de Droit Int. Privé*, n. 192.

[82] Cf. canon 1926.

[83] Cf. canon 1927.

[84] Cf. Van Hove, *De Legibus*, n. 220; Onclin, *De Legis Indole*, p. 338.

[85] "[Peregrini] Neque [adstringuntur] legibus territorii in quo versantur, iis exceptis quae . . . actuum sollemnia determinant; . . . "—canon 14, § 1, 2°.

positive will of the universal legislator expressed in this canon. Some authors, indeed, base this obligation upon the necessity of public order.[86] This application of the principle, "the law of the place governs the act," was adopted by the Code from Civil Law.[87] The practical reasons advanced by civil jurists for the requirements of given solemnities for the juridical effect of certain acts are that the proof of the act may be facilitated and the liberty of the parties protected against fraud and duress.[88] They distinguish between private acts and public acts.[89] Only in acts of a public character, such as the contract of marriage, is the obligation derived from public order; in private acts, as for instance in the case of private contracts, the law determining formalities is for the protection of the individual. Although the private individual may waive the protection of the formalities of law when only his own interest is at stake, his intention to observe these formalities is presumed unless otherwise evident.[90] Those canonists, who maintain that the obligation to observe the particular laws determining the formalities of the act is derived from the necessity of public order, adopt this distinction between public and private acts. The stranger is, according to this distinction, obliged to observe only those formalities determined for a public act.[91]

However, the reason for this distinction is not evident in the Code. The text of the canon states in general terms that the stranger is bound by the particular laws of the place which determine the solemnities of acts. By this general statement of the Code, it follows that every particular law which determines a special formality of an act should be observed by everyone in the place. Moreover, if the obligation of observing solemnities of acts pertained to public acts, and was derived in every instance from public order, it would be sufficiently

[86] Cf. Van Hove, *De Legibus*, n. 219; Ojetti, *Commentarium in Cod*, I, 116.

[87] Cf. Claeys Bouuaert-Simenon, *Manuale Iuris Can.*, I, 93, nota 5; Toso, *Comm. Minora*, I, 71.

[88] Cf. Weiss, *Traité de Droit Int. Privé*, III, 115, 116; Surville, *Cours de Droit Int. Privé*, n. 186; Hannan, *The Canon Law of Wills*, n. 353.

[89] Cf. Weiss, *Traité de Droit Int. Privé*, III, 116.

[90] Cf. Weiss, *Traité de Droit Int. Privé*, III, 118.

[91] Cf. Van Hove, *De Legibus*, n. 219: "Si autem de iure communi nulla forma specialis requiritur, seu agitur de actu privato, a peregrinis regulae particulares non videntur servandae." Cf. also Ojetti, *Commentarium in Cod.*, I, 116.

provided for under that title. Finally, the pre-Code doctrine knew of no such distinction between private and public acts. Hence, there is an obligation upon the stranger to observe all of the particular laws of the place where he is which determine the solemnities of acts. Since the requirement of certain solemnities can not be said in every case to be a matter of concern for public order, the obligation of the stranger to observe all of the particular laws of the place which determine the solemnities of acts is not sufficiently based upon the necessity of public order, but upon the positive will of the legislator expressed in canon 14, § 1, 2°.[92]

In determining the exact meaning of the term *solemnities of acts,* civil jurists distinguish between the intrinsic and the extrinsic elements in a juridical act. The intrinsic element consists in the requisites for the validity or licitness of the act, considered apart from its external manifestation. Some of these requisites are the capacity of the subject, his consent, and the conditions for the validity of the consent.[93] The extrinsic element refers to the external manifestation of the juridical act. Its purpose is to establish the existence of the act and the freedom of the party placing the act. It consists in the written document of the act, in the presence of witnesses or of a public official, or in other means of manifestation.[94] The term *solemnities of an act* is limited to this external element.[95]

Most frequent among the examples of particular laws which determine the solemnities of acts are laws regarding contracts. Those laws regarding the contract of marriage have been treated in the previous title. Solemnities may be determined by particular Canon Law

[92] Cf. Onclin, *De Legis Indole,* p. 352.

[93] The laws regulating this element are personal in Canon Law. In those countries where the juridical system is based on English Common Law, however, the principle of strict territoriality of law generally applies to this element also. Cf. *Restatement of Conflict of Laws,* § 333; *supra,* pp. 107, 108.

[94] Cf. Weiss, *Traité de Droit Int. Privé,* III, 109; Surville, *Cours de Droit Int. Privé,* n. 185.

[95] Cf. Weiss, *Traité de Droit Int. Privé,* III, 110; Pillet, *Principes du Droit International Privé* (Paris, 1903), p. 473—cited hereafter as *Principes du Droit Int. Privé;* Surville, *Cours de Droit Int. Privé,* n. 185; Story, *Conflict of Laws,* §§ 160, 161; Van Hove, *De Legibus,* n. 219; Claeys Bouuaert-Simenon, *Manuale Iuris Can.,* I, n. 164.

to protect the Church from injury caused by the alienation of church property.[96] The written permission of the ordinary of the place is a solemnity required for any act out of the ordinary course of church administration.[97] The particular laws applying the general laws of procedure in ecclesiastical trials are laws which determine the solemnities of acts.[98] Finally, those Civil Laws treated in the previous title which are given canonical sanction in the Code, are, for the most part, laws which determine the solemnities of acts.

§ 6. *Obligation Arising from Public Order*

The only remaining exceptional obligation of the stranger to observe the particular laws of the place of his temporary residence is the obligation to observe those laws which secure public order in the place. The proximate basis of this obligation is the positive will of the legislator expressed in canon 14, § 1, 2°.[99] Searching for a more fundamental basis for this obligation, canonists appeal to the natural law. It is unjust for the stranger to remain in a place to the detriment of the inhabitant. The natural law forbids harm done to others.[100]

But a distinction should be made here between the obligation which arises from the natural law to avoid scandal in every instance and the obligation which arises from public order. The obligation to avoid scandal primarily regards private good. It urges in every instance. A law which was not of itself enacted to oblige strangers, and which generally does not bind them, may in rare instances have to be observed by the stranger to avoid scandal arising from exceptional circumstances. Public order, however, regards the public good.[101] The ob-

[96] Cf. canons 1530, § 2; 1533; 1540-1542. Note that frequently in this matter the same law may be considered from two different aspects. Thus here a law determining a solemnity of an act to protect the property of the Church is also a law which is extra-territorial because its violation would bring harm upon the territory.

[97] Cf. canon 1527.

[98] Cf. Van Hove, *De Legibus*, n. 219.

[99] "[Peregrini] Neque [adstringuntur] legibus territorii in quo versantur, iis exceptis quae ordini publico consulunt . . . "—canon 14, § 1, 2°.

[100] Cf. Vermeersch, *Theologia Moralis*, I, n. 259; Vermeersch-Creusen, *Epitome Iuris Canonici*, I, n. 110; Onclin, *De Legis Indole*, pp. 336, 337; Deschepper, "De subjecto legis particularis,"—*Coll. Brug.*, XXIV (1924), 56.

[101] The exact difference between public order and public good will be treated in the following chapter.

ligation arising from public order prescinds from special circumstances.[102] It is a direct result of the exceptional subjection of the stranger to the legislative jurisdiction of the local legislator. The social order and the public good of the territory sometimes demand that the legislator enact a law to be observed by the habitual resident and the temporary visitor alike.[103] Hence the obligation arising from scandal is based entirely upon the natural law. It is outside the scope and intention of the law whose observance it urges. And it depends entirely upon the accidental circumstances. The obligation arising from public order, although based in last analysis upon the natural law, is more properly said to be based upon the native *legislative* jurisdiction of the local legislator. It is a consequence of his duty to legislate for the good of the habitual inhabitants of the territory, his natural and ordinary subjects. Public order is the very object and scope of the law which secures it, and which because of it must be observed. It binds the stranger to observe the law directly and in every circumstance.

Outside of these six titles of exceptional subjection to the local legislator, the stranger cannot be obliged to observe the particular laws of the place of his temporary residence. The general rule is that the particular laws of the place of his temporary residence do not bind the stranger. The exceptional obligation to observe them must either be self-evident or demonstrated. When either the particular law does not evidently bind the stranger, or the legislator has not clearly indicated his decision that the law binds the stranger, the latter is free from the obligation of observing the law. If on the other hand, the particular law does evidently bind the stranger because of one of the six titles explained above, or the legislator has issued an authentic declaration to that effect, the stranger has a real obligation to observe that law while he is in the territory where it is in force.

[102] Cf. Van Hove, *De Legibus*, n. 126.

[103] Cf. Ryan, *Episcopal Jurisdiction*, p. 104.

Chapter VIII

OBLIGATION TO OBSERVE THE LAWS WHICH SECURE PUBLIC ORDER

Both canonists[1] and civil jurists[2] admit the obscurity in the term *public order*. Its meaning must be described rather than defined. Moreover, the protection of public order is often dependent upon the changing circumstances of time and place.[3] Therefore, the legislator should indicate clearly in the law which he enacts to secure public order his intention to place upon strangers an obligation to observe it.[4]

Article I. Meaning of the Term *Laws Which Secure Public Order* (*Leges Quae Ordini Publico Consulunt*)

The origin of the term *public order*, used in canon 14, is a matter of conjecture. It was used in ecclesiastical literature but rarely before the Code. Its appearance in the more standard works on ecclesiastical law dates from the edition of De Angelis' work, *Praelectiones Iuris Canonici*, and was used in only a few other works before the Code of Canon Law.[5] Van Hove[6] and other canonists following his suggestion[7] see the influence of the XIX Century Italian and French jurists

[1] Cf. Van Hove, *De Legibus*, n. 215; Claeys Bouuaert-Simenon, *Manuale Iuris Can.*, I, n. 164; Vermeersch, *Theologia Moralis*, I, n. 286; Leroux, "Le sujet des lois ecclésiastiques,"—*REL*, XVI (1924-1925), 339, note 1.

[2] Cf. Weiss, *Traité de Droit Int. Privé*, III, 96.

[3] Cf. Van Hove, *De Legibus*, n. 216; Van Hove, "Leges quae ordini publico consulunt,"—*ETL*, I, (1924), 157; Onclin, *De Legis Indole*, pp. 336, 337; Le Picard, "La notion d'ordre public en droit canonique,"—*NRT*, LV (1928), 364; Roelker, "The traveler and local statutes,"—*The Jurist*, II (1942), 111; Weiss, *Traité de Droit Int. Privé*, III, 96; Pillet, *L'Ordre Public en Droit International Privé* (Grenoble-Paris, 1890), p. 40—hereafter cited as *L'Ordre Public*; Surville, "De la personnalité des lois envisagée comme principe fondamental du droit international privé,"—*JDIP*, XVI (1889), 535.

[4] Cf. Roelker, "The traveler and local statutes,"—*The Jurist*, II (1942), 110.

[5] Cf. *supra*, pp. 61, 62.

[6] *De Legibus*, n. 214; "Leges quae ordini publico consulunt,"—*ETL*, I (1924), 155, 156.

[7] Cf. Le Picard, "La notion d'ordre public en droit canonique,"—*NRT*, LV (1928), 354; Onclin, *De Legis Indole*, p. 344; Toso, "De ordine publico,"—*Jus Pont.*, X (1930), 342.

upon the choice of this term in the Code. There is much to indicate the correctness of this deduction. Authorities upon Private International Law since the late XIX Century, especially of the school of Mancini, used this term to indicate those laws of the country so necessary for its welfare that they had to be observed by aliens. The influence of this school of Private International Law was very noticeable upon the formation of canon 14.[8]

Whatever the origin of the term may be, whether from the isolated works of a few pre-Code canonists and moralists, or from the common use of the term by the civil jurists, it is certain that much aid can be derived from the doctrine of the civil jurists in its interpretation. On the other hand, although the term public order is new in Canon Law, it is a formula used to express a doctrine widely prevalent before the Code.[9] Those particular laws which were indicated before the Code by Sanchez and his followers as obligatory on the stranger are referred to in the Code by the term public order.[10] Thus the pre-Code doctrine must also be used as a norm in the interpretation of the term *laws which secure public order.*

Due not only to the brevity of the term, but also to the intrinsic obscurity of the matter, canonists are not in agreement concerning the meaning of public order. A number of canonists interpret the term as practically synonymous with public good.[11] Others with a negative approach, restrict the term public order to those laws which must be

[8] Cf. *supra*, pp. 42, 43.

[9] Cf. Le Picard, "La notion d'ordre public en droit canonique,"—*NRT*, LV (1928), 355; Onclin, *De Legis Indole*, p. 335; Van Hove, *De Legibus*, n. 216; Van Hove, "Leges quae ordini publico consulunt,"—*ETL*, I (1924), 155-158; Michiels, *Normae Generales*, I, 317; Kinane, " 'Peregrini' and the laws which take care of public order,"—*Irish Ecclesiastical Record*, VLIII (1934), 117—hereafter cited by the initials *IER*.

[10] Cf. *supra*, pp. 60-62.

[11] Cf. Augustine, *Canon Law*, I, 92; Cocchi, *Comm. in Codicem*, I, n. 53; Molien, "Lois,"—*Dictionaire de Théologie Chrétienne* (ed. A. Vacant, E. Mangenot, 14 vols., Paris: Librarie Letouzey et Ané, 1903—), IX (1926), col. 894—hereafter this work is cited by the initials *DTC*; Antoine, "Étrangers,"—*DTC*, V (1913), col. 986; Kinane, " 'Peregrini' and the laws which take care of public order,"—*IER*, XLIII (1934), 119.

observed by all to prevent common injury to the community.[12] These authors, who have given a more extensive treatment to this concept, interpret it as referring to those laws which have as their purpose to maintain an order essential in the community, an order which cannot be violated by anyone, because it affects the entire community and each member of it indiscriminately.[13]

§ 1. *Generic Element in the Concept of Public Order*

The juridical concept of public order has as its genus public good. All laws are designed for the common good of society.[14] The manner in which law prescribes for the common good of society is the basis of the distinction between laws designed for the public good and laws designed for the private good. The object of laws for the public good is that which does not come under the ownership of any private individual, but primarily and of itself belongs to the entire community, as such, and immediately serves the use or interest of the entire community. Private good is that which immediately and primarily pertains to the ownership of private individuals, and proximately serves their interest. Laws regarding private good are designed for the common good only reductively and secondarily, because by the improvement of the condition of the individual, who is part of the society, the whole society is improved.[15]

This distinction between public and private good is recognized in numerous places in the Code where it uses the adjective, "public,"[16] to designate that which pertains to the interest, utility, or welfare of the

[12] Cf. Vermeersch-Creusen, *Epitome Iuris Canonici*, I, n. 110; Wernz-Vidal, *Ius Canonicum*, I, n. 156; Vermeersch, *Theologia Moralis*, I, n. 286; Claeys Bouuaert-Simenon, *Manuale Iuris Can.*, I, n. 164; Simenon, "Territorialitas legum,"—*REL*, XXI (1929-1930), 185.

[13] Cf. Van Hove, "Leges quae ordini publico consulunt,"—*ETL*, I (1924), 158; Van Hove, *De Legibus*, n. 216; Onclin, *De Legis Indole*, pp. 333-337; Leroux, "Le sujet des lois ecclésiastiques,"—*REL*, XVI (1924-1925), 338, 339; Le Picard, "La notion d'ordre public en droit canonique,"—*NRT*, LV (1928), 362; Michiels, *Normae Generales*, I, 318.

[14] Cf. S. Thomas, *Summa Theologica*, Ia IIae, Q. XC, A. II, c.; Suarez, *De Legibus*, Lib. I, c. VII, nn. 1, 4.

[15] Cf. Suarez, *De Legibus*, *Lib.* I, c. VII, n. 7; Michiels, *Normae Generales*, I, 143, 319.

[16] Cf. canons 1188, § 2, 1°; 1291; 1379, § 2; 1586; 1933, § 3; 1935, 2.

entire community.[17] The distinction between public and private good is especially emphasized in the laws governing ecclesiastical procedure.[18] Thus, when the public good is at stake, as in the defense of the rights of minors, ecclesiastical moral persons, and poor and inexperienced persons, and in cases involving scandal and the removal of public harm or social disturbance, the judge may proceed in virtue of his office, without the presentation of an introductory bill of complaint, interrogate the parties, and even supply deficient proof.[19] The office of the promoter of justice is chiefly concerned with the public good.[20] He is required by law to intervene in all criminal cases, in marriage cases involving an impediment by its very nature public, in the concession of the *restitutio in integrum* to minors, and in the recourse against the rejection of the introductory bill of complaint.[21] Outside of these cases, he is to intervene in contentious trials whenever, in the judgment of the ordinary, the public good demands it,[22] such as in cases involving the existence of pious foundations, the rights of the Church, and the free bestowal of benefices.[23]

From all of these examples in the Code, the concept of public good as opposed to private good can be determined as that which substantially affects the whole society as such,[24] that which at once substan-

[17] Cf. Glaser, "Variation des Wortsinnes und Kodexauslegung,"—*Theologisch-praktische Quartalschrift*, LXXXIII (1930), 146, 147.

[18] Cf. Le Picard, "La notion d'ordre public en droit canonique,"—*NRT*, LV, (1928), 357, 358.

[19] Cf. canons 1648, §2; 1687; 1618; 1619; 1742, § 1; Lega-Bartoccetti, *Commentarius in Iudicia Ecclesiastica Iuxta Codicem Iuris Canonici* (3 vols., Romae: Anonima Libraria Cattolica Italiana, 1938-1941), I, 232—hereafter cited as Lega-Bartoccetti, *Iudicia Ecclesiastica;* Noval, *De Iudiciis*, n. 203; Le Picard, "La notion d'ordre public en droit canonique,"—*NRT*, LV (1928), 357, 358.

[20] Cf. Roberti, *De Processibus* (2 vols., Romae: Apud Aedes Facultatis Iuridicae ad S. Apollinaris, 1926), I, n. 122.

[21] Cf. canons, 1586; 1971, § 1, 2°; 1688, § 2; 1709, § 3.

[22] Cf. canon 1506.

[23] Cf. *Normae S. R. Tribunalis, Arts*, 26, 27—*AAS*, XVI (1924), 457; Roberti, *De Processibus*, I, n. 122; Noval, *De Iudiciis*, n. 203; Glynn, *The Promoter of Justice, His Rights and Duties* (The Catholic University of America Canon Law Studies, n. 101, Washington, D. C.: The Catholic University of America, 1936), p. 90—hereafter cited as *The Promoter of Justice*.

[24] "Causae boni publici dicuntur illae in quibus relatio iuridica substantialis societatis uti talis interest."—Roberti, *De Processibus*, I, n. 169.

tially affects the interest and welfare of each member of the community.

So far, in its being distinguished from private good and in its substantial and immediate relation to the entire community, and to all of the members of the society indiscriminately, the concept of public order is one with the concept of public good.

§ 2. *Difference Between Public Order and Public Good*

Although the juridical concepts, public order and public good, are generically the same in that both connote a substantial and immediate relationship to the entire community, they are not coextensive.[25] The term public good pertains to whatever tends to further the welfare of the community, whatever is of interest to all members of the community. It does not invariably imply the note of social necessity, but applies equally well to what is to the common advantage of all, without being in any sense indispensable. Finally, it depends very often upon the circumstances, so that what is of public good on one occasion may not be on another.[26]

The concept of public order, however, is less extensive than that of public good. Whatever pertains to public order pertains to public good. But not every thing that pertains to public good can be said to pertain to public order. Public order is comprehended under the term public good. Its relation to public good is like that of species to genus.

Whereas the Code uses the term *public good* in numerous places, the term *public order* appears uniquely in canon 14. This choice of distinctive terminology suggests the intention of the Code to place a specific limitation on the concept of public order. Although the term was probably derived from Civil Law, the framers of the Code must have chosen it because of its peculiar exactness to express the concept they desired. Order is composed of three elements: multiplicity, uni-

[25] Several authors seem to use these terms synonymously—cf. *supra*, p. 138.

[26] Cf. Noval, *De Iudiciis*, n. 203; Glynn, *The Promoter of Justice*, pp. 85-88; Lega, *De Delictis*, p. 21; Onclin, *De Legis Indole*, p. 333; Van Hove, *De Legibus*, n. 216; Le Picard, "La notion d'ordre public en droit canonique,"—*NRT*, LV (1928), 363.

formity, and purpose or objective.[27] Uniformity is the formal element in the concept of order. It is required by the purpose for which the order is designed. Any divergence from the uniformity of the multiple constitutents of the order hinders the accomplishment of this purpose. For example, suppose a group of match sticks are placed in order to form a design. The removal of one of these match sticks immediately results in the destruction of the design, or at least in its disfiguration. This necessary uniformity to attain the purpose of the order is the dominant note in the concept of order. Order, it is true, is the effect of all law.[28] But the special use of the term *order* in canon 14 places special emphasis upon this dominant effect, uniformity of conduct. Public order is that complete uniformity of conduct in the society which is of immediate interest and concern to the whole society, to all the members individually.

Such a strict uniformity of conduct can be imposed upon everyone in the territory, upon strangers as well as members, only when the purpose of the regulation is necessary so that each member might attain his objective as a member of that society. Or negatively, such strict uniformity of conduct can only be required of all in the territory when any divergence from it renders the objective of the society more difficult of attainment for all of the members in it. For the stranger is not a member of the community. He is not striving to attain the particular objective of that society in which he is a stranger. Therefore, he cannot be forced to cooperate positively and constantly in the particular efforts of the society to attain its goal. His subjection to local authority is, therefore, only transitory and limited.[29] His only obligation to the society wherein he is a stranger is to refrain from hindering the attainment of its particular purpose. To hinder here does not mean to render impossible. For example, an act which objectively gives scandal, may not actually lead a certain bystander into sin. It

[27] Cf. S. Thomas, *Commentarium in De Divinis Nominibus* (*Opera Omnia,* vol. XXIX, Parisiis: Apud Ludovicum Vivès, 1889), C. IV, lec. 1; Marling, *The Order of Nature* (Washington, D. C.: The Catholic University of America, 1934), pp. 31, 32.

[28] Cf. Kinane, " 'Peregrini' and the laws which take care of public order,"—*IER,* XLIII (1934), 119.

[29] Cf. *supra*, pp. 119, 120.

will, however, place that person in the occasion of sin and thereby render his personal sanctification the more difficult. The local legislator has, by native right, authority over the stranger only in his function as guardian of the public welfare of his habitual subjects. Therefore a strict uniformity of action can be imposed on all in the territory, including strangers, only when the objective desired is immediately and directly necessary for the good of all the members of the society, only when every deviation from this strict uniformity of itself endangers each member's attainment of his purpose in the society. In this lies the distinction between public order and public good: in the necessary connection of the object of the regulation with the attainment of the purpose of the society so that a strict uniformity of conduct is required to secure that object.

This specific characteristic of necessity in the concept of public order is emphasized by the civil jurists from whom the term was probably derived. Mancini[80] and Laurent[81] held that public order pertained to that law which organizes and conserves the civil society. Fiore distinguished public order from public law. He taught that public order, or social law, referred to whatever is indispensable for safeguarding the interests of the collectivity and for the maintenance of those moral principles which are fundamental in the public law of the state and in the moral sentiments of the people.[82] Pillet states that the laws which secure public order are the resumé of the essential conditions for the peaceful existence of the society, and might as correctly be called laws for the security and safety of the state.[83] Public order, he states,

[80] "Les règles générales du droit international privé,"—*JDIP*, I (1874), 297.

[81] "Études sur le droit international privé,"—*JDIP*, V (1878), 338.

[82] "Limitation des lois étrangères,"—*JDIP*, XXXV (1908), 359, 360, 364.

[83] "Il faut aussi protéger la société contre les abus que les particuliers pourraient faire de leur liberté au détriment de tous. Les dispositions ayant cet objet se reconnaîtront à un caractère différent, elles visent la protection de tous et non pas seulement de certains et apparaissent sous la forme d'une réglémentation général. On les appelle souvent lois d'ordre public et cette dénomination, quoique l'on puisse dire, est assez expressive car, de même qu'une règle d'ordre concerne à la fois tous les membres du groupe pour lequel elle est faite, une loi d'ordre public s'adresse au même titre à toutes les personnes comprises dans la juridiction de l'État qui l'a promulguée. Dans une étude précédente nous avons adopté l'expression de lois de garantie sociale. Elle désigne les mêmes lois, mais en les plaçant plus directement au

is that which concerns the whole community and is of interest to and benefits all and not just certain members of the community.[84] Surville states that laws of public order include all laws which have as their purpose to assure the good order, the welfare of the country, the security of the citizens and of property.[85] Despagnet expressively calls laws of public order the fortress in the legislation in each country, the fundamental principles upon which the state is based, the indispensable principles for its good organization.[86] In fine, the civil jurists who followed the teachings of Mancini restrict the meaning of the term public order to those things which are indispensable for the peace and good order in the state, for the very purpose of the state, and therefore require a uniformity of conduct by all persons in the territory.

This same interpretation of the term public order, and its distinction from public good is in conformity with the different expressions used by the pre-Code authors after the XVI Century to indicate the obligation of the stranger to observe certain laws of the place where he temporarily is. Sanchez restricted this exceptional obligation to those laws whose transgression results in harm to the community. Laymann,

point de vue de leur objet, ayant l'avantage de mieux indiquer que les lois de cette sorte sont le résumé des conditions essentielles à l'existence paisible d'une société. On peut user indifféremment de l'un et l'autre termes."—*Principes du Droit Int. Privé,* n. 134; cf. *Traité de Droit Int. Privé,* I, n. 37; *L'Ordre Public,* pp. 17-24.

[84] *Principes du Droit Int. Privé,* n. 374.

[85] "La notion de l'ordre public englobe, d'abord, toutes les lois qui ont pour but d'assurer le bon ordre et la salubrité dans le pays, toutes celles qui s'y proposent la securité des personnes et des propriétés."—*Cours de Droit Int. Prive,,* pp. 49, 50; cf. "De la personnalité des lois envisagée comme principe fondamental du droit international privé,"—*JDIP,* XVI (1889), 536.

[86] "Ce sont ses dispositions législatives, sorte de fortresse dans la législation de chaque pays que l'on ne peut évader, qui constituent les règles dites *d'ordre public,* et donc l'observation, dans chaque État suffit pour assurer le respect de la souveraineté, bien que l'on accepte sur d'autres points l'application d'une loi étrangère."

"La nécessité de se soumettre à ces règles d'ordre public se conçoit sans peine. L'État, personne morale, indépendant par nature, perd son caractère essentiel s'il ne s'oppose pas à l'application de règles qui sont en contradiction avec ce qu'il considère, dans sa libre souveraineté, comme l'expression même des principes fondamentaux sur lesquels il prétend se baser et indispensable du maintien de sa bonne organisation."—"L'ordre public en droit international privé."—*JDIP, XVI* (1889), 5.

using a positive approach, more significantly stated that the stranger must observe only those laws which were enacted for the special good and utility of the society, or for the peaceful commerce with the inhabitants.[37] Schmalzgrueber, emphasizing the element of necessity, states that strangers are bound to observe the particular laws of the territory which are especially enacted for the good of the territory because of the necessity of the society.[38] Génicot uses a formula similar to that of the jurists when he speaks of laws which are to be observed by all in order that the common good may not be destroyed.[39] De Angelis, Tanquerey and Marc employ the same terms as the jurists when they hold that the stranger is bound by the laws of the place which are designed to secure the *public order* or the *security of the place.*[40]

Many commentators on the Code have indicated that the difference between public order and public good lies in the element of necessity in the former. Vermeersch and Creusen state that public order is secured by those laws which are enacted to avert a common danger, rather than to promote a common good.[41] Simenon[42] and Claeys Bouuaert[43] more explicitly state that those laws secure public order which are enacted to avert scandal or the disturbance of the social order. These negative interpretations emphasize the necessity of the observance of the laws which secure public order, of the uniformity of conduct. They do not, however, indicate that only negative laws, prohibitions, secure public order. A positive law can have as its purpose the avoidance of scandal, and of the disturbance of the social order. Be-

[37] Cf. *supra*, pp. 60, 61.

[38] "Peregrinos obligari legibus particularibus loci, si illae specialiter latae sint in bonum illius loci ob necessitatem reipublicae."—*Jus Ecclesiasticum Universum*, I, Tit. II, n. 42.

[39] "Leges quae sint omnibus servandae ne bonum commune pereat."—*Theologia Moralis*, I, n. 96.

[40] Cf. *supra*, p. 62. Notable are their synonymous use of the two terms *public order* and *security of the place*. Pillet taught that these two expressions were interchangeable. Cf. *supra*, p. 143, note 33; Roelker, "The traveler and local statutes,"—*The Jurist*, II (1942), 107, 108.

[41] Cf. Vermeersch-Creusen, *Epitome Iuris Canonici*, I, n. 110; Vermeersch, *Theologia Moralis*, I, n. 286; also, Wernz-Vidal, *Ius Canonicum*, I, n. 156; Jone, *Kanonischen Rechtes*, I, 33.

[42] "Territorialitas legum,"—*REL*, XXI (1929-1930), 185.

[43] Claeys Bouuaert-Simenon, *Manuale Iuris Can.*, I, n. 164.

cause of the danger of limiting these laws to purely negative laws, other authors more correctly give a positive description of public order.[44] Van Hove,[45] Michiels,[46] and several others[47] distinguish public order from public good because of its fundamental necessity for the public welfare of the society, and its immediate relationship to the essential welfare of all the members of the community.

In brief, then, two elements constitute public order: public necessity and a strict uniformity of conduct on the part of everyone in the territory which is required to provide for that public necessity. The Code by stressing the word *order* in canon 14 emphasizes its characteristic note, namely strict uniformity. A strict uniformity of conduct, however, cannot be required of all, including strangers, except when such conduct is necessary for the particular society to attain its purpose; that is when such conduct is of itself[48] necessary for each member in

[44] Il [l'étranger] est donc tenu d'observer les lois, qu'elles soient prohibitives ou préventives, comme c'est le cas ordinaire, ou même qu'elles exigent un concours positif, si elles ont pour but d'écarter un 'damnum commune'."—Van Hove, "Leges quae ordini publico consulunt,"—*ETL*, I (1924), 157.

[45] "Ce sont celles qui ont pour but de maintenir un ordre essentiel dans la communauté, un ordre qui ne peut être troublé par personne, parce que cet ordre intéresse la communauté toute entière, c'est-à-dire à tout le moins tout membre quelconque de la communauté."—"Leges quae ordini publico consulunt,"—*ETL*, I 1924), 158;

"Differentia inter ordinem publicum et bonum publicum videtur esse in gradu maiore vel minore quo observantia legis est necessaria ad bonum publicum. Illae leges quae ab omnibus sunt servandae ne bonum publicum pereat, omnes, etiam peregrinos, ligant; quae ad bonum publicum necessariae non sunt, a peregrinis servari non debent."—*De Legibus*, n. 216.

[46] "Leges ordinem illum tuentes, munientes, illae solae, sed omnes dicendae sunt, quae non solummodo, si observenur, communitati positivam utilitatem conferunt, sed quae ita *necessariae* sunt ut ipsis omissis vel a quocumque in peculiari communitatis territorio versanti, sive incola aut advena sit, sive sit extraneus, transgressis, ipsa communitas, ipsum regimen et securitas subditorum in periculo sint, seu commune damnum patiantur."—*Normae Generales*, I, 318.

[47] Cf. Deschepper, "De obligatione peregrinorum et vagorum,"—*Coll. Brug.*, XXIV (1924), 155; Cappello, *Summa Iuris Canonici*, I, n. 80; Teodori, "Peregrini quoad censuras,"—*Appollinaris*, IV (1931), 141; Onclin, *De Legis Indole*, p. 333; Toso, "De ordine publico,"—*Jus Pont.*, X (1930), 342, 343; Wernz-Vidal, *Ius Canonicum*, I, n. 156; Beste, *Introd. in Codicem*, p. 72.

[48] By this is meant that the *natural* result of the violation of public order is an obstacle to the achievement of the purpose of the society. In certain accidental cir-

the society to be unhindered in his pursuit of the minimum of his objectives as a member of the society. In Canon Law, public order refers only to those objectives in the particular ecclesiastical society which are the minimum requirements for its good organization and the sanctification of its members, and which are made more difficult of attainment unless a strict uniformity of conduct is imposed on all in the territory.

§ 3. *Laws Which Secure Public Order*

So far the emphasis has been placed upon the juridical meaning of the term public order. An analysis has disclosed that this term refers to those necessary conditions in the society which require a strict uniformity of conduct on the part of all in the society for their unhindered fulfillment.

There is a further limitation on the juridical meaning of the text in the Code which establishes the exceptional obligation of the stranger arising from public order. The stranger is bound to observe those *laws which secure* this public order so essential for the welfare of the entire community. In each civil society the civil legislator determines those principles of government which are to be considered essential.[49] Although the juridical meaning of the term public order is in principle the same in both Canon and Civil Law, its application is only analogous because of the difference in the purposes of the two societies.[50] In the Church the principles of public order are based on divine and universal Canon Law. There can be no thought of a public order that contradicts these principles. But particular laws can determine the essential public order of the Church as it is applied to the accidentals of time and place. Particular laws may secure public order in the particular ecclesiastical society.[51]

Wherefore, the Code states that particular laws which secure public order are to be observed by the strangers in the territory. Here it must

cumstances, some of the members may still be unhindered by this violation of the public order in the attainment of their purpose in the society.

[49] Cf. Despagnet, "L'ordre public en droit international privé,"—*JDIP*, XVI (1889), 5; Van Hove, "Leges quae ordini publico consulunt,"—*ETL*, I (1924), 157.

[50] Cf. Van Hove, "Leges quae ordini publico consulunt,"—*ETL*, I (1924), 157.

[51] Cf. Van Hove, *De Legibus*, n. 216; Onclin, *De Legis Indole*, p. 337.

be noted that the Code uses the verb *consulunt*.[52] The grammatical meanings of the verb *consulere* when used with the dative case are: to take counsel for, to look to, to consult, to respect, to regard, to secure, to have a certain sollicitude for which seeks to protect.[53] Laws which secure (*consulunt*) public order, therefore, must be restricted to those laws whose whole force and complete object is immediately concerned with public order. Indeed, in Private International Law, only those laws which are absolutely indispensable for public order and have no other purpose than to maintain it are admitted to be laws of public order.[54] To impose upon a stranger a law which did not have as its entire object the preservation of public order would be an injustice unless justified by some other title of subjection. The law which secures public order must be so indispensable for that order that every

[52] Cf. canon 14, § 1, 2°.

[53] "Neutrorum more consulere est consultare, deliberare ac deliberando habere rationem et curam alicujus rei (It. *consultare, déliberare, aver cur di qualche cosa deliberandò*; Fr. *deliberer, se consulter, en consultant avoir soin de*; Hisp. *consultar, deliberar, proveer*; Germ. *sich berathen, Rath suchen en finden, Rath halten und berschliessen, berathend für etwas sorgen;* Angl. *to consult, deliberate, to provide for, take care of.*) . . . Cum Dativo personae aut rei significat habere rationem et curam alicujus personae aut rei, tuere, providere, prospicere . . . —Sic *consulere saluti suae* et *consulere rebus suis,* saepe dicitur in extremis periculis et re desperata, cum quis omnia facit sui unius tuendi causa, relicta aliorum cura . . . "—J. Facciolati, Aeg. Forcellini et J. Furlanetti, *Lexicon Totius Latinitatis* (ed. 2., 4 vols., cura F. Corradini, Patavii, 1864-1887), I, 823. Cf. *Thesaurus Linguae Latinae Editus Auctoritate et Consilio Academiarum Quinque Germanicarum Berolinensis Gottingensis Lipsiensis Monacensis Vindobonensis* (8 vols., Lipsiae, 1900—) IV (1904-1909), col. 577-579; Leverett, *Lexicon of the Latin Language* (2.ed. Philadelphia, 1850), pp. 201. 202.

[54] "L'on ne devra admettre comme lois d'ordre public que celles auxquelles il sera nécessaire d'attribuer ce caractère. En d'autres termes, il ne suffira pas qu'une loi soit conforme à l'ordre public ou même propre à assurer son maintien, pour qu'elle soit réellement d'ordre public; il faudra qu'elle soit indispensable à cet ordre public, que l'absence de ses dispositions ait pour résultat de détruire l'ordre public. Le caractère exceptionnel des lois d'ordre public étant donné, ce sont des idées qui s'imposent. S'il est évident, d'une part, qu'une disposition légale essentielle au maintien de l'ordre public doit recevoir une application absolue, il n'est pas moins certain que donner le même effet à une loi qui n'offre pas ce caractére, aboutit à léser sans nécessite les intérêts particuliers qui eussent été garantis par l'application des principes, c'est-à-dire une injustice."—Pillet, *L'Ordre Public,* p. 18; cf. *Principes du Droit Int. Privé,* p. 374; Weiss, *Traité de Droit Int. Privé,* III, 100, 101.

violation of it naturally results in a violation of the public order, and a danger to the attainment of the purpose of the society, or in the case of the ecclesiastical society, an obstacle to the sanctification of the members.[55] That injury to the public order which may accidentally result from the violation of a law by an individual act in certain particular circumstances is prevented by other titles of exceptional subjection to the local legislator, which have been treated in the previous chapter. The exceptional injury done to the public order may be taken care of by the local ordinary in virtue of his exceptional powers of coercion according to canon 2222. Legislative jurisdiction should provide not for the exceptional and the accidental, but for the normal and the natural results of human conduct. Hence the Code, when establishing this reason for the exceptional subjection to local laws, states that the stranger is bound to observe the particular laws of the territory *which* secure public order, *not when* they secure public order.[56]

Lest this interpretation become too strict, it is to be noted that the laws which secure public order are often founded upon the presumption of a general danger, namely, the presumption that harm will result to the public order from every violation of the law. Just as exceptional cases may be presented to show harm done to the public order by the violation of a law whose intrinsic purpose and entire scope is not the protection of that order, so, too, the exceptional case may be presented where, due to special circumstances, the individual violation of a law which is designed to secure public order does not actually result in harm to that order. However, in virtue of canon 21, the stranger is bound to observe those laws which really secure public order, even in special circumstances when the violation of the law may have no effect on public order.

[55] "Requiritur tamen ut tales leges, attentis specialibus circumstantiis, ex ipso suo scopo, ordini publico consulunt. Perturbatio ordinis publici debet sequi quamcumque violationem legis; non potest pendere a circumstantiis omnino particularibus alicuius actus in individuo spectati."—Van Hove, *De Legibus*, n. 216; cf. Michiels, *Normae Generales*, I, 318; Onclin, *De Legis Indole*, p. 337; Le Picard, "La notion d'ordre public en droit canonique,"—*NRT*, LV (1928), 362; Deschepper, "De obligatione peregrinorum et vagorum,"—*Coll. Brug.*, XXIV (1924), 156.

[56] Cf. Van Hove, *De Legibus*, n. 216.

Laws which secure public order, then, are limited to only those laws which have as their entire and sole purpose the maintenance of that order, that strict uniformity of conduct, which is indispensable for the good organization of the particular ecclesiastical society, and which is required to attain those conditions in which the individual members of the society are normally enabled to work out their personal sanctification without the danger of being hindered by the activities of those around them.

Article II. Laws Which Obviously Secure Public Order

Those laws which are designed to secure public order can be identified by the clear statement of the text of the law itself, by an authentic interpretation given by the legislator, or by an investigation of the particular statute by the traveler himself.[57] In the absence of a clear statement in the text of the law[58] that it is designed to secure public order, the stranger must seriously examine whether or not the statute can be reasonably considered a law of public order. Once he has exercised due care to identify these laws, his judgment whether he is obliged to observe the law or not prevails until an authentic interpretation is given.[59]

On the other hand, the legislator, in making a law or giving an authentic interpretation cannot justly and legitimately oblige strangers to observe a law on the grounds of public order which does not actually pertain to public order. A law, to be just, must have as its intrinsic purpose (*finis operis*) something useful for the common good.[60] The only common good in whose attainment the stranger must cooperate is the public order of the community. The legislator cannot arbitrarily decide that this or that law is required for the public order of his community. The object and the content of the law, not the intention of the legislator, determines its necessity for the public order. Unless

[57] Cf. Roelker, "The traveler and local statutes,"—*The Jurist,* II (1942), 110-115.

[58] Such a clear statement is greatly to be desired in all laws designed to secure public order. Examples of expressions indicating these laws may be found in canons 290; 301, § 2; 343, § 1; 1320. Cf. Roelker, "The traveler and local statutes,"—*The Jurist,* II (1942), 110; Cance, *Code de Droit Canonique,* I, n. 43.

[59] Cf. Claeys Bouuaert-Simenon, *Manuale Iuris Can.,* I, n. 164; Beste, *Introductio in Cod.,* p. 72; Roelker, "The traveler and local statutes,"—*The Jurist,* II (1942), 110-115.

[60] Cf. Suarez, *De Legibus,* I, c. VII, n. 9.

the law objectively and because of its content secures public order, it cannot be reasonably and justly imposed upon strangers as a law of public order.

As a consequence, both the legislator and the subject of the law have a duty to determine which laws pertain to public order and which do not. Although the requirements of public order vary in different circumstances, certain laws, where they are in force, by their very content and in every circumstance obviously secure public order.

§ 1. *Laws Concerning the Organization of Public Offices and Powers*

The laws which determine the local organization of public offices and powers most obviously secure public order in both Civil[61] and Canon Law.[62] The particular regulation of the rights and duties of incumbents in public office, or of the exercise of public power, and of the relationship of the faithful with their ecclesiastical superiors is essential to the organization of the territory and the unhindered attainment of its ultimate purpose. When the occasion presents itself, strangers are obliged by reason of public order to observe all of these local laws which regard the bestowal and acceptance of benefices, offices and functions, the administration of public property and the performance of public duties in the territory, and the administration of judicial power.[63]

[61] Cf. Surville, "De la personnalité des lois envisagée comme principe fondamental du droit international privé,"—*JDIP*, XVI (1899), 536; Surville, *Cours de Droit Int. Privé*, p. 51; Weiss, *Traité de Droit Int. Privé*, III, 101; Pillet, *L'Ordre Public*, p. 51; Despagnet, "L'ordre public en droit international privé,"—*JDIP*, XVI (1889), 5.

[62] Cf. Van Hove, *De Legibus*, n. 216; Van Hove, "Leges quae ordini publico consulunt,"—*ETL*, I (1924), 159; Michiels, *Normae Generales*, I, 320; Coronata, *Inst. Iuris Can.*, I, n. 16; Cappello, *Summa Iuris Can.*, I, n. 80; Berutti, *Inst. Iuris Can.*, I, n. 61; Onclin, *De Legis Indole*, pp. 339, 340; Toso, "De ordine publico,"—*Jus Pont*., X (1930), 342; Le Picard, "La notion d'ordre public en droit canonique."—*NRT*, LV (1928), 356.

[63] Cf. Van Hove, "Leges quae ordini publico consulunt,"—*ETL*, I (1924), 159; Le Picard, "La notion d'ordre public en droit canonique,"—*NRT*, LV (1928), 356; Onclin, *De Legis Indole*, p. 339.

§ 2. *Laws Regarding Good External Order*

Of secondary importance to the regulation of public power, perhaps, but equally binding upon the strangers in the territory, are those laws which provide for good external order in the Church.[64] Such, for example, are the local regulations regarding the public exercise of divine worship,[65] the time and manner of ringing church bells, and the care of both church and cemetery,[66] the collection of alms,[67] the making of announcements,[68] the care, decoration and furnishing of the church and the sacred vestments and vessels for use at the altar,[69] the assignment of seats in the church for the faithful,[70] and the orderly and reverent conduct of sacred processions.[71] The local regulations regarding all of these things are essential, not only to avoid confusion in the exercise of public worship, but also to make sure that nothing unbecoming, nothing liable to give scandal, should enter into the corporate worship of God by the community. They constitute an order that is vital to the entire community, and therefore must be observed uniformly by all, even strangers, within the community.[72]

§ 3. *Laws Regarding Immovable Property in the Territory* (Res Sitae)

Laws regarding immovable property in the territory[73] are considered in Private International Law to be absolutely territorial because they

[64] Cf. Van Hove, *De Legibus*, n. 216; "Leges quae ordini publico consulunt,"—*ETL*, I (1924), 159; Michiels, *Normae Generales*, I, 320; Wernz-Vidal, *Ius Canonicum*, I, n. 156; Cappello, *Summa Iuris Canonici*, I, n. 80; Eichmann, *Kirchenrechts*, I, n. 64; Jone, *Kanonischen Rechtes*, I, 33; Ojetti, *Commentarium in Cod.*, I, 116; Onclin, *De Legis Indole*, p. 340; Le Picard, "La notion d'ordre public en droit canonique,"—*NRT*, LV (1928), 356.

[65] Cf. canon 1184, 1°.

[66] Cf. canon 1184, 2°.

[67] Cf. canons 1184, 3°; 1503; 621-624; 691, §§ 3, 5.

[68] Cf. canon 1184, 3°.

[69] Cf. canon 1184, 4°, 5°.

[70] Cf. canons 1184, 4°; 1262; 1263.

[71] Cf. canon 1295.

[72] Cf. canon 1261, § 2: "Si loci Ordinarius leges pro suo territorio hac in re [divino cultu] tulerit, etiam religiosi omnes, exempti quoque, obligatione tenentur easdem servandi . . . "

[73] It has been already pointed out that immovable property is the basis for the extra-territorial obligation of laws. Here immovable property is considered as the

are designed to secure public order.[74] From the time of the decretalists, laws directly affecting property located in the territory were commonly held to bind strangers indirectly as often as they entered into a juridical relationship involving such property.[75] There is no explicit legislation in the Code which reaffirms this common doctrine of the pre-Code authors.[76] Modern canonists, however, unhesitatingly classify laws regarding immovable property as laws which secure public order.[77] Indeed, it is of necessity for the good organization of the society that the immovable property be regulated by a uniform legislation in the territory.[78] Moreover, the public importance of the legislation for immovable property in the Church is further evidenced from the fact that the Church directly legislates for no other property except ecclesiastical property and that property destined for pious or charitable purposes.

§ 4. *Laws Enacted Specifically for Strangers*

The clear statement in the law is an indication for the subject that the law is designed to secure public order. Certain pre-Code authors[79] taught that the local legislator could enact laws specifically for strangers as conditions upon which they were allowed to stay within the

object of the acts of strangers. Thus here is an example of a class of laws which can be under different aspects both extra-territorial and absolutely territorial.

[74] Cf. Surville, *Cours de Droit Int. Privé*, p. 52; Surville, "De la personnalité des lois envisagée comme principe fondamental du droit international privé."—*JDIP*, XVI (1889), 537; Pillet, *L'Ordre Public*, p. 27; Pillet, *Principes de Droit Int. Privé*, pp. 385-389; Weiss, *Traité de Droit Int. Privé*, III, 103.

[75] Cf. Wernz, *Jus Decretalium*, I, n. 107; *supra*, pp. 34, 58, 59.

[76] Cf. Van Hove, "Leges quae ordini publico consulunt,"—*ETL*, I (1924), 160; Kinane, "'Peregrini' and the laws which take care of public order,"—*IER*, *XLIII* (1934), 125.

[77] Cf. Van Hove, *De Legibus*, n. 216; "Leges quae ordini publico consulunt,"—*ETL*, I (1924), 160; Jone, *Kanonischen Rechtes*, I, 33; Cicognani, *Ius Canonicum*, II, 104; Michiels, *Normae Generales*, I, 320; Torrubiano Ripoll, *De Derecho Canónico*, I, n. 102; Maroto, *Inst. Iuris Can.*, I, n. 102; Onclin, *De Legis Indole*, p. 340; Kinane, "'Peregrini' and the laws which take care of public order,"—*IER*, XLIII (1934), 125; Le Picard, "La notion d'ordre public en droit canonique,"—*NRT*, LV (1928), 356, 357.

[78] Cf. Van Hove, "Leges quae ordini publico consulunt,"—*ETL*, I (1924), 160; Weiss, *Traité de Droit Int. Privé*, III, 103.

[79] Cf. Wernz, *Ius Decretalium*, I, n. 107; *supra* p. 52.

territory. This position has also found favor among a number of authors since the Code.[80] Such a general affirmation, however, must be rejected.[81] According to the principle of canon 201, § 1, jurisdiction can be directly exercised only over subjects. Strangers are subject to the local legislator only in those exceptional cases specified in the universal law. The universal law, however, does not give the local legislator power to enact laws restricting the right of travelers to pass through or visit in his territory. Indeed, as Van Hove points out,[82] the local ordinary can establish particular regulations to be complied with by a visiting priest before he is habitually admitted to celebrate Mass in the diocese,[83] or he can refuse to allow a visiting cleric to remain longer in his territory, for a just cause,[84] or as an ecclesiastical penalty.[85] But these restrictions regard only clerics, and the latter two suppose a just cause and regard singular cases. They do not empower the local ordinary to enact preventative laws.

The local legislator can enact laws specifically affecting strangers only when the public order demands it.[86] When such a law is enacted, therefore, it is presumed to be a law designed to secure public order. On the other hand, as Onclin[87] points out, such a law of itself binds

[80] Cf. Maroto, *Inst. Iuris Can.*, I, n. 201, p. 312, nota 2; Cocchi, *Comm. in Codicem*, I, n. 56; Cappello, *Summa Iuris Canonici*, I, n. 80; Torrubiano Ripoll, *De Derecho Canónico*, I, n. 102; Merkelbach, *Theologia Moralis*, I, n. 358; Jone, *Kanonischen Rechtes*, I, 33.

[81] Cf. Van Hove, *De Legibus*, n. 218; "Leges quae ordini publico consulunt,"—*ETL*, I (1924), 166; Michiels, *Normae Generales*, I, 321, 322; Onclin, *De Legis Indole*, p. 344; Esswein, *Extrajudicial Powers*, pp. 79, 80; Kinane, "'Peregrini' and the laws which take care of public order,"—*IER*, XLIII (1934), 122.

[82] "Leges quae ordini publico consulunt,"—*ETL*, I (1924), 167.

[83] Cf. canon 804, § 3; 1303, §§ 2-4; *supra*, pp. 126, 127.

[84] Cf. canon 144.

[85] Cf. canon 2298, n. 7; Esswein, *Extrajudicial Powers*, p. 80.

[86] Cf. Van Hove, *De Legibus*, n. 218; "Leges quae ordini publico consulunt,"—*ETL*, I (1924), 166; Michiels, *Normae Generales*, I, 322; Onclin, *De Legis Indole*, p. 344; Ayrinhac, *General Legislation*, n. 102; Vermeersch-Creusen, *Epitome Iuris Canonici*, I, n. 110; Beste, *Introd. in Codicem*, p. 72; Wernz-Vidal, *Ius Canonicum*, n. 156; Cicognani, *Ius Canonicum*, II, 104; Vermeersch, *Theologia Moralis*, I, n. 286.

[87] "Igitur Ordinariis integrum non est peregrinos subiicere legibus specialibus, sed tantum legibus quae ordini publico consulunt; hae autem leges subditos et peregrinos pariter obligant."—*De Legis Indole*, p. 345.

the habitual subjects equally as much as strangers. A particular law intended exclusively for strangers, outside of the cases provided for in canons 804, § 3, and 1303, §§ 2-4 would find application only in that rare occasion in which the public order could be violated only by strangers.

Article III. Laws Which Are Not of Obvious Public Order

Between those laws which, as discussed in the previous article, secure public order because of the very nature of their content and in every case, and those laws which obviously do not pertain to public order in any way because they pertain to the inner sanctity of the faithful or to purely private matters, there are classes of laws which may be designed to secure public order in given circumstances. Because they are not of *obvious* public order, it is in regard to these laws that the legislator should expressly indicate in the text of the law his judgment that on account of the circumstances they are designed to secure public order and are thereby binding on all in the territory, including strangers.

§ 1. *Special Obligations Imposed on the Clergy*

A number of diocesan statutes are enacted under the title *De Obligationibus Clericorum* which cause particular concern to the visiting priest when he investigates his subjection to these laws. Many of these laws are designed to promote the inner sanctity of the clergy and their perseverance in the study of ecclesiastical sciences.[88] These laws, although indirectly very useful and even necessary for the common good, are designed primarily and directly for the good of individuals. They do not pertain to public order.[89]

Canon 136 specifies that clerics are to wear the clerical garb according to the legitimate custom of the place and the prescriptions of the

[88] Cf. canons 124-126; 129-131.

[89] Cf. Michiels, *Normae Generales,* I, 321; Van Hove, "Leges quae ordini publico consulunt,"—*ETL,* I (1924), 161; Onclin, *De Legis Indole,* p. 341; Claeys Bouuaert-Simenon, *Manuale Iuris Can.,* I, n. 164; Jone, *Kanonischen Rechtes,* I, 33; Le Picard, "La notion d'ordre public en droit canonique,"—*NRT,* LV (1928), 356; Simenon, "Territorialitas legum,"—*REL,* XXI (1929-1930), 185; Kinane, "'Peregrini' and the laws which take care of public order,"—*IER,* XLIII (1934), 123.

local ordinary. This obligation is generally recognized as, of itself, grave, although admitting a parvity of matter.[90] The gravity of the obligation of wearing the clerical garb is indicated by the penalties prescribed in the Code for its violation.[91] The Sacred Congregation of the Council, in a circular letter issued in 1926,[92] instructed local ordinaries to threaten visiting priests with an *ipso facto* suspension if they should lay aside the clerical garb without a reasonable and just cause. A decree of the same congregation, published in 1931,[93] states that those priests who, contrary to lawful custom and to the prescriptions of the place, publicly wear garments which are thoroughly secular naturally diminish the respect of Catholics toward the clerical state and expose themselves to the danger of acting in a manner unbecoming their state in life. In short, the obligation of wearing the clerical dress is based in itself upon public order.

Although substantially the obligation of wearing the clerical garb is based on public order, the particular manner in which this obligation is to be carried out varies in different territories. A response of the Sacred Consistorial Congregation to the Archbishop of Quebec in 1916[94] clearly states that the visiting priest is free to conform either to the customs of his own diocese or to those of the diocese where he is visiting in the matter of wearing the clerical garb. This interpretation has not been changed by the instructions of the Sacred Congregation of the Council since the Code.[95] Creusen indicates that the local ordinary cannot impose the clerical garb of his territory upon visiting clerics unless they remain long enough in his territory to acquire a

[90] Cf. Coronata, *Inst. Iuris Can.*, I, n. 195; Beste, *Introd. in Codicem*, p. 187; Vermeersch-Creusen, *Epitome Iuris Can.*, I, n. 254; Cappello, *Summa Iuris Canonici*, I, n. 238; Fallon, "The obligation of wearing the clerical dress during holidays,"—*IER*, XIL (1939), 499. 500.

[91] Cf. canons 136, § 3; 188, 7°; 2379.

[92] S.C.C., litt. circ., 1 iul. 1926—*AAS*, XVIII (1926), 312.

[93] S.C.C., decr., 28 iul. 1931—*AAS*, XXIII (1931), 336.

[94] S.C.Consist. (ad archiep. Quebecen.), 31 mar. 1916—*AAS*, VIII (1916), 148.

[95] Cf. Fallon, "The obligation of wearing the clerical dress during holidays,"—*IER*, XIL (1939), 500; Darmanin, "Annotationes,"—*Jus Pont.*, XVII (1937), 278; Balt, *Commentarium Iuris Can.*, I, n. 71; Onclin, *De Legis Indole*, p. 344; Van Hove, "Leges quae ordini publico consulunt,"—*ETL*, I (1924), 161; Vermeersch-Creusen, *Epitome Iuris Canonici*, I, n. 254.

quasi-domicile.[96] Visiting priests, then, are bound because of public order to observe the local laws regarding the obligation of wearing the clerical garb, but may fulfill this obligation according to the manner of their own diocese if they choose.

Finally many local statutes are enacted to restrain clerics from occupations or recreations which are unbecoming[97] or foreign to[98] the clerical state. It is to be noted first of all that the universal law does not forbid the participation of the clergy in all secular recreations and pursuits, but only those which bring discredit upon or lessen the dignity of the clergy.[99] A statute which would indiscriminately forbid all such occupations would be against the Code and would unlawfully deprive the clergy of certain pursuits to which they have a right. Moreover, particular statutes in this matter are often designed to foster clerical sanctity and to increase the reverence of the people for their priests. The failure to observe such statutes by the visiting priest does not necessarily result in injury to the public order.[100] Certain local prohibitions against attending the theater or driving or riding in an automobile are not laws of obvious public order.[101] Generally, therefore, statutes regulating this matter do not bind strangers. However, due to special circumstances of the place, whether because of abuses to be eradicated or because of the high esteem with which the clergy is cherished by the laity, laws regulating this matter may truly be necessary for public order. Laws, for instance, restricting priests from taking part in political controversies or public demonstrations[102] may

[96] "L'habit ecclésiastique prescrit est celui qu'autorisent la coutume et les préscriptions de l'Ordinaire du pays dont le prêtre est originaire. Aux clercs qui n'ont pas même un quasi-domicile, les Ordinaires ne peuvent imposer, sauf raison grave, d'adopter l'habit ecclésiastique du diocèse."—"L'obligation de l'habit ecclésiastique,"—*NRT*, LVIII (1931), 821.

[97] Canons 139; 140.

[98] Canon 139.

[99] "Spectaculis, choreis et pompis *quae eos dedecent, vel quibus clericos interesse scandalo sit*, . . . "—canon 140 (Italics inserted). Cf. Van Hove, *De Legibus*, n. 216.

[100] Cf. Van Hove, *De Legibus*, n. 216; Michiels, *Normae Generales*, I, 321; Onclin, *De Legis Indole*, p. 342; Van Hove, "Leges quae ordini publico consulunt,"—*ETL*, I (1924), 162; Kinane, " 'Peregrini' and the laws which take care of public order,"—*IER*, XLIII (1934), 124.

[101] Cf. Roelker, "The traveler and local statutes,"—*The Jurist*, II (1942), 113.

[102] Cf. canon 141, § 1.

well be laws of public order. Kinane, in showing that the laws of the Council of Maynooth, which forbid clerics to attend the races, circuses, plays, operas, and similar performances, are laws of public order, states:

> In a Catholic community such as ours, whose ideal of the clerical state is so high, and whose sentiments so easily revolt at any unbecoming action on the part of ecclesiastics, these laws have for their object, not so much the promotion of greater sanctity amongst the clergy, as the preservation of clerical decorum and the maintenance of clerical prestige amongst the community generally. . . . In non-Catholic communities, on the other hand, these reasons hardly hold, or at least, hold only in a modified way, so that it would seem more likely that in such places the prohibitions in question would have the personal sanctification of individuals for their primary object.[103]

To apply the more concrete description of public order derived in the first article of this chapter, such prohibitions are objectively laws of public order only when the normal inhabitant, and not just a few of the more sensitive persons in the territory, would feel a certain disgust or shame in observing a cleric violating them. Then the efficacy of the leadership of the clergy in the community would be subject to a general detriment by the single non-observance of the law. It is an accepted fact that the normal person fails to distinguish between the person and the group. He judges whole classes by the impressions made by single representatives of the class. When these circumstances obtain, and in most dioceses of the United States they do not often obtain, the non-observance of such laws has a serious effect on all, is a matter of public order.

The authentic decision as to whether the violation of a law would involve public order or not rests with the ordinary of the place.[104] However, no law in this matter can legitimately oblige the stranger

[103] " 'Peregrini' and the laws which take care of public order,"—*IER*, XLIII (1934), 124; cf. also Canestri, "De lege cum sanctione poenali lata in peregrinos,"—*Appollinaris*, VII (1934), 97.

[104] Cf. canon 17; S.C.C., litt. circ., 1 iul. 1926—*AAS*, XXVIII (1926), 312; Blat, *Commentarium Iuris Can.*, I, n. 71.

unless it objectively pertains to public order.[105] Because the visiting priest is usually ignorant of the special circumstances which make such a law necessary for public order, his obligation to observe it should be clearly expressed in the law, and the law itself should be sufficiently promulgated in the territory by being posted in the church sacristies, published in diocesan directories, and the like.[106]

§ 2. *Special Obligations Imposed on the Faithful*

The distinction between the notion of scandal and the notion of public order has been clearly indicated. If, however, the violation of a law causes real scandal of its very nature and in every instance, such a law would be necessary to safeguard public order.

A particular law prohibiting dangerous books[107] may bind strangers in the territory because of the subject matter of the books. Because canon 1395, § 1 restricts the particular legislation prohibiting books to the subjects of the legislator,[108] certain authors[109] hold that strangers cannot be bound by these particular prohibitions. Such, however, is not the significance of the canon. The phrase "for their subjects" indicates that the particular prohibitions enacted by local legislators do not affect the universal Church.[110] Strangers are true, although exceptional, subjects of the local legislator when public order is involved. Before the Code, strangers could be subject to the obligation imposed by the particular prohibition of books.[111] A particular book or publication may indeed be of such a nature that it will cause harm in the locality by its circulation and its use. In such a case, the law forbidding its purchase and use may be necessary for public order.

[105] Cf. Van Hove, "Leges quae ordini publico consulunt,"—*ETL,* I (1924), 162.

[106] Cf. Decretum Vicariatus Urbis, 25 maii 1918—*AAS,* X (1918), 300.

[107] Cf. canon 1395, § 1.

[108] "Ius et officium libros ex iusta causa prohibendi competit . . . *pro suis subditis* Conciliis quoque particularibus et locorum Ordinariis."—canon 1395, § 1 (Italics inserted).

[109] Cf. Coronata, *Inst. Iuris Can.,* II, n. 960; Augustine, *Commentary,* VI (1937), 455; Blat, *Commentarium Iuris Can.,* III, 2-6 (2.ed., 1934), n. 284; Noldin-Schmitt, *De Praeceptis,* n. 704; Berutti, *Inst. Iuris Can.,* IV (1940), n. 149; Eichmann, *Kirchenrechts,* II, 100.

[110] Cf. Van Hove, "Leges quae ordini publico consulunt,"—*ETL,* I (1924), 162.

[111] Cf. Wernz,*Ius Decretalium,* III, 111, nota 82; De Meester, *Iuris Canonici Compendium,* III, n. 1354.

Although the universal law contains no general legislation specifically regarding the attendance of the faithful at determined theatrical productions or cinemas, the principles that regulate the prohibition of books apply here, according to canon 20, to determine the obligation of the stranger to observe particular laws prohibiting attendance at these amusements. The harmful effect of these amusements varies greatly in different localities according to the culture and habits of the people. The judgment of this harmful effect has been expressly entrusted to the local ordinaries.[112] It is chiefly by discouraging attendance at these productions that the ordinary is enabled to curb their exhibition within his territory and thus protect the public morals and prevent the dissemination of false doctrine.

An increasing number of recent diocesan statutes constitute legislation concerning radio broadcasting. The Code, promulgated in 1917, contains no legislation on this point. However, because of the very extensive field of influence in the whole territory that can be exerted by the radio, those particular laws regarding the use of the radio may be of extreme importance to public order. The universal law requires the previous censorship of all books, written even by lay persons, which regard sacred Scripture, theology, and other ecclesiastical sciences, ethics, and other religious and moral subjects.[113] Moreover, the permission of the lawful superior is required for all the published works of clerics, and for the works of lay persons which appear in publications ordinarily hostile to the Catholic religion or good morals.[114] The use of the radio as a means of communication is even more powerful than that of the printed word. Public order is involved in the use of the radio to express views or to deliver addresses or sermons on any of the subjects noted above, by clerics on any subject and by lay persons on broadcasts sponsored by those habitually hostile to the Church and good morals.

Although the Code entrusts the previous censorship of books to the proper local ordinary of the author, to the ordinary of the place of

[112] Pius XI, litt. encycl., "*Vigilanti cura,*" 29 iunii 1936—*AAS*, XXVIII (1936), 261; cf. *AER*, XCV (1936), 124.

[113] Cf. canon 1385, § 1.

[114] Cf. canon 1386.

publication, or to the ordinary of the place where the book is printed,[115] the more exact parallel legislation to the case of radio broadcasting is in the legislation on preaching. Permission to preach is to be obtained from the ordinary of the place where the sermon is to be delivered.[116] With these parallel laws of the Code as norms of interpretation, it follows that the local laws regulating radio broadcasting in any of those cases which require the previous censorship of books or the permission of the lawful superiors are laws which are designed to secure public order, and the visitor is bound by them as often as he plans to broadcast over a radio station located in that territory.

§ 3. *Penal Laws*

A number of authors since the Code maintain that all penal laws bind strangers because they are designed to secure public order.[117] This position is based upon the principle of procedure that a tribunal acquires competence by reason of the commission of a delict in the territory,[118] and upon the theory that the primary and only intrinsic purpose of the penal system in the Church is the restoration of the social order.[119] It has been demonstrated that the latter theory fails to take into consideration the specific purpose of the Church, namely to secure the salvation of the individual souls entrusted to it by its divine Founder. Therefore it enjoys not intrinsic but only extrinsic probability, because of the weighty authority supporting it. The former basis of this position, that the commission of a delict determines judicial competence,[120] was the reason set forth by the decretalists and the pre-Code authorities for the subjection of the stranger to all the penal laws of the territory.[121] But the only fact established by the commis-

[115] Cf. canon 1385, § 2.

[116] Cf. canon 1341.

[117] Cf. Maroto,*Inst. Iuris Can.*, I, n. 201; Cicognani, *Ius Canonicum,* II, 103; Cocchi, *Commentarium in Cod.*, I, n. 56; Toso, *Comm. Minora,* I, 34; Ojetti, *Commentarium in Cod.*, I, 116; Torrubiano Ripoll, *De Derecho Canónico,* I, n. 102; Eichmann, *Kirchenrechts,* I, 65; Prümmer, *Manuale Theologiae Moralis,* I, 131; Merkelbach, *Theologia Moralis,* I, n. 358; Noldin-Schmitt, *De Principiis,* n. 152; Roberti, *De Delictis et Poenis,* n. 60.

[118] Cf. Maroto, *Inst. Iuris Can.*, I, n. 201; Cicognani, *Ius Caninicum,* II, 103; Toso, *Comm. Minora,* I, 34.

[119] Cf. *supra,* pp. 106, 107.

[120] Cf. canons 1565, § 1; 1566, §§ 1, 2.

[121] Cf. *supra,* pp. 32, 33, 37, 60.

sion of a delict is the competence of the court, not the application of the law.[122] If the title of competence established the law to be applied in the case, the court of the second instance would apply its own law rather than that of the court of the first instance in the adjudication of a case.[123] Indeed, canon 1566 presupposes subjection to the particular penal law. It does not establish it. There is no delict committed except by him who is already subject to the law,[124] and without a delict there is no title of competence.[125]

Michiels distinguishes between medicinal and vindictive penalties. The primary purpose of medicinal penalties is the correction of the delinquent, according to canon 2241, § 1. Therefore from the mere fact that they are penal laws one cannot conclude that they secure public order. Vindictive penalties, however, are directly intended to expiate the delict according to canon 2286. That means, according to Michiels, that they are to secure public order. Hence penal laws sanctioned by vindictive penalties of their very nature secure public order and thereby bind strangers.[126]

Although this distinction is appealing at first glance, it places too much emphasis upon the immediate purpose of vindictive penalties, the expiation of the offense and the restoration of the injured social order.[127] That vindictive penalties sanction laws which have as their object the public good may well be sustained. There is, however, a much more restricted extension to the term, public order, than there is to the term, public good. The principal intrinsic purpose of the penal laws in the Church, even those sanctioned by vindictive penalties, is the correction of the delinquent.[128]

[122] Cf. Van Hove, *De Legibus*, n. 217; Michiels, *Normae Generales*, I, 322; Esswein, *Extrajudicial Powers*, p. 80; Onclin, *De Legis Indole*, p. 350; Van Hove, "Leges quae ordini publico consulunt,"—*ETL*, I (1924), 162; Kinane, "'Peregrini' and the laws which take care of public order,"—*IER*, XLII (1934), 123.

[123] Cf. Van Hove, *De Legibus*, n. 217; "Leges quae ordini publico consulunt,"—*ETL*, I (1924), 163.

[124] Cf. canon 2195, § 1.

[125] Cf. Van Hove, *l.c.*; Onclin, *De Legis Indole*, p. 350.

[126] Cf. *Normae Generales*, I, 323, 324.

[127] Cf. Roelker, "The traveler and local statutes,"—*The Jurist*, II (1942), 118, 119.

[128] Cf. *supra*, p. 107.

The subjection of the stranger to the local penal laws is found in canon 2226, § 1.[129] He is subject to the penalty who is subject to the imperative or prohibitive elements of the same penal law. The stranger is liable to the penalty attached to particular laws only when he is otherwise bound to observe those laws by reason of public order, the solemnity of acts, or by some other reason of subjection treated in Chapter VII of this study.

If, however, the particular legislator attaches a penalty to an already existing divine or universal law, the penal sanction becomes as though a new particular law.[130] From the obligation of the stranger to observe the divine or universal law, one cannot argue his subjection to the particular penal sanction which has been attached. The stranger is liable to the penalty attached by authority of the local legislator only when the divine or universal law is designed to secure public order, or otherwise concerns those matters which render the stranger subject to the local legislator.

The consideration of these various classes of laws which may or may not be designed for public order in the concrete circumstances has illustrated the variability of the requirements for public order in different localities. It must also be noted that the requirements for public order may change over a period of time in the same locality. It is unjust to impose upon strangers a law which at a previous time was found necessary to secure public order, but which is no longer necessary because of the change in circumstances.

[129] "Poenae adnexae legi aut praecepto obnoxius est qui lege aut praecepto tenetur, nisi expresse eximatur."—canon 2226, § 1. Cf. Van Hove, *De Legibus,* n. 217; Cappello, *Summa Iuris Canonici,* I, n. 80; Cappello, *De Censuris,* n. 19; Claeys Bouuaert-Simenon, *Manuale Iuris Can.,* I, n. 164; Chelodi, *Ius Poenale,* n. 26; Jone, *Kanonischen Rechtes,* I, 33; Wernz-Vidal, *Ius Canonicum,* VII (1937), n. 240; Berutti, *Inst. Iuris Can.,* I, n. 86; Onclin, *De Legis Indole,* p. 350; Van Hove, "Leges quae ordini publico consulunt,"—*ETL,* I (1924), 165; Kinane, "'Peregrini' and the laws which take care of public order,"—*IER,* XLII (1934), 122; Teodori, "Peregrini quoad censuras,"—*Consult. Iuris Can.,* I (1934), 278; Roelker, "The traveler and local statutes,"—*The Jurist,* II (1942), 118, 119; Crnica, *Modificationes in Tractatu de Censuris per Codicem Introductae,* p. 20; Coronata, *Inst. Iuris Can.,* IV, n. 1712; Sole, *De Delictis et Poenis,* n. 106; Vermeersch-Creusen, *Epitome Iuris Canonici,* I, n. 110; Esswein, *Extrajudicial Powers,* p. 81.

[130] Cf. Van Hove, "Leges quae ordini publico consulunt,"—*ETL,* I (1924), 165, 166; Lega, *De Delictis,* pp. 160, 161.

Chapter IX

THE OBLIGATION OF THE TRAVELER AND UNIVERSAL LAW: THE OBLIGATION OF VAGRANTS

Article I. The Obligation of the Traveler and Universal Law

Canon 14, § 1, 3° states the obligation of the traveler relative to universal law. This number may be considered in two parts: the traveler is obliged to observe all of the universal laws in force in the territory where he is visiting; but he is not obliged to observe those laws which are not in force in the territory in which he is visiting, even though they may be in force in his own territory.[1]

§ 1. *General Principles Governing the Obligation of the Traveler to Observe Universal Laws*

A number of commentators on the Code see in this number of canon 14 an application of the general presumption of the territoriality of law established in canon 8, § 2.[2] Although universal laws theoretically bind everywhere according to canon 13, § 1, in practice there are exceptions whereby the universal law is sometimes not in force in particular localities. Therefore canon 8, § 2 has a useful application to universal laws considered practically and concretely. This application of canon 8, § 2 is also in harmony with the pre-Code doctrine. The controversies which chiefly centered upon the *Tametsi* decree before the Code demonstrated the existence of both personal and territorial universal laws.[3] In the very formation of the law now expressed in canon 8, § 2, the presumption in favor of territoriality of law was removed from exclusive application to particular laws and applied to laws in general. Moreover, the application of canon 8, § 2 to universal laws is a consistent and logical explanation of canon 14, § 1, 3°.[4] Un-

[1] "At legibus generalibus tenentur [peregrini], etiamsi hae suo in territorio non vigeant, minime vero si in loco in quo versantur non obligent."—canon 14, § 1, 3°.

[2] Cf. Michiels, *Normae Generales*, I, 313-315; Maroto, *Inst. Iuris Can.*, I, n. 201; Berutti, *Inst. Iuris Can.*, I, n. 55; Blat, *Commentarium Iuris Can.*, I, n. 71; Cance, *Code de Droit Canonique*, n. 37; Claeys Bouuaert-Simenon, *Manuale Iuris Can.*, I, n. 154; Beste, *Introd. in Codicem*, p. 63.

[3] Cf. *supra*, p. 47.

[4] Cf. Michiels, *Normae Generales*, I, 314.

less certainly personal, universal laws are to be considered territorial. Therefore in places where they are not in force, the traveler is not bound to observe them unless they are both certainly personal and bind in his own territory. Because the traveler is subject to the Supreme Legislator everywhere, whenever he is in a territory where the universal law is in force, he is immediately bound to observe it.

Although the application of canon 8, § 2 to universal law is supported by weighty and practical arguments, it is not enough to explain canon 14, § 1, 3°. Some universal laws are certainly personal, such as those which determine the capacity of persons and those which impose upon their subjects purely personal obligations. When these laws are in force in his proper territory, the traveler has the obligation of still observing them outside his territory if canon 14, § 1, 3° is to be interpreted only by canon 8, § 2. The complete interpretation of canon 14, § 1, 3° must therefore be placed upon a different basis. Michiels[5] explains this difficulty by stating that the traveler bound by a personal universal law is presumed still bound by the law when in a territory where it is not in force until he can demonstrate his exemption by showing the territoriality of the local exception. Although in practice few cases will be found where the local exception from the universal law is not territorial, this explanation places a greater limit upon the canon than its text implies.

Therefore, the majority of canonists[6] place the complete basis of canon 14, § 1, 3° upon the territorial character of the local exemption rather than upon the presumption in favor of the territoriality of universal law. By a positive concession of the universal legislator expressed in canon 14, § 1, 3°, the local exemption from the universal law, whether it is derived from a concordat, a local dispensation, a general

[5] *Normae Generales,* I, 314.

[6] Cf. Van Hove, *De Legibus,* n. 221; Maroto, *Inst. Iuris Can.,* I, n. 201; Wernz-Vidal, *Ius Canonicum,* I, n. 153; Beste, *Introd. in Codicem,* p. 72; Cance, *Code de Droit Canonique,* n. 43; Cicognani, *Ius Canonicum,* II, 104, 105; Ojetti, *Commentarium in Cod.,* I, 118; Chelodi-Bertagnoli, *Ius de Personis* n. 65; Ayrinhac, *General Legislation,* n. 104; Berutti, *Inst. Iuris Can.,* n. 60; Cappello, *Summa Iuris Canonici,* I, n. 80; Balt, *Commentarium Iuris Can.,* I, n. 71; Onclin, *De Legis Indole,* p. 323; Deschepper, "De obligatione peregrinorum et vagorum,"—*Coll. Brug.,* XXIV (1924), 156.

indult, a privilege, or a particular custom, is to be considered as though a territorial privilege regarding travelers.

Therefore it benefits all of those in the territory, whether habitual residents or travelers. On the other hand, it does not benefit anyone after he has left the territory.[7] In a word, because canon 14, § 1, 3° establishes as a territorial privilege all exceptions from the universal law enjoyed throughout the territory, the traveler is bound to observe all the universal laws and only those universal laws in force where he is.

This explanation of canon 14, § 1, 3° is to be preferred because it allows for the full force of the canon. It does not exclude personal universal laws from its application. The text of the canon is expressed in general terms without any such restrictions regarding personal universal laws. Moreover, if canon 14, § 1, 3° were only a logical application of canon 8, § 2, it would be unnecessary, for it would be already provided for in the latter canon.

§ 2. *Applications of Canon* 14, § 1, 3°

Although the interpretation of canon 14, §1, 3° must be given full extent according to its text, there are many universal laws which impose upon subjects an obligation to be fulfilled in their own territory. These laws are in effect the same as particular laws in the sense that they are enacted to benefit the particular territory of the subject. They are universal in the sense that they are imposed upon all the members of the Church belonging to a class. Since the non-observance of these laws does harm in the proper territory of the traveler bound by them, he is still obliged to observe them notwithstanding any general exemption that may be enjoyed in the place where he actually may be.[8]

Other applications of this number of canon 14 need little explanation. A traveler in Canada, for instance, on the 15th of August is not bound to observe the holy day established by universal law,[9] because by special privilege the feast is transferred in Canada to the following

[7] Note that purely personal privileges are not affected by canon 14, § 1, 3°. They are governed by canon 74 and benefit their recipients everywhere.

[8] Cf. Maroto, *Inst. Iuris Can.*, I, n. 201; p. 214, nota (2).

[9] Cf. canon 1247, § 1.

Sunday.[10] On the other hand, a traveler from Canada in the United States would be bound to observe the feast of the Assumption because the universal law remains in full force regarding that feast in the United States.

What has been pointed out in a previous chapter[11] concerning the obligation of a traveler leaving or entering a territory during the time allowed for the fulfillment of a law applies equally well here.

§ 3. *Obligation of the Traveler when the Universal Law is Substituted by a Particular Law*

A special problem is presented when the universal law is not in force in a territory, but another obligation is established in the same matter by a particular law. When the obligation of the universal law is completely and substantially suspended in the territory, it is evident that the traveler is not bound to observe it. Neither is he bound to observe a particular law that may be in force to take the place of the suspended universal law. These conclusions follow from canon 14, § 1, 2° and 3°. A difficulty is presented regarding the universal law of abstinence during Lent on Fridays and Saturdays[12] in those places where particular indults have transferred the Saturday abstinence to the previous Wednesday.

Three situations are possible. On Wednesday the traveler may be in the territory where the universal law is in force, and on Saturday of the same week he may be in the territory where the indult is in force. In this situation he is free from the obligation of abstinence on both Wednesday and Saturday. He does not have to abstain on Wednesday, because he is in the territory where the universal law is in force. And on Saturday he is in the place where the indult excuses him from Saturday abstinence.[13]

In the second situation, he observed the obligation of abstinence on Wednesday according to the indult in effect in the place where he was,

[10] Cf. Beste, *Introd. in Codicem*, p. 72.

[11] Cf. *supra*, pp. 89, 90.

[12] Cf. canon 1252, § 2.

[13] Cf. Van Hove, *De Legibus*, n. 222; Vermeersch, *Theologia Moralis*, I, n. 287; Onclin, *De Legis Indole*, p. 323; Noldin-Schmitt, *De Principiis*, n. 152; Bucceroni, *Theologia Moralis*, I, n. 287; Leroux, "Le sujet des lois ecclésiastiques,"—*REL*, XVI (1924-1925), 340.

and then arrived for Saturday in a place where the universal law is in force. In this situation he is not bound to fulfill the obligation again on Saturday. No one is bound to fulfill the same obligation twice.[14]

The third situation contemplates the case where the traveler remains the whole week in a territory which enjoys the indult of Wednesday abstinence. The authors are not in agreement concerning the obligations of the traveler to observe the law of abstinence in this situation.[15] To settle the doubts arising in the diocese of Namur and certain other dioceses of France and Belgium, the Sacred Congregation of the Council was asked on which of the two days, Wednesday or Saturday, were travelers obliged to observe the law of lenten abstinence. The Sacred Congregation responded that, provided scandal be avoided, travelers were to observe one day or the other according to their choice.[16] This resolution was prefaced by an opinion of the consultors of the Sacred Congregation in which they distinguished between the substance of the universal law of lenten abstinence and the manner of its observance. The indults which were referred to did not affect the substance of the law, namely the obligation of two days of abstinence a week. They only changed one of the days on which this law could be observed in the territory. Bouscaren reports this opinion of the consultors as follows:

> Non-residents are obliged to observe the substance of the law of abstinence for Lent, that being a general law (c. 14, § 1, 3°). Since, however, they are not bound to observe particular laws of the territory in which they are, they are not obliged as local residents are, to observe abstinence on Wednesday instead of Saturday; but they must abstain on either Wednesday or Saturday (in addition to Friday), in places where Wednesday has been substituted for Saturday as a day of abstinence.[17]

[14] Cf. Michiels, *Normae Generales,* I, 226; Van Hove, *De Legibus,* n. 221; Noldin-Schmitt, *De Principiis,* I, n. 152; Leroux, "Le sujet des lois ecclésiastiques,"—*REL,* XVI (1924-1925), 338, 340; Teodori, "Peregrini quoad leges servandas,"—*Consult. Iuris Can.,* I (1934), 19.

[15] Cf. Creusen, "Casuistique de Carême,"—*NRT,* LI (1924), 159, 160.

[16] S.C.C., *Namurcen. et aliorum,* 9 feb. 1924—*AAS,* XVI (1924), 94, 95.

[17] *The Canon Law Digest* (2 vols. and Supplement 1941) Milwaukee: The Bruce Publishing Co., 1934-1941), I, 54.

This resolution directly applies only to the indults in question.[18] The Sacred Congregation has no authority to interpret the canons of the Code.[19] The interpretation given by the consultors, since it was not a direct part of the resolution, has only the force of a doctrinal interpretation.

For these reasons, some canonists[20] still maintain that, except in those territories directly affected by the resolution of the Sacred Congregation, travelers are not obliged to abstain on either Wednesday or Saturday in those places which enjoy the indult of Wednesday abstinence. The universal law, they maintain, by comparison with canon 1247, states the substance of the law of lenten abstinence when it specifies two days on which abstinence is obligatory. Therefore, by substituting another day for the abstinence, the particular indult changes not only the manner but also the substance of the universal law. Therefore, adhering strictly to the principles of canon 14, § 1, 2° and 3°, the traveler need not fast on either Wednesday or Saturday in those places where the indult is in force, and where the interpretation of the Sacred Congregation does not apply.

The more common opinion of the authorities,[21] however, adopts the interpretation of the Sacred Congregation of the Council. Although it is not an authentic interpretation of the Code, it offers the safe norm for action.[22] Moreover, the solution depends, in last analysis, upon the interpretation of the indult, and not upon the interpretation of the law. If the indult substantially removes the obligation of the universal

[18] Cf. canon 17, § 3.

[19] Cf. Benedict XV, motu proprio, "*Cum iuris canonici,*" 5 sept. 1917—*AAS*, IX (1917), 483.

[20] Cf. Van Hove, *De Legibus*, n. 222; Creusen, "Usage des indults d'abstinence par les étrangers,"—*NRT*, LI (1924), 252; Onclin, *De Legis Indole*, p. 361.

[21] Cf. Vermeersch-Creusen, *Epitome Iuris Canonici*, II, n. 567; Berutti, *Inst. Iuris Can.*, I, 80, nota I; Claeys Bouuaert-Simenon, *Manuale Iuris Can.*, I, n. 164; Cicognani, *Ius Canonicum*, II, 105; Coronata, *Inst. Iuris Can.*, II, n. 827, p. 145, nota 1; Jone, *Kanonischen Rechtes*, I, 33; II, 415; Blat, *Commentarium Iuris Can.*, III, 2-6 (2.ed., 1934), n. 119; Ayrinhac, *Administrative Legislation in the New Code of Canon Law* (London-New York-Toronto: Longmans Green and Co., 1930), p. 116; Vermeersch, *Theologia Moralis*, I, n. 287; Leroux, "Le sujet des lois ecclésiastiques," —*REL*, XVI (1924-1925), 340.

[22] Cf. Vermeersch-Creusen, *Epitome Iuris Canonici*, I, n. 122.

law, the traveler is not bound to observe the universal law at all. Nor is he bound to observe the particular law which may be substituted for it in the territory. If, however, the indult leaves the universal law substantially intact, and only affects an accidental determination of the obligation, then the freedom of the traveler is limited to that accidental determination by the particular law. Since the indults which permit the substitution of Wednesday for Saturday in the law of lenten abstinence are all obtained from the same Congregation,[23] the most reasonable interpretation of these indults is in accordance with the interpretation given by the Congregation itself for those indults in force in Belgium and France.

Although the interpretation given by the Sacred Congregation of the Council is to be theoretically preferred for all of the indults, the interpretation given by Van Hove and Creusen can be sustained in practice. All of these indults are habitual faculties. They are to be given a broad interpretation in law.[24] Therefore, wherever there has not been given an authentic interpretation of the indults to the contrary, the traveler cannot be held strictly bound to observe the law of abstinence on Wednesday or on Saturday where the indult is in effect. In the United States the indult for the substitution of Wednesday instead of Saturday as the day of abstinence during Lent is given individually to each diocese.[25] A traveler, then, in the United States, in a diocese other than his own, need not, according to the broader interpretation, observe the law of abstinence on Wednesday or Saturday during Lent.

Article II. The Obligation of the Vagrant

The final consideration in regard to the obligation of the traveler to observe Canon Law is concerned with the obligation of him who has no domicile or quasi-domicile, the vagrant. The importance of a domicile or quasi-domicile, as has been pointed out, is chiefly in regard to

[23] Cf. canon 250, § 2.

[24] Cf. canons 66, § 1; 60; Van Hove, *De Privilegiis*, nn. 154, 158.

[25] Cf. Ap. Del., United States, 2 feb. and 21 apr., 1932—*HPR*, XXXIV (1934), 1083; Bouscaren, *Canon Law Digest*, II, 159; Towmey, "To abstain from flesh meat," —*AER*, C (1939), 109, 110; Hannan, "Lenten Regulations,"—*The Jurist*, I (1941), 144, 145.

particular laws. Hence the vagrant is subject to the universal law in the same manner in which all other travelers are subject to it.[26] The obligation of the vagrant to observe particular laws in the territory where he is has been a controverted question until the promulgation of the Code. The authors who followed Suarez extended the principle of absolute territoriality of law to include the vagrant.[27] Sanchez and his followers made an exception to their general rule of the exemption of the stranger to demonstrate the obligation of the vagrant to observe all of the particular laws in force in the territory where he was. The reasons advanced for this were purely reasons of expediency rather than juridical arguments.[28] Laymann, and those who shared his views on the matter, demonstrated that there was no difference between the vagrant and any other stranger in the territory according to strict juridical reasoning. This opinion became the more common opinion before the Code.[29]

This more common opinion must be admitted as the more juridically sound. The vagrant is no more a member of the local community where he happens to be than any other traveler. He has no permanent bond with the habitual members in the community. He does not intend to remain in the community and to work in union with the members of the community for the common objective. From the strict principles of law, therefore, he cannot be held to cooperate positively in the attainment of the objective of the community any more than other travelers. He cannot be held completely subject to the local authority, the authoritative expression of the local bond of union among the members of the community.

On the other hand, he is as permanently a member of that community where he is as he is of any community. The authority of the community where the vagrants are, as Ryan says, "is the only authority which can at any given time and in any given place practically serve the purpose of the Church in their regard."[30] For this practical rea-

[26] "Vagi obligantur legibus . . . generalibus . . . quae vigent in loco in quo versantur."—canon 14, § 2.

[27] Cf. *supra,* p. 53.

[28] Cf. *supra,* pp. 63, 64.

[29] Cf. *supra,* p. 64.

[30] *Episcopal Jurisdiction,* p. 103.

son, the Code establishes the vagrants in the same juridical status as the habitual subjects of the territory.[81] Vagrants therefore are bound to observe all of the laws in force in the territory where they are, whether those laws are universal or particular.[82]

[81] Cf. canons 94, § 2; 881, § 1; 1097, § 1; 1563; Van Hove, *De Legibus*, n. 224; Michiels, *Normae Generales*, I, 328; Wernz-Vidal, *Ius Canonicum*, I, n. 153; Vermeersch-Creusen, *Epitome Iuris Canonici*, I, n. 111; Claeys Bouuaert-Simenon, *Manuale Iuris Canonici*, I, n. 165; Cicognani, *Ius Canonicum*, II, 105; Ayrinhac, *General Legislation*, n. 104; Berutti, Inst. Iuris Can., I, n. 60; Cappello, *Summa Iuris Canonici*, I, n. 83; Toso, *Comm. Minora*, I, 34; Beste, *Introd. in Codicem*, p. 72; Leroux, "Le sujet des lois ecclésiastiques,"—*REL*, XVI (1924-1925), 338; Deschepper, "De obligatione peregrinorum et vagorum,"—*Coll. Brug.*, XXIV (1924), 157; Vindex, "Domicilium et quasi-domicilium eorumque effectus in Codice Juris Canonici,"—*Jus Pont.*, VI (1926), 157.

[82] "Vagi obligantur legibus tam generalibus quam particularibus quae vigent in loco in quo versantur."—canon 14, § 2.

CONCLUSIONS

1. The canonical evidence in the period before Gratian does not indicate a definite discipline regarding the obligations of the traveler.

2. In establishing a presumption in favor of the territoriality of laws, the Code adopts the doctrine of Pacelli that the obligation of law depends upon the will of the legislator.

3. It cannot be sustained that diocesan subjects in the exempt places of regulars are juridically absent from the surrounding diocese.

4. Canon 14, § 1, 1° has rendered the pre-Code fiction of moral presence unnecessary by the recognition of personal laws and of the extra-territorial obligation of laws whose violation does harm in the territory.

5. The assigning of scandal as a reason for strangers' obeying laws of public order is not universally applicable.

6. The juridical concept of *public order* is less extensive than the concept of *public good.*

7. The juridical concept of public order in the Church may be described as that strict uniformity of conduct on the part of everyone in the community, which is indispensable for the good organization of the ecclesiastical society, or which is required in order that the individual members of the society may attain their personal sanctification unhindered by the actions of those around them.

8. Laws which secure public order are only those laws the entire and only purpose of which is to secure that strict uniformity of conduct as described in conclusion seven.

9. Penal laws are not necessarily laws which secure public order; neither are penal laws necessary indications of laws which secure public order, or of laws the violation of which by an absent subject will cause harm to the territory.

BIBLIOGRAPHY

Sources

Acta Apostolicae Sedis, Commentarium Officiale, Romae, 1909—

Acta Sanctae Sedis, 41 vols., Romae, 1865-1908.

Antiquae Collectiones Decrtalium cum Antonii Augustini Episcopi Ilerdensis Notis, Ilerdae, 1576.

Bullarum Diplomatum et Privilegiorum Sanctorum Romanorum Pontificum, Taurinensis Editio, 25 vols., Augustae Taurinorum, 1857-1872.

Codex Iuris Canonici Pii X Pontificis Maximi iussu digestus Benedicti Papae XV auctoritate promulgatus, Romae: Typis Polyglottis Vaticanis, 1917.

Codicis Iuris Canonici Fontes cura Emi. Petri Card. Gasparri Editi, 9 vols., Romae (postea Civitate Vaticana): Typis Polyglottis Vaticanis, 1923-1939. Vols. VII, VIII, et IX ed. cura et studio Emi. Iustiniani Card. Sarédi.

Collectanea S. Congregationis de Propaganda Fide, 2.ed., 2 vols., Romae, 1907.

Corpus Iuris Canonici, ed. Lipsiensis 2., post Aemilii Ludovici Richter curas instruxit Aemilius Friedberg, 2 vols., Lipsiae: Ex Officina Bernhardi Tauchnitz, 1879-1881. Editio anastatice repitita, 1928.

Corpus Iuris Civilis, 3 vols., Berolini, 1928-1929. *Institutiones*, quas recognovit P. Krueger; *Digesta*, quae recognovit T. Mommsen et retractavit P. Krueger; *Codex Instinianus*, quem recognovit et retractavis P. Krueger.

Corpus Scriptorum Ecclesiasticorum Latinorum, 68 vols., Pragae, Vindobonae, Lipsiae, 1866—.

Decreta Authentica Congregationis Sacrorum Rituum ex actis eiusdem collecta eiusque auctoritate promulgata, 6 vols., Romae, 1898-1927.

Decretales D. Gregorii Papae IX, una cum Glossa Restitutae, Romae, 1582.

Decretum Gratiani Emendatum et Notationibus Illustratum Una cum Glossis, Venetiis, 1605.

Denzinger, Henr., et Bannwart, Clem., *Enchiridion Symbolorum, Definitionum, et Declarationum de Rebus Fidei et Morum*, 16. et 17.ed., Friburgi Brisgoviae: Herder, 1928.

Girard, Paul Frédéric, *Textes du Droit Romain*, 5.ed., Arthur Russeau, Paris: Librairie Nouvelle de Droit et de Jurisprudence, 1923.

Jaffé, Philippus, *Regesta Pontificum Romanorum ab Condita Ecclesia ad Annum post Christum Natum MCXCVIII*, 2 vols. in 1, Lipsiae, 1885-1888.

Jus Pontificium de Propaganda Fide, Vol. II, ed. R. de Martinis, Romae, 1909.

Liber Sextus Decretalium Bonifacii Papae VIII, Clementis Papae V Constutiones, Extravagantes tum Viginti Ioannis Papae XXII, Haec Omnia cum suis Glossis suae Integritati Restituta, Venetiis, 1591.

Mansi, Joannes D., *Sacrorum Conciliorum Nova et Amplissima Collectio*, 53 vols. in 59, Parisiis, Lipsiae, Arnhem, 1901-1927.

Monumenta Germaniae Historica, Legum Series I, Tom. I, ed. H. Pertz, Hannoverae, 1835; *Legum Sectio II, Capitularia Regum Francorum,* Tom. I, ed. A. Boretius, Hannoverae, 1877; *Legum Sectio III, Concilia Aevi Merovingici,* rec. F. Maassen, Hannoverae, 1893; Tom. II, rec. A. Werminghoff, Hannoverae, 1908.

Monumenta Germaniae Historica, Epistolae Karolini Aevi, Tom. VI, Pars II, Fasc. I, ed. Ernestus Perles, Hannoverae, 1912.

Monumenta Germaniae Historica, Epistolarum Series II, Tom. I, Pars I, ed. P. Ewald, Berolini, 1887.

Potthast, Augustus, *Regesta Pontificum Romanorum inde ab a. post Christum natum MCXCVIII ad a. MCCCIV,* 2 vols., Berolini, 1874-1875.

Reference Works

Abbott, Frank F.-Johnson, Allen C., *Municipal Administration in the Roman Empire,* Princeton: Princeton University Press, 1926.

Acta Congressus Iuridici Internationalis, 5 vols., Romae: Apud Custodiam Librariam Pont. Instituti Utriusque Iuris, 1935-1937.

Aertnys, J., *Theologia Moralis Secundum Doctrinam S. Alfonsi de Ligorio,* 7.ed. aucta et emendata, 2 vols., Paderbornae, 1906.

Alford, Culver B., *Jus Civile Matrimoniale in Statibus Foederatis Americae Septentrionalis cum Jure Canonico Comparatum,* Romae: Anonima Libraria Cattolica Italiana—New York: P. J. Kenedy & Sons, 1938.

Angelus Clavasensus, *Summa Angelica de Casibus Conscientialibus cum Additionibus Jacobi Ungarelli . . . necnon Augustino Patavino,* Venetiis, 1510.

Antoninus, B., St., *Summae Sacrae Theologiae, Iuris Pontificii, et Caesarei,* 4 vols., Venetiis, 1571.

Aquinas, Thomas, St., *Opera Omnia,* 34 vols., Parisiis: Apud Ludovicum Vivès, 1880-1889.

Arriaga, Rodrigo de, *Disputationes Theologicae in [Summam] Divi Thomae,* 8 vols., Antverpiae, 1643-1655.

Augustine, Charles, [Bachofen], *A Commentary on the New Code of Canon Law,* 8 vols., St. Louis: Herder, 1931-1938. Vol. I, 6.ed., 1931; Vol. II, 6.ed., 1936; Vol. VI, 3.ed., 1931.

Ayrinhac, H. A., *Administrative Legislation in the New Code of Canon Law,* London-New York-Toronto: Longmans Green and Co., 1930.

——, *General Legislation in the New Code of Canon Law,* London-New York-Toronto: Longmans Green and Co., 1933.

Ayrinhac, H. A.—Lydon, P. J., *Penal Legislation in the New Code of Canon Law,* Revised ed., New York: Benziger, 1936.

Azpilcueta, Martinus (Navarrus), *Enchiridion sive Manuale Confessariorum et Poenitentium,* Wirceburgi, 1593.

Azorius, Ioannes Lorcitanus, *Institutionum Moralium Pars Prima,* 2.ed., Brixiae, 1617.

Bachofen, Charles Augustine, *Compendium Jurium Religiosorum*, Neo-Eboraci-Cincinnati-Chicagiae, 1903.

——, *Summa Juris Ecclesiastici Publici*, Romae, 1910.

Baldus de Ubaldis, *Commentarium in . . . Codicis Libros*, 9 vols. in 7, Venetiis, 1572.

Ballerini, Antonius—Palmieri, Dominicus, *Opus Theologicum Morale in Busembaum Medullam*, 3.ed., 7 vols., Prati, 1898.

Barbosa, Augustinus, *Collectanea Doctorum tam Veterum quam Recentiorum in Jus Pontificium Universum*, 5 vols. in 4, Lugduni, 1656.

——, *Pastoralis Solicitudo, sive De Officio et Potestate Episcopi Tripartita Descriptio*, 4 vols. in 2, Lugduni, 1628.

Bargilliat, M., *Praelectiones Juris Canonici*, 24.ed., 2 vols., Parisiis, 1907.

Baronius, Caesar, *Annales Ecclesiastici*, 23 vols. in 37, Bari, 1865-1883.

Bartholomew of Brescia (Brixiensis), cf. *Decretum Gratiani una cum Glossis*.

Bartolus à Saxaferrato, *Omnia Quae Extant Opera*, 11 vols., Venetiis, 1590-1595.

Baviera, Giovanni, *Il Diritto Internazionale dei Romani*, Modena, 1898.

Benedicti XIV (Prosperus Lambertinus), *De Synodo Dioecesana*, 2.ed., 2 vols., Parmae, 1764.

——, *Institutiones Ecclesiasticae Prosperi Lambertini postea Benedicti XIVi*, ed. ab Ildelphonsa a S. Sarolo, Romae, 1747.

Bernard of Parma (de Botone), cf. *Decretales Gregorii IX una cum Glossis*.

Berutti, Christophorus, *Institutiones Iuris Canonici*, 4 vols., Taurini-Romae: Marietti, 1936-1940. Vol. I, 1936; Vol. III, 1936; Vol. IV, 1940; Vol. XI, 1938.

Beste, Udalricus, *Introductio in Codicem*, Collegeville, Minn.: St. John's Abbey Press, 1938.

Billuart, F. C., *Summa Sancti Thomae*, nova ed., 9 vols. in 8, Parisiis, [no date].

Black, Henry Campbell, *Black's Law Dictionary*, 3.ed., by the Publisher's Editorial Staff, St. Paul Minn.: West Publishing Co., 1933.

Blat, Albertus, *Commentarium Textus Codicis Iuris Canonici*, 6 vols., Romae: Ex Typographia Pontificia in Instituto Pii IX, 1921-1938. Vol. I, 1.ed., 1921; Vol. II, 2.ed., 1921; Vol. III, pars 2-6, 2.ed., 1934.

Böckhn, Placidus, *Commentarius in Jus Canonicum Universum*, 5 vols. in 3, Salisburgi-Parisiis, 1776.

Boich, Henricus, *In V Libros Decretalium Commentaria*, Venetiis, 1574.

Bonacina, Martin, *Operum de Morali Theoligia, Tomi Tres*, 3 vols., Venetiis, 1687.

Bouquillon, Thomas, *Theologia Moralis Fundamentalis*, 2.ed., Brugis, 1890.

Bouscaren, T. L., *The Canon Law Digest*, 2 vols. and Supplement 1941, Milwaukee: Bruce Publishing Co., 1934-1941.

Bucceroni, J., *Institutiones Theologiae Moralis*, 3.ed., 2 vols., Romae, 1898.

Busembaum, H., *Medulla Theologiae Moralis*, ed. ult. S. Congr. de Prop. Fide, 2 vols., Tornaci, [1865].

Cance, Adrien, *Le Code de Droit Canonique*, 16.ed., 3 vols. Paris: J. Gabalda et Fils, 1928-1930.

Cappello, Felix M., *Summa Iuris Canonici,* 3 vols., Romae: Apud Aedes Universitatis Gregorianae, 1936-1939. Vol. I, 3.ed., 1938; Vol. II, 3.ed., 1939; Vol. III, 1936.

——, *Summa Iuris Publici Ecclesiastici,* 3.ed., Romae: Apud Aedes Universitatis Gregorianae, 1932.

——, *Tractatus Canonico-Moralis de Censuris iuxta Codicem Iuris Canonici,* 3.ed., Taurinorum Augustae: Marietti, 1933.

——, *Tractatus Canonico-Moralis De Sacramentis,* 3 vols. in 6, Taurinorum Augustae: Marietti-Apud Aedes Universitatis Gregorianae. Vol. I, et Vol. II, pars I, 3.ed., 1938; Vol. II, pars II, 1.ed., 1932; Vol. II, pars III, 1.ed., 1935; Vol. III, pars I-II, 4.ed., 1939.

Castropalao, Ferd., *Opera Omnia in Septem Tomos Divisa,* 7 vols., in 3, Lugduni, 1682.

Cavagnis, Felix, *Institutiones Iuris Publici Ecclesiastici,* 4.ed., 3 vols., Romae, 1906.

Cerato, Prosdocimus, *Censurae Vigentes Ipso Facto A Codice Iuris Canonici Excerptae,,* 2.ed., Patavii: Typis Seminarii, 1921.

Chelodi, Ioannes, *Ius Poenale et Ordo Procedendi in Iudiciis Criminalibus Iuxta Codicem Iuris Canonici,* 4.ed. recognita et aucta a Vigilio Dalpiaz, Tridenti: Libreria Moderna Editrice A. Ardesi, 1935.

Chelodi, I—Bertagnolli, E., *Ius de Personis Iuxta Codicem Iuris Canonici Praemisso Tractatu De Principiis et Fontibus I.C.,* 2.ed., Tridenti: Libr. Edit. Tridentum, 1927.

Cicognani, Hamletus I, *Ius Canonicum Primo Studii Anno in Usum Auditorum Excerpta,* 2 vols., Romae: Ex Officina Typographica Ausonia-Ex Schola Typographica "Pio X," 1925.

Cicognani, A.—O'Hara, J.—Brennan, F., *Canon Law,* Second resived edition, Philadelphia: Dolphin Press, 1935.

Claeys Bouuaert, F.—Simenon, G., *Manuale Juris Canonici ad Usum Seminariorum,* 3 vols., Vol. I, 3.ed., Gandae et Leodii: J. De Meester et Fils, 1930.

Cocchi, Guidus, *Commentarium in Codicem Iuris Canonici ad Usum Scholarum,* 5 vols. in 8, Taurinorum Augustae: Marietti, 1932-1940. Vol. I, 5.ed., 1938; Vol. II, 4.ed., 1937; Vols. III-V, 3.ed., 1932; Vol. VI, 3.ed., 1933; Vol. VII, 3.ed., 1940; Vol. VIII, 4.ed., 1938.

Coninck, Aegidius de, *Commentarium in Universam Doctrinam D. Thomae, De Sacramentis et Censuris,* 2.ed., 2 vols., Antverpiae, 1619.

Coronata, Matthaeus Conte a, *De Locis et Temporibus Sacris,* Taurinorum Augustae: Marietti, 1922.

——, *Institutiones Iuris Canonici ad Usum Utriusque Cleri et Scholarum,* 5 vols., Taurini: Marietti, 1933-1939. Vols. I-II, 2.ed., 1939; Vol. III, 1933; Vol. IV, 1935; Vol. V, 1936.

Costello, John M., *Domicile and Quasi-Domicile,* The Catholic University of America Canon Law Studies, n. 69, Washington, D. C.: The Catholic University of America, 1930.

Covarruvias, Didacus, *Opera Omnia,* 2 vols., Coloniae, 1679.

Cozza, Laurentius, *Tractatus Dogmatico-Moralis de Jejunio Ecclesiastico in Tres Partes Distributus,* Romae, 1724.

Creusen, J., *Religieux et Religieuses d'après le Droit Ecclésiastique,* 3.ed., Bruxelles: Dewit, 1924.

Crnica, Antonius, *Modificationes in Tractatu de Censuris per Codicem Iuris Canonici Introductae,* S. Mauritii Agaunensis, 1919.

D'Angelo, Sosius, *Jus Digestorum,* 2 vols., Romae: Athenaeum Pontificii Seminarii Romani ad "S. Appollinaris," 1927-1928.

D'Annibale, Iosephus, *Summula Theologiae Moralis,* 3.ed., 3 vols., Romae, 1891.

Dargin, Edward V., *Reserved Cases According to the Code of Canon Law,* The Catholic University of America Canon Law Studies, n. 20, Washington, D. C.: The Catholic University of America, 1924.

De Angelis, Phillipus, *Praelectiones Iuris Canonici ad Methodum Decretalium Gregorii IX Exactae,* 9 vols., Romae-Parisiis, 1877-1891..

De Herdt, P. J. B., *Sacrae Liturgiae Praxis Juxta Ritum Romanum,* 8.ed., 3 vols., Lovanii, 1888-1889.

De Ligorio, St. Alfonsus M., *Theologia Moralis,* nova ed., 2 vols., Vesuntione, 1928.

De Luca, I. B., *Theatrum Veritatis et Iustitiae,* 16 vols. in 9, Coloniae, 1706.

De Lugo, Joannes, *Disputationes Scholasticae et Morales,* nova ed., J. B. Fournials, 8 vols., Parisiis: Apud Ludovicum Vivès, 1868-1869.

De Meester, A., *Juris Canonici et Juris Canonico-Civilis Compendium,* nova ed., 3 vols. in 4, Brugis: Sumptibus et Typis Societatis Sancti Augustini, 1921-1928.

Diana, Antoninus, *Resolutiones Morales,* 8.ed., Lugduni, 1635.

Dictionaire de Théologie Chrétienne, ed. A. Vacant, E. Mangenot, 14 vols.; Librarie Letouzey et Ané, 1903.

Dominicus a Sancto Geminiano, *Commentaria Propria Diligentissime Castigata in Decretum,* Venetiis, 1504.

Durantis (Durandus) Gulielmus, *Speculum Iuris Cum Additionibus Iohannis Andreae et Baldi,* Francofurti, 1592.

Eichmann, Eduard, *Lehrbuch des Kirchenrechts auf Grund des Codex Iuris Canonici,* 4.ed., 2 vols., Paderborn: Verlag Ferdinand Schöningh, 1934.

Engel, Ludovicus, *Collegium Universi Juris Canonici,* 9.ed., Venetiis, 1860.

Esswein, Anthony A., *The Extrajudicial Coercive Powers of Ecclesiastical Superiors,* The Catholic University of America Canon Law Studies, n. 127, Washington, D. C.: The Catholic University of America Press, 1941.

Facciolati, J.—Forcellini, Aeg.—Furlanetti, J., *Lexicon Totius Latinitatis,* 2.ed., 4 vols., Patavii, 1864-1887.

Fanfani, Ludovicus, *De Iure Parochorum ad Norman Codicis Iuris Canonici,* 2.ed., Taurini-Romae, Marietti, 1936.

——, *De Iure Religiosorum ad Norman Codicis Iuris Canonici,* 2.ed., Taurini-Romae: Marietti, 1925.

Feije, Henricus Joannes, *De Impedimentis et Dispensationibus Matrimonialibus,* 3.ed., 2 vols., Lovanii, 1885.

Felinus Sandeus, Cf. Sandeus.

Ferry, William A., *Stole Fees,* The Catholic University of America Canon Law Studies, n. 59, Washington, D. C.: The Catholic University of America, 1930.

Ferraris, F. Lucius, *Prompta Bibliotheca, Canonica, Juridica, Moralis, Theologica, necnon Ascetica, Polemica, Rubricistica Historica*, ed. novissima, 9 vols., Romae, 1885-1899 (Vol. V, 1889).

Filliucius, Vincentius, *Quaestionum Moralium de Christianis Officiis in Casibus Conscientiae Tomi Duo*, 2 vols., Lugduni, 1633-1634. Vol. I, 1634; Vol. II, 1633.

Fournier, Paul—Le Bras, Gabriel, *Histoire des Collections Canoniques en Occident depuis les Fausses Décrétales jusqu'au Decret de Gratien*, 2 vols., Paris: Recueil Sirey, 1931.

Gasparri, Petrus, *Tractatus Canonicus de Matrimonio*, 3.ed., 2 vols., Parisiis-Lugduni, 1900.

——, *Tractatus Canonicus de Matrimonio*, ed. nova ad mentem Codicis I.C., 2 vols., [Civitate Vaticana]: Typis Polyglottis Vaticanis, 1932.

Génicot, Eduardus, *Theologiae Moralis Institutiones*, 2 vols., Lovanii, 1896.

Génicot, E.—Salsmans, I., *Institutiones Theologiae Moralis*, 2 vols., Bruxellis: Alb. De Wit, 1927.

Gibalini, Joseph, *Scientia Canonica*, 2 vols., Lugduni, 1670.

Girard, Paul Frédéric, *Manuel Élémentaire de Droit Romain*, 8.ed., Paris: Librairie Arthur Rousseau, 1929.

——, *Textes de Droit Romain*, Paris: Librairie Arthur Rousseau, 1923.

Glynn, John C., *The Promoter of Justice*, The Catholic University of America Canon Law Studies, n. 101, Washington, D. C.: The Catholic University of America, 1936.

Gonzalez-Tellez, Emmanuel, *Commentaria Perpetua in Singulos Textus Quinque Librorum Decretalium Gregorii IX*, 5 vols. in 4, Venetiis, 1649.

Guilfoyle, Merlin J., *Custom*, The Catholic University of America Canon Law Studies, n. 105, Washington, D. C.: The Catholic University of America, 1937.

Gury, P. Ioannes, *Compendium Theologiae Moralis*, ed. Romana, 2 vols., Romae, 1872.

Hannan, Jerome D., *The Canon Law of Wills*, Philadelphia: The Dolphin Press, 1935.

Herincx, Gulielmus, *Summa Theologiae Scholasticae et Moralis in Quatuor Partes Distributa*, 2.ed., 4 vols. in 3, Antverpiae, 1680.

Hinschius, Paul, *Das Kirchenrecht der Katholiken und Protestanten in Deutschland*, 6 vols., Berlin, 1869-1897. Vol. IV, 1888.

Hollweck, Joseph, *Die kirchlichen Strafgesetze*, Mainz, 1899.

Hostiensis, Cardinalis (Henricus de Segusio), *Commentaria in V Libros Decretalium*, 5 vols. in 3, Venetiis, 1581.

Huber, Ulric, *Praelectionum Juris Civilis Tomi Tres Secundum Institutiones et Digesta Justiniani*, 3 vols., Maceratae, 1838-1839.

Innocent IV (Sinibaldus Fliscus), *Apparatus Decretalium Innocentii Papae IV*, Venetiis, 1481.

Joannes Andreae, *In Sextum Librum Decretalium Novella Commentaria*, Venetiis, 1581.

——, cf. *Liber Sextus Decretalium Bonifacii Papae VIII . . . cum Suis Glossis.*

Joannes Teutonicus, cf. *Decretum Gratiani . . . una cum Glossis.*

Jone, Heribert, *Gesetzbuch des Kanonischen Rechtes*, 3 vols., Paderborn: Ferdinand Schöningh, 1939-1941.

Keller, Charles F., *Mass Stipends,* The Catholic University of America Canon Law Studies, n. 27, Washington, D. C.: The Catholic University of America, 1925.

Kuttner, S., *Repertorium der Kanonistik* (1140-1234), *Prodromus Corporis Glossatorum,* Studi e Testi, Città Del Vaticano: Biblioteca Apostolica Vaticana, 1937.

La Croix, Claudius, *Theologia Moralis, Postremo vero Multis Locupletata et Studiosis Proposita a R.P. Francisco Antonio Zacharia,* 3 vols., Ravenna-Venetiis, 1771.

Lainé, A., *Introduction au Droit International Privé,* Paris, 1888.

Lancellotus, Io. Paulus, *Institutiones Iuris Canonici Quibus Ius Pontificium Singulari Methodo Libris Quatuor Comprehenditur,* Lugduni, 1579.

Laymann, Paul, *Theologia Moralis in V Libros Distributa,* ed. prima Patavina, 2 vols., Patavii, 1733.

Leage, R. W.—Ziegler, C. H., *Roman Private Law Founded on the Institutes of Gaius and Justinian,* 2.ed. London: Macmillan and Co., Ltd., 1937.

Lega, Michael, *Praelectiones in Textum Iuris Canonici—De Delictis et Poenis,* 2.ed., Romae, 1910.

——, *Praelectiones in Textum Iuris Canonici—De Iudiciis Ecclesiasticis,* Vol I, *De Iudiciis Ecclesiasticis Civilibus,* 2.ed., Romae, 1905.

Lega, M.—Bartoccetti, V., *Commentaria in Iudicia Ecclesiastica Iuxta Codicem Iuris Canonici,* 3 vols., Romae: Anonima Libraria Cattolica Italiana, 1938-1941.

Lehmkuhl, Augustinus, *Theologia Moralis,* 11.ed., 2 vols., Friburgi Brisgoviae, 1910.

Lessius, Leonardus, *De Justitia et Jure Ceterisque Virtutibus Cardinalibus Libri Quatuor,* 4.ed., Antverpiae, 1617.

Leurenius, Petrus, *Forum Ecclesiasticum in quo Jus Canonicum Universum . . . in iis quae Utrique Juri, Canonico et Civili Communia sunt Explanantur,* 5 vols. in 3, Venetiis, 1729.

Leverett, F. P., *Lexicon of The Latin Language,* 2.ed., Philadelphia, 1850.

Mackintosh, James, *Roman Law in Modern Practice,* Edinburgh: Green and Son, Ltd., 1934.

Marc, Clemens, *Institutiones Morales Alphonsianae,* 2 vols., Romae, 1885.

Marc-Gestermann-Raus, *Institutiones Morales Alphonsianae,* 19.ed., 2 vols., Lugduni: Lutetiae Parisiorum, 1933.

Marling, Joseph M., *The Order of Nature,* Washington, D. C.: The Catholic University of America, 1934.

Maroto, Philip, *Institutiones Iuris Canonici ad Norman Novi Codicis,* 2 vols., Vol. I, 3.ed., Romae: Apud Commentarium Pro Religiosis, 1921.

Medina, Bartholomeus, *Expositio in Primam Secundae Angelici Doctoris D. Thomae Aquinatis,* 3.ed., Venetiis, 1590.

Meili, F., *International Civil and Commercial Law as Founded upon Theory, Legislation, and Practice,* Trs. and supplemented by Arthur K. Kuhn, London, 1905.

——, *Über das historische Debut Doktrin des internationalen Privat-und Strafrechts,* Leipzig, 1899.

Merkelbach, Benedictus H., *Summa Theologiae Moralis ad Mentem D. Thomae et Norman Iuris Novi,* 2.ed., 3 vols., Parisiis: Typis Desclée, De Brouwer et Soc., 1935-1939.

Michiels, Gommarus, *Normae Generales Iuris Canonici, Commentarium Libri I Codicis Iuris Canonici,* 2 vols., Lublin: Universitas Catholica, 1929.

Migne, Jacques Paul, *Patrologiae Cursus Completus, Series Latina,* 221 vols., Parisiis, 1844-1864.

Mommsen, Theodor, *Römisches Strafrecht,* Leipzig, 1899.

Moretti, Aloisius, *De Sacris Functionibus Episcopo Celebrante—Assistente—Absente,* 4 vols., Taurini: Marietti, 1936-1939.

Navarrus, cf. Azpilcueta.

Neumeyer, Karl, *Die gemeinrechtliche Entwickelung des internationalen Privat-und Strafrechts bis Bartolus,* 2 vols., München, Berlin, und Leipzig, 1901-1916.

Noldin, H., *Summa Theologiae Moralis,* 3 vols., Oeniponte, 1905.

Noldin, H.—Schmitt, A., *De Praeceptis Dei et Ecclesiae,* 22.ed., Oeniponte: Typis et Sumptibus Fel. Rauch, 1934.

——, *De Principiis Theologiae Moralis,* 26.ed., Oeniponte: Typis et Sumptibus Fel. Rauch, 1939.

Noval, Joseph, *Commentarium Codicis Iuris Canonici—Liber IV, De Processibus, Pars I, De Iudiciis,* Augustae Taurinorum: Marietti, 1920.

Ojetti, B., *Commentarium In Codicem Iuris Canonici,* 4 vols., Romae: Apud Aedes Universitatis Gregorianae, 1927-1931. Vol. I, 1927; Vol. II, 1928; Vol. III, 1930; Vol. IV, 1931.

——, *Synopsis Rerum Moralium et Iuris Pontificii Alphabetico Ordine Digesta,* Romae, 1909.

Onclin, Gulielmus, *De Territoriali vel Personali Legis Indole,* Universitas Catholica Lovaniensis Dissertationes ad Gradum Magistri in Facultate Theologica vel in Facultate Iuris Canonici consequendum conscripta, Series II, tomus 31, Gembloci: J. Duculot, 1938.

Ottaviani, Alaphridus, *Institutiones Iuris Publici Ecclesiastici,* 2.ed., 2 vols., [Civitate Vaticana]: Typis Polyglottis Vaticanis, 1935-1936.

Paludanus (Pierre de la Palu), *Lucubrationum Opus in IV Sententiarum,* Paris, 1518.

Panormitanus (Nicolaus de Tudeschis), *Commentaria in Quinque Libros Decretalium,* 5 vols. in 7, Venetiis, 1588.

Passerini, Petrus, *Commentarium in Primum Librum Sexti Decretalium,* Venetiis, 1648.

Phillimore, Sir Rob't Jos., *Commentaries upon International Law,* 4 vols., London, 1854-1861. Vol. IV, 1861.

Pichler, Vitus, *Jus Canonicum secundum Quinque Decretalium Titulos Explicatum,* 2 vols., Ravenna, 1741.

Pickering, Octavius, *Reports of Cases Argued and Determined in the Supreme Judicial Court of Massachusetts,* vol. XXIII, Boston, 1842.

Pignatelli, Jacobus, *Consultationes Canonicae,* 12 vols. in 6, Coloniae Allobrogum, 1700.

Pillet, Antoine, *L'Ordre Public en Droit International Privé,* Grenoble-Paris, 1890.

——, *Principes du Droit International Privé,* Paris, 1903.

——, *Traité Pratique de Droit International Privé,* 2 vols., Grenoble: Imprimérie Joseph Allier—Paris: Librarie de la Societé du Recueil de Sirey, 1923.

Pontius, Basilius, *De Sacramento Matrimonii Tractatus*, 2.ed., Bruxelles, 1627.

Poste-Whittuck, *Gaii Institutiones, Or Institutes of Roman Law by Gaius*, 4.ed., Oxford, 1904.

Prümmer, Dominicus, *Manuale Iuris Canonici*, 4. et 5.ed., Friburgi Brisgoviae: Herder, 1927.

——, *Manuale Theologiae Moralis*, 8.ed., 3 vols., Friburgi Brisgoviae: Herder, 1935-1936.

Reiffenstuel, Anacletus, *Ius Canonicum Universum*, 5 vols. in 7, Parisiis, 1864-1870. Vol. IV, 1867.

——, *Theologia Moralis*, 7.ed., 2 vols., Mutinae, 1714.

Reilly, Peter, *Residence of Pastors*, The Catholic University of America Canon Law Studies, n. 97, Washington, D. C.: The Catholic University of America, 1935.

Restatement of the Law of the Conflict of Laws, American Law Institute at Washington, D. C., May 11, 1934, St. Paul, Minn.: American Law Institute Publishers, 1934.

Rivet, L., *Institutiones Iuris Ecclesiastici Privati*, 3 vols., Romae, 1916.

Roberti, Franciscus, *De Delictis et Poenis*, 2.ed., 1 vol. in 2, Apud Custodiam Librariam Pontificii Instituti Utriusque Iuris, [1938].

——, *De Processibus*, 2 vols., Romae: Apud Aedes Facultatis Iuridicae ad S. Appollinaris, 1926.

Rufinus, *Die Summa Decretorum des Magister Rufinus*, ed. Heinrich Singer, Paderborn, 1902.

Ryan, Gerald A., *Principles of Episcopal Jurisdiction*, The Catholic University of America Canon Law Studies, n. 120, Washington, D. C.: The Catholic University of America Press, 1939.

Sa, Emanuelis, *Aphorismi Confessariorum ex variis Doctorum Sententiis Collecti*, ed. novissima, Lugduni, 1669.

Sabetti, Aloysius, *Compendium Theologiae Moralis*, 3.ed. ab auctore recognita ad normam Conc. Plen. Balt. III, atque recentiorum Congr. Rom. decretorum, Neo-Eboraci et Cincinnati, 1888.

Salmanticenses, *Cursus Theologiae Moralis*, 6 vols., Venetiis, 1728.

Sanchez, Thomas, *De Sancto Matrimonii Sacramento*, Antwerpiae, 1626.

——, *Opus Morale in Praecepta Decalogi*, 2 vols., Parmae, 1723.

Sandeus, Felinus, *Commentarium in Quinque Libros Decretalium*, 4 vols., Romae, 1661.

——, *Consilia seu Responsa*, Lugduni, 1553.

Santi, Franciscus, *Praelectiones Juris Canonici Juxta Ordinem Decretalium Gregorii IX*, 2 vols., Ratisbonae, Neo-Eboraci et Cincinati, 1886.

Sartori, Cosmas, *Enchiridion Canonicum seu Sanctae Sedis Responsiones post editum Codicem J. C. datae*, Vicetiae: ex Typographica Commerciali, 1938.

Savigny, K. F., *System des heutigen römischen Rechts*, 8 vols., Berlin, 1840-1849. Vol. VII, 1849.

Savigny-Cathcart, *History of Roman Law in the Middle Ages*, Vol. I, Edinburgh, 1829.

Schaefer, Timotheus, *De Religiosis ad Norman Codicis Iuris Canonici,* 3.ed., Roma: Typis Polyglottis Vaticanis, 1940.

Schmalzgrueber, Franciscus, *Jus Ecclesiasticum Universum,* 5 vols. in 12, Romae, 1843-1845.

Schmier, Franciscus, *Jurisprudentia Canonico-Civilis, seu Jus Canonicum Universum,* Venetiis, 1754.

Schroeder, H. J., *Disciplinary Decrees of the General Councils,* St. Louis: Herder, 1937.

Sherman, Charles P., *Roman Law in the Modern World,* 2.ed., 3 vols., New York: Baker, Voorhis & Co., 1924.

Sole, Jacobus, *De Delictis et Poenis,* Romae-[R]Atisbonae-Coloniae Agrippinae--Neo-Eboraci-Cincinnati: Pustet, 1920.

Soto, Dominicus de, *Commentariorum in Quartum Sententiarum,* 2 vols., Venetiis, 1569.

Story, Joseph, *Commentaries on the Conflict of Laws Foreign and Domestic,* 5 ed., Boston, 1857.

Suarez, Franciscus, *Opera Omnia,* 26 vols., Parisiis: Apud Ludovicum Vivès, 1856-1866. Vol. V, *De Legibus,* 1856; Vol. XIII, *De Virtute Religionis,* 1859; Vol. XXIII, *De Censuris,* 1861.

Surville, F., *Cours Élémentaire de Droit International Privé,* 7.ed., Paris: Rousseau & Cie., 1925.

Sylvius, Franciscus, *Commentarii in Totam Primam Secundae S. Thomae Aquinatis,* 2 vols., Ventiis, 1726.

Tanquerey, Ad., *Synopsis Theologiae Moralis et Pastoralis,* 3.ed., 2 vols., Neo-Eboraci, Cincinnati, Chicagiae, 1907.

——, *Theologia Moralis et Fundamentalis,* 9.ed., Parisiis-Tornaci-Romae: Desclée et Socii, 1931.

Tarquini, Camillo, *Juris Ecclesiastici Publici Institutiones,* Romae, 1862.

Theologia Dogmatica, Polemica, Scholastica et Moralis in Alma Universitate Wirceburgensi, Vol. III, *De Beatitudine, De Actibus Humanis, De Legibus, De Jure et Justitia, Auctore Ignatio Neubauer,* 2.ed., Lutetiae Parisiorum, 1852.

Thesaurus Linguae Latinae Editus Auctoritate et Consilio Academiarum Quinque Germanicarum Berolinensis Gottingensis Lipsiensis Monacensis Vindobonensis, 8 vols., Lipsiae, 1900—. Vol. IV, 1904-1909.

Torrubiano Ripoll, Jaime, *Novísimas Instituciones de Derecho Canónico,* 2.ed., 2 vols., Madrid: Otero-Portella, 1934.

Toso, Albertus, *Ad Codicem Iuris Canonici Commentaria Minora,* 5 vols., Romae: Marietti-Tiferni Tiberini: ex officina Typogr. Vinciana, 1921-1927, Vol. I, 2.ed., Tiferni Tiberini: ex officiana Typogr. Vinciana, 1921.

Van Hove, A., *Commentarium Lovaniense in Codicem Iuris Canonici,* 1 vol. in 5 toms. Mechliniae-Romae: H. Dessain, 1928-1939. Tom. I, *Prolegomena,* 1928; Tom. II, *De Legibus Ecclesiasticis,* 1930; Tom. III, *De Consuetudine, De Temporis Supputatione,* 1933; Tom. IV, *De Rescriptis,* 1936; Tom. V, *De Privilegiis, De Dispensationibus,* 1939.

Vasquez, G., *Commentarium ac Disputationum in Iam IIae Sancti Thomae*, ed noviss., 4 vols., Lugduni, 1631.

Veranus, Cajetanus Felix, *Juris Caninici Universi Commentarius*, 3 vols., Monachi, 1703.

Vermeersch, Arthurus, *Theologia Moralis, Principia, Responsa, Consilia*, 4 vols., Vol. I, 2.ed., Roma: Università Gregoriana 1926.

Vermeersch, A.—Creusen I, *Epitome Iuris Canonici*, 3 vols., Mechliniae-Romae: H. Dessain, 1934-1937. Vol. I, 6.ed., 1937; Vols. II, III, 5.ed., 1934, 1936.

Vernier, C.—Frank, R. A., *American Family Laws*, 5 vols. and 1938 supplement, Stanford University, Cal.: Stanford University Press, 1931-1938.

Voet, Joannes, *Commentarium ad Pandectas*, ed. quinta Veneta, 7 vols., Bassani, 1827-1828. Vol. III, 1827.

Weiss, André, *Traité Élémentaire du Droit International Prive*, 2.ed., Paris, 1890.

——, *Traité Théorique et Pratique de Droit International Privé*, Vol. III, 12.ed., *Le Conflict des Lois*, Paris, 1912.

Wenger, Leopold, *Institutes of the Roman Law of Civil Procedure*, revised ed., trs. by Otis Harrison Fisk, New York: Veritas Press, 1940.

Wernz, Franciscus X., *Ius Decretalium ad Usum Praelectionum in Scholis Textus Canonici Sive Iuris Decretalium*, 3.ed., 6 vols. in 8, Prati, 1913-1915. Vol. I, 1913.

Wernz, F. X.—Vidal, P., *Ius Canonicum*, 7 vols. in 8, Romae: Apud Aedes Universitatis Gregorianae, 1923-1938. Vol. I, 1938; Vol. II, 2.ed., 1928; Vol. VII, 2.ed., 1937.

Westlake, J., *A Treatise on Private International Law, or The Conflict of Laws, with Principal Reference to its Practice on the English and other Systems of Jurisprudence*, London, 1858.

Wehrlé, R., *De la Coutume dans le Droit Canonique*, Paris: Recueil Sirey, 1928.

Willems, Pierre, *Le Sénat de la République Romaine*, 2.ed., 2 vols., Paris, 1885.

Zallinger, Jac. Ant., *Institutiones Juris Ecclesiastici*, 5 vols., Romae, 1823.

Zoesius, Henricus Jacobus, *Commentarius in Jus Canonicum sive ad Decretales Gregorii IX*, Venetiis, 1757.

Articles

Antoine, C., "Étrangers,"—*DTC*, V (1913), coll. 982-989.

Beale, J. H., "Marriage and the domicil,"—44 *Harvard Law Review* (1930-1931), 501-529.

Canestri, A., "De lege cum sanctione poenali lata in peregrinos,"—*Apollinaris*, VII (1934), 97-102.

Chénon, E., "La loi pérégrine à Rome,"—*Bulletin du Comité des Travaux Historiques et Scientifiques*, 1890, 212-245.

Creusen, I, "Casuistique de Carême,"—*NRT*, LI (1924), 155-163.

——, "L'Obligation de l'habit ecclésiastique,"—*NRT*, LVIII (1931), 818-821.

——, "Usage des indults d'abstinence par les étrangers,"—*NRT*, LI (1924), 250-253.

Darmanin, A., "Annotationes,"—*Jus Pont.*, XVII (1937), 278.

——, "De reservatione peccatorum iure Codicis Piano-Benedictino,"—*Angelicum*, V (1928), 55-70, 213-214, 539-554.

Deschepper, R., "De indole personali legum episcopalium,"—*Coll. Brug.*, XXIII (1923), 219-222.

——, "De obligatione peregrinorum et vagorum,"—*Coll. Brug.*, XXIV (1934), 153-158.

——, "De subjecto legis ecclesiasticae particularis,"—*Coll. Brug.*, XXIV (1924), 53-56.

——, "De territorialitate et personalitate legum ecclesiasticarum,"—*Coll. Brug.*, XXIII (1923), 199-203.

Despagnet, F., "L'ordre public en droit international privé,"—*JDIP*, XVI (1889), 5-21, 207-222.

"Developments in the law—Conflict of laws,"—50 *Harvard Law Review* (1936-1937), 1119-1206.

Donnelly, F. B., "Compulsory blood tests before Marriage,"—*AER*, CI (1939), 9-21.

Donovan, J. P., "Is the interpretation of canon 900 also dated?"—*HPR*, XLII, (1942), 431-436.

Fallon, M. J., "The obligation of wearing the clerical dress during holidays,"—*IER*, XIL (1939), 449-450.

Felici, P., "De seminario in aliena dioecesi rusticanti,"—*Apollinaris*, XII (1939), 264.

Fiore, P., "De la limitation de l'autorité des lois étrangères et de la détermination des lois d'ordre public,"—*JDIP*, XXXV (1908), 351-366.

Glaser, J., "Variation des Wortsinnes und Kodexauslegung,"—*Theologisch-praktische Quartalschrift*, LXXXIII (1930), 146-149.

Hannan, J. D., "Lenten regulations,"—*The Jurist*, I (1941), 143-146.

Hilling, N., "Die Bedeutung der iurisdictio voluntaria und involuntaria im römischen Recht und im kanonischen Recht des Mittelalters und der Neuzeit,"—*AKKR*, CV (1925), 449-473.

——, "Über den Gebrauch des Ausdrucks iurisdictio im kanonischen Recht während der ersten Hälfte des Mittelalters,"—*AKKR*, CXVIII (1938), 165-170.

Kereckhove, M., Van de, "De notione jurisdictionis in jure Romano,"—*Jus Pont.*, XVI (1936), 49-65.

——, "De notione jurisdictionis apud decretistas et priores decretalistas,"—*Jus Pont.*, XVIII (1938), 10-14.

Kinane, J., " 'Peregrini' and the laws which take care of public order,"—*IER*, XLIII (1934), 113-125.

Kuttner, S., "Wer war der Decretalist 'Abbas antiquus'?"—*Zeitschrift der Savigny Stiftung für Rechtsgeschichte*, LVII (1937), 471-487.

Larraona, A., "Adnotationes,"—*CpR*, XII (1931), 11-13.

——, "De potestate dominativa publica in iure canonico,"—*Acta Congressus Iuridici Internationalis*, IV (1937), 145-180.

Laurent, F., "Études sur le droit international privé,"—*JDIP*, V (1878), 308-344.

Le Picard, R., "La notion d'ordre public en droit canonique,"—*NRT*, LV (1928), 352-372.

Leroux, E., "Le sujet des lois ecclésiastiques,"—*REL* XVI (1924-1925), 329-341.

Mancini, P., "Les règles générales du droit international privé,"—*JDIP*, I (1874), 221-319.

Molien, A., "Lois,"—*DTC*, IX (1926), coll. 871-910.

Moore, T. V., "Marriage and venereal disease,"—*AER*, CIII (1940), 27-53.

Noval, J., "De ratione corrigendi ac puniendi sive in judicio sive extra jure Codicis J.C.,"—*Jus Pont.*, I-II (1921-1922), 147-156; III (1923), 36-40, 204-210.

Ramos, D., "De conditione saecularium in domibus religiosorum,"—*CpR*, VI (1925), 28-33.

Roelker, E. G., "The traveler and local statutes,"—*The Jurist*, II (1942), 105-119.

Simenon, G., "Territorialitas legum,"—*REL*, XXI (1929-1930), 184-187.

Surville, F., "De la personnalité des lois envisagée comme principe fondamental du droit international privé,"—*JDIP*, XVI (1889), 528-538.

Teodori, I, "Peregrini quoad censuras,"—*Consult. Iuris Can.*, I (1934), 276-279—*Apollinaris*, IV (1931), 139-141.

——, "Peregrini quoad leges servandas,"—*Consult. Iuris Can.*, I (1934), 17-19—*Apollinaris*, III (1930), 316-318.

Toso, A., "De ordine publico,"—*Jus Pont.*, X (1930), 342, 343.

——, "Annotationes,"—*Jus Pont.*, III (1923), 7.

Toutain, J., "Etudes sur l'organization municipale du Haut-empire. De la distinction faite par Aulu-Gelle entre les municipes et les colonies des provinces à l'époque impériale,"—*Mélanges d'Archéologie et d'Histoire, École Français de Rome*, XVI (1896), 315-329.

Twomey, L. J., "To abstain from flesh meat,"—*AER*, C (1939), 109-131.

Van Hove, A., "Leges quae ordini publico consulunt,"—*ETL*, I (1924), 153-167.

——, "La territorialité et la personnalité des lois en droit canonique depuis Gratien (vers 1140), jusqu'à Jean Andrea (†1348),"—*TVR*, III (1922), 277-332.

Vermeersch, A., "Annotationes,"—*Periodica*, X (1922), 255, 256.

——, "De locis in quibus episcopi indulgentias concedere possunt,"—*Periodica*, XIX (1930), 25*, 26*.

Vindex, "Domicilium et quasi-domicilium eorumque effectus in Codice Juris Canonici,"—*Jus Pont.*, VI (1926), 34-55, 112-126, 154-158.

Periodicals

Angelicum, Romae, 1924—

Apollinaris, Romae, 1928—

Archiv für katholisches Kirchenrecht, Innsbruck, 1857-1861; Mainz, 1862—

Bulletin du Comité des Travaux Historiques et Scientifiques, Section des Sciences Économiques et Sociales, Paris, 1883-1902.

Collationes Brugenses, Brugis Flandorum, 1896—

Commentarium pro Religiosis (later *Commentarium pro Religiosis et Missionariis*), *Romae*, 1920—

Consultationes Iuris Canonici, Romae, 1934—

Ecclesiastical Review, The (originally *The American Ecclesiastical Review*), Philadelphia, 1889—
Ephemerides Theologicae Lovanienses, Lovanii, 1924—
Harvard Law Review, Cambridge, Mass., 1887—
Homiletic and Pastoral Review, The, New York, 1900—
Irish Ecclesiastical Record, Dublin, 1864—
Journal du Droit International Privé et de la Jurisprudence Comparée, Paris, 1874—
Jurist, The, Washington, D. C., 1941—
Jus Pontificium, Romae, 1921—
Mélanges d'Archéologie et d'Histoire, École Française de Rome, Paris, 1881—
Monitore Ecclesiastico, Il, Roma, 1876—
Nouvelle Revue Théologique, Paris, 1869—
Periodica de Re Canonica et Morali utili Praesertim Religiosis et Missionariis, Bruges, 1905—
Revue Ecclésiastique de Liége, Leodii, 1908—
Theologisch-praktische Quartalschrift, Linz, 1832—
Tijdschrift Voor Rechtgeschiednis—Revue d'Histoire du Droit, Haarlem, 1919—
Zeitschrift der Savigny Stiftung für Rechtsgeschichte, Weimar, 1880—

Abbreviations

AAS—*Acta Apostolicae Sedis*
AER—*American Ecclesiastical Review*
AKKR—*Archiv für katholisches Kirchenrecht.*
ASS—*Acta Sanctae Sedis.*
C—*Codex Iustinianus.*
Coll. Brug.—*Collationes Brugenses.*
CpR—*Commentarium pro Religiosis et Missionariis.*
CSEL—*Corpus Scriptorum Ecclesiasticorum Latinorum.*
Consult. Iuris Can.—*Consultationes Iuris Canonici.*
D—*Digesta Iustinianum.*
Decreta Authentica—*Congregationis Sacrorum Rituum . . . promulgata.*
DTC—*Dictionaire de Théologie Chrétienne.*
ETL—*Ephemerides Theologicae Lovanienses.*
Fontes—*Codicis Iuris Canonici Fontes cura . . . Gasparri editi.*
HPR—*Homiletic and Pastoral Review.*
IER—*Irish Ecclesiastical Record.*
JDIP—*Journal du Droit International Privé et de la Jurisprudence Comparée.*
JE—Jaffé, *Regesta Pontificum Romanorum*—section edited by Ewald.
JK—Jaffé, *Regesta Pontificum Romanorum*—section edited by Kalenbrunner.
JL—Jaffé, *Regesta Pontificum Romanorum*—section edited by Loewenfeld.
Jus Pont.—*Jus Pontificium.*
Mansi—*Sacrorum Conciliorum Nova et Amplissima Collectio.*
MPL—Migne, *Patrologia Latina.*

N—*Novellae Justinianae*
NRT—*Nouvelle Revue Théologique.*
PCI—*Pontificia Commissio Ad Codicis Canones Authentice Interpretandos.*
Periodica—*Periodica de Re Canonica et Morali Utili praesertim Religiosis et Missionariis.*
Potthast—*Regesta Pontificum Romanorum.*
REL—*Revue Ecclésiastique de Liége.*
S.C.C.—*Sacra Congregatio Concilii.*
S.C.Consist.—*Sacra Congregatio Consistorialis.*
S.C. De Prop. Fide.—*Sacra Congregatio De Propaganda Fide.*
S.C. de Sacr.—*Sacra Congregatio De Disciplina Sacramentorum.*
S.C.S. Off.—*Sacra Congregatio Sancti Officii.*
S.R.C.—*Sacra Congregatio Sacrorum Rituum.*
TVR—*Tijdschrift Voor Rechtgeschiednis*—*Revue d'histoire du Droit.*

BIOGRAPHICAL NOTE

JOHN LEO HAMMILL was born on October 26, 1913, at Massena, New York. After completing his primary and secondary education in the public schools of Canton, New York, he entered Wadhams Hall College, Ogdensburg, New York, in the fall of 1930. His Theological course was begun in the fall of 1934 at the Grand Seminary, Montreal, Quebec. The following year he was transferred to complete his Theological studies in the Sulpician Seminary, Washington, D. C. At the same time he enrolled in the School of Philosophy at the Catholic University of America, where he received the degree of the Master of Arts in June, 1939. He was ordained to the sacred priesthood on June 3, 1939, in Ogdensburg, New York. In September of that year he entered the School of Canon Law at the Catholic University of America. He received the degree of the Baccalaureate in Canon Law in June, 1940, and the degree of the Licentiate in Canon Law in June, 1941.

ALPHABETICAL INDEX

CANON LAW STUDIES

1. Freriks, Rev. Celestine A., C.PP.S., J.C.D., Religious Congergations in Their External Relations, 121 pp. 1916.
2. Galliher, Rev. Daniel M., O.P., J.C.D., Canonical Elections, 117 pp., 1917.
3. Borkowski, Rev. Aurelius L., O.F.M., J.C.D., De Confraternitatibus Ecclesiasticis, 136 pp., 1918.
4. Castillo, Rev. Cayo, J.C.D., Direstación Historico-Canonica sobre la Potestad del Cabildo en Sede Vacante o Impedida del Vicario Capitular, 99 pp., 1919 (1918).
5. Kubelbeck, Rev. William J., S.T.B., J.C.D., The Sacred Penitentiara and its Relations to Faculties of Ordinaries and Priests, 129 pp., 1918.
6. Petrovits, Rev. Joseph, J.C., S.T.D., J.C.D., The New Church Law On Matrimony, X-461 pp., 1919.
7. Hickey, Rev. John J., S.T.B., J.C.D., Irregularities and Simple Impediments in the New Code of Canon Law, 100 pp., 1920.
8. Klekotka, Rev. Peter J., S.T.B., J.C.D., Diocesan Consultors, 179 pp., 1920.
9. Wanenmacher, Rev. Francis, J.C.D., The Evidence in Ecclesiastical Procedure Affecting the Marriage Bond, 1920 (Printed 1935).
10. Golden, Rev. Henry Francis, J.C.D., Parochial Benefices in the New Code, IV-119 pp., 1921 (Printed 1925).
11. Koudelka, Rev. Charles J., J.C.D., Pastors, Their Rights and Duties According to the New Code of Canon Laws, 211 pp., 1921.
12. Melo, Rev. Antonius, O.F.M., J.C.D., De Exemptione Regularium, X-188 pp., 1921.
13. Schaaf, Rev. Valentine Theodore, O.F.M., S.T.B., J.C.D., The Cloister, X-180 pp., 1921.
14. Burke, Rev. Thomas Joseph, S.T.D., J.C.D., Competence in Ecclesiastical Tribunals, IV-117 pp., 1922.
15. Leech, Rev. George Leo, J.C.D., A Comparative Study of the Constitution, "Apostolicae Sedis" and the "Codex Juris Canonici," 179 pp., 1922.
16. Motry, Rev. Hubert Louis, S.T.D., J.C.D., Diocesan Faculties According to the Code of Canon Law, II-167 pp., 1922.
17. Murphy, Rev. George Lawrence, J.C.D., Delinquencies and Penalties in the Administration and Reception of the Sacraments, IV-121 pp., 1923.
18. O'Reilly, Rev. John Anthony, S.T.D., J.C.D., Ecclesiastical Sepulture in the New Code of Canon Law, II-129 pp., 1923.
19. Michalicka, Rev. Wenceslas Cyrill, O.S.B., J.C.D., Judicial Procedure in Dismissal of Clerical Eempt Religious, 107 pp., 1923.
20. Dargn, Rev. Edward Vincent, S.T.B., J.C.D., Reserved Cases According to the Code of Canon Law, IV-103, pp. 1924.
21. Godfrey, Rev. John A., S.T.B., J.C.D., The Right of Patronage According to the Code of Canon Law, 153 pp., 1924.

22. Hagedorn, Rev. Francis Edward, J.C.D., General Legislation on Indulgences, II-154 pp., 1924.
23. King, Rev. James Ignatius, J.C.D., The Administration of the Sacraments to Dying Non-Catholics, V-141 pp., 1924.
24. Winslow, Rev. Francis Joseph, O.F.M., J.C.D., Vicars and Prefects Apostolic, IV-149 pp., 1924.
25. Correa, RRev. Jose Servelion, S.T.L., J.C.D., La Potestad Legislativa de la Iglesia Catolica, IV-127 pp., 1925.
26. Dugan, Rev. Henry Francis, A.M., J.C.D., The Judiciary Department of the Diocesan Curia, 87 pp., 1925.
27. Keller, Rev. Charles Frederick, S.T.B., J.C.D., Mass Stipends, 167 pp., 1925.
28. Paschang, Rev. John Linus, J.C.D., The Sacramentals According to the Code of Canon Laws, 129 pp., 1925.
29. Piontek, Rev. Cyrillus, O.F.M., S.T.B., J.C.D., De Indulto Exclaustrationis necnon Saeculariationis, XIII-289 pp., 1925.
30. Kearney, Rev. Richard Joseph, S.T.B., J.C.D., Sponsors at Baptism According to the Code of Canon Law, IV-127 pp., 1925.
31. Bartlett, Rev. Chester Joseph, A.M., LL.B., J.C.D., The Tenure of Parochial Property in the United States of America, V-108 pp., 1926.
32. Kilker, Rev. Adrian Jerome, J.C.D., Extreme Unction, V-425 pp., 1926.
33. McCormick, Rev. Robert Emmett, J.C.D., Confessors of Religious, VIII-266 pp., 1926.
34. Miller, Rev. Newton Thomas, J.C.D., Founded Masses According to the Code of Canon Law, VII-93 pp., 1926.
35. Roelker, Rev. Edward G., S.T.D., J.C.D., Principles of Privilege According to the Code of Canon Law, XI-166 pp., 1926.
36. Bakalarczyk, Rev. Richardus, M.I.C., J.U.D., De Novitiatu, VIII-208 pp., 1927.
37. Pizzuti, Rev. Lawrence, O.F.M., J.U.L., De Parochis Religiosis, 1927 (Not printed).
38. Bliley, Rev. Nicholas Martin, O.S.B., J.C.D., Altars According to the Code of Canon Law, XIX-123 pp., 1927.
39. Brown, Mr. Brendan Francis, AA.B., LL.M., J.U.D., The Canonical Juristic Personality with Special Reference to Its Status in the United Statee of America, V-212 pp., 1927.
40. Cavanaugh, Rev. William Thomas, C.P., J.U.D., The Reservation of the Blessed Sacrament, VIII-101 pp., 1927.
41. Doheny, Rev. William J., C.S.C., A.B., J.U.D., Church Property: Modes of Acuisition, X-118 pp., 1927.
42. Feldhaus, Rev. Aloysius H., C.PP.S., J.C.D., Oratories, IX-141 pp., 1927.
43. Kelly, Rev. James Patrick, A.B., J.C.D., The Jurisdiction of the Simple Confessor, X-208 pp., 1927.
44. Neuberger, Rev. Nicholas J., J.C.D., Canon 6 or the Relation of the Codex Juris Canonici to the Preceding Legislation, V-95 pp., 1927.

45. O'Keefe, Rev. Gerald Michael, J.C.D., Matrimonial Dispensations, Powers of Bishops, Priests and Confessors, VIII-232 pp., 1927.
46. Quigley, Rev. Joseph, A.B., A.M., J.C.D., Condemned Societies, 139 pp., 1927.
47. Zaplotnik, Rev. Johannes Leo, J.C.D., De Vicariis Foraneis, X-142 pp., 1927.
48. Duskie, Rev. John Aloysius, A.B., J.C.D., The Canonical Status of the Orientals in the United States, VIII, 196 pp., 1928.
49. Hyland, Rev. Francis Edward, J.C.D., Excommunication, Its Nature, Historical Development and Effects, VIII-181 pp., 1928.
50. Reinmann, Rev. Gerald Joseph, O.M.C., J.C.D., The Third Order Secular of Saint Francis, 201 pp., 1928.
51. Schenk, Rev. Francis J., J.C.D., The Matrimonial Impediments of Mixed Religion and Disparity of Cult, XVI-318 pp., 1929.
52. Coady, Rev. John Joseph, S.T.D., J.U.D., A.M., The Appointment of Pastors, VIII-150 pp., 1929.
53. Kay, Thomas Henry, J.C.D., Competence in Matrimonial Procedure, VIII-164 pp., 1929.
54. Turner, Rev. Sidney Joseph, C.P., J.U.D., The Vow of Poverty, XLIX-217 pp., 1929.
55. Kearney, Rev. Raymond A., A.B., S.T.D., J.C.D., The Principles of Delegation, VII-149 pp., 1929.
56. Conran, Rev. Edward James, A.B., J.C.D., The Interdict, V-163 pp., 1930.
57. O'Neil, Rev. William H., J.C.D., Papal Rescripts of Favor, VII-218 pp., 1930.
58. Bastnagel, Rev. Clement Vincent, J.U.D., The Appointment of Parochial Adjutants and Assistants, XV-257 pp., 1930.
59. Ferry, Rev. William A., A.B., J.C.D., Stole Fees, V-135 pp., 1930.
60. Costello, Rev. John Michael, A.B., J.C.D., Domicile and Quasi-Domicile, VII-201 pp., 1930.
61. Kremer, Rev. Michael Nicholas, A.B., S.T.D., J.C.D., Church Support in the United States, VI-1930.
62. Angulo, Rev. Luis, C.M., J.C.D., Legislación de la Iglesia sobre la intención en la aplicación de la Santa Misa, VII-104 pp., 1931.
63. Frey, Rev. Wolfgang Norbert, O.S.B., A.B., J.C.D., The Act of Religious Profession, VIII-174 pp., 1931.
64. Roberts, Rev. James Brendan, A.B., J.C.D., The Banns of Marriage, XIV-140 pp., 1931.
65. Ryder, Rev. Raymond Aloysius, A.B., J.C.D., Simony, IX-151 pp., 1931.
66. Campagna, Rev. Angelo, Ph.D., J.U.D., Il Vicario Generale del Vescovo, VII-205 pp., 1931.
67. Cox, Rev. Joseph Godfrey, A.B., J.C.D., The Administration of Seminaries, VI-124 pp., 1931.
68. Gregory, Rev. Donald J., J.U.D., The Pauline Privilege, XV-165 pp., 1931.
69. Donohue, Rev. John F., J.C.D., The Impediment of Crime, VII-110 pp., 1931.
70. Dooley, Rev. Eugene A., O.M.I., J.C.D., Church Law On Sacred Relics, IX-143 pp., 1931.

71. Orth, Rev. Raymond Clement, O.M.C., J.C.D., The Approbation of Religious Institutes, 171 pp., 1931.

72. Pernicone, Rev. Joseph M., A.B., J.C.D., The Ecclesiastical Prohibition of Books, XII-267 pp., 1932.

73. Clinton, Rev. Connell, A.B., J.C.D., The Paschal Precept, IX-108 pp., 1932.

74. Donnelly, Rev. Francis B., A.M., S.T.L., J.C.D., The Diocesan Synod, VIII-125 pp., 1932.

75. Torente, Rev. Camilo, C.M.F., J.C.D., Las Processiones Sagradas, V-145 pp., 1932.

76. Murphy, Rev. Edwin J., C.PP.S., J.C.D., Suspension Ex Informata Conscientia, XI-122 pp., 1932.

77. Mackenzie, Rev. Eric F., A.M., S.T.L., J.C.D., The Delict of Heresy in its Commission, Penalization, Absolution, VII-124 pp., 1932.

78. Lyons, Rev. Avitus E., S.T.B., J.C.D., The Collegiate Tribunal of First Instance, XI-147 pp., 1932.

79. Connolly, Rev. Thomas A., J.C.D., Appeals, XI-195 pp., 1932.

80. Sangmeister, Rev. Joseph V., A.B., J.C.D., Force and Fear as Precluding Matrimonial Consent, V-211 pp., 1932.

81. Jaeger, Rev. Leo A., A.B., J.C.D., The Administration of Vacant and Quasi-Vacant Episcopal Sees in the United States, IX-229 pp., 1932.

82. Rimlinger, Rev. Herbert T., J.C.D., Error Invalidating Matrimonial Consent, VII-79 pp., 1932.

83. Barrett, Rev. John D. M., S.S., J.C.D., A Comparative Study of the Third Plenary Council of Baltimore and the Code, IX-221 pp., 1932.

84. Carberry, Rev. John J., Ph.D., S.T.D., J.C.D., The Juridical Form of Marriage, X-177 pp., 1934.

85. Dolan, Rev. John L., A.B., J.C.D., The Defensor Vinculi, XII-157 pp., 1934.

86. Hannan, Rev. Jerome D., A.M., S.T.D., LL.B., J.C.D., The Canon Law of Wills, IX-517 pp., 1934.

87. Lemieux, Rev. Delisle A., A.M., J.C.D., The Sentence in Ecclesiastical Procedure, IX-131 pp., 1934.

88. O'Rourk, Rev. James J., A.B., J.C.D., Parish Registers, VII-109 pp., 1934.

89. Timlin, Rev. Bartholomew, O.F.M., A.M., J.C.D., Condional Matrimonial Consent, X-381 pp., 1934.

90. Wahl, Rev. Francis X., A.B., J.C.D., The Matrimonial Impediments of Consanguinity and Affinity, VI-125 pp., 1934.

91. White, Rev. Robert J., A.B., LL.B., S.T.B., J.C.D., Canonical Ante-Nuptial tial Promises and the Civil Law, VI-152 pp., 1934.

92. Herrera, Rev. Antonio Parra, O.C.D., J.C.D., Legislación Ecclesiástica sobre el Ayuno y la Abstinencia, XI-191 pp., 1935.

93. Kennedy, Rev. Edwin J., J.C.D., The Special Matrimonial Process in Cases of Evident Nullity, X-165 pp., 1935.

94. Manning, Rev. John J., A.B., J.C.D., Presumption of Law in Matrimonial Procedure, XI-111 pp., 1935.

95. Moeder, Rev. John M., J.C.D., The Proper Bishop for Ordination and Dimisorial Letters, VII-135 pp., 1935.
96. O'Mara, Rev. William A., A.B., J.C.D., Canonical Causes for Matrimonial Dispensations, IX-155 pp., 1935.
97. Reilly, Rev. Peter, J.C.D., Residence of Pastors, IX-81 pp., 1935.
98. Smith, Rev. Mariner T., O.P., S.T.L., J.C.D., The Penal Law for Religious, VII-169 pp., 1935.
99. Whalen, Rev. Donald W., A.M., J.C.D., The Value of Testimonial Evidence in Matrimonial Procedure, XIII-297 pp., 1935.
100. Cleary, Rev. Joseph F., J.C.D., Canonical Limitations on the Alienation of Church Property, VIII-141 pp., 1936.
101. Glynn, Rev. John C., J.C.D., The Promoter of Justice, XX-337 pp., 1936.
102. Brennan, Rev. James H., S.S., A.M., S.T.B, J.C.D., The Simple Convalidation of Marriage, VI-135 pp., 1937.
103. Brunini, Rev. Joseph Bernard, J.C.D., The Clerical Obligations of Canons 139 and 142, X-121 pp., 1937.
104. Connor, Rev. Maurice, A.B., J.C.D., The Administrative Removal of Pastors, VIII-159 pp., 1937.
105. Guilfoyle, Rev. Merlin Joseph, J.C.D., Custom, XI-144 pp., 1937.
106. Hughes, Rev. James Austin, A.B., A.M., J.C.D., Witnesses in Criminal Trials of Clerics, IX-140 pp., 1937.
107. Jansen, Rev. Raymond J., A.B., S.T.L., J.C.D., Canonical Provisions for Catechetical Instruction, VII-153 pp., 1937.
108. Kealy, Rev. John James, A.B., J.C.D., The Introductory Libellus in Church Court Procedure, XI-121 pp., 1937.
109. McManus, Rev. James Edward, C.SS.R., J.C.D., The Administration of Temporal Goods in Religious Institutes, XVI-196 pp., 1937.
110. Moriarity, Rev. Eugene James, J.C.D., Oaths in Ecclesiastical Courts, X-115 pp., 1937.
111. Rainer, Rev. Eligius George, C.SS.R., J.C.D., Suspension of Clerics, XVII-249 pp., 937.
112. Reilly, Rev. Thomas F., C.SS.R., J.C.D., Visitation of Religious, VI-195 pp., 1938.
113. Moriarty, Rev. Francis E., C.SS.R., J.C.D., The Extraordinary Absolution from Censures, XV-334 pp., 1938.
114. Connolly, Rev. Nicholas P., J.C.D., The Canonical Erection of Parishes, X-132 pp., 1938.
115. Donovan, Rev. James Joseph, J.C.D., The Pastor's Obligation in Prenuptial Investigation, XII-322 pp., 1938.
116. Harrigan, Rev. Robert J., M.A., S.T.B., J.C.D., The Radical Sanation of Invalid Marriages, VIII-208 pp., 1938.
117. Boffa, Rev. Conrad Humbert, J.C.D., Canonical Provisions for Catholic Schools, X-211 pp., 1939.

118. Parsons, Rev. Anscar John, O.F.M. Cap., J.C.D., Canonical Elections, XII-236 pp., 1939.
119. Reilly, Rev. Edward Michael, A.B., J.C.D., The General Norms of Dispensation, X-156 pp., 1939.
120. Ryan, Rev. Gerald Aloysius, A.B., J.C.D., Principles of Episcopal Jurisdiction, XII-172 pp., 1939.
121. Burton, Rev. Francis James, C.S.C., A.B., J.C.D., A Commentary on Canon 1125, X-222 pp., 1940.
122. Miaskiewicz, Rev. Francis Sigismund, J.C.D., Supplied Jurisdiction Accordng to Canon 209, XII-340 pp., 1940.
123. Rice, Rev. Patrick William, A.B., J.C.D., Proof of Death in Prenuptial Investigation, VIII-156 pp., 1940.
124. Anglin, Rev. Thomas Francis, M.S., J.C.D., The Eucharistic Fast, VIII-183 pp., 1941.
125. Coleman, Rev. John Jerome, J.C.D., The Minister of Confirmation, VI-153 pp. 1941.
126. Downs, Rev. John Emmanuel, A.B., J.C.D., The Concept of Clerical Immunity, XI-163 pp., 1941.
127. Esswein, Rev. Anthony Albert, J.C.D., Extrajudicial Penal Powers of Ecclesiastical Superiors, X-144 pp., 1941.
128. Farrell, Rev. Benjamin Francis, M.A., S.T.L., J.C.D., The Rights and Duties of the Local Ordinary Regarding Congregations of Women Religious of Pontifical Approval, V-195 pp., 1941.
129. Feeney, Rev. Thomas John, A.B., S.T.L., J.C.D., Restitutio in Integrunm, VI-169 pp., 1941.
130. Findlay, Rev. Stephen William, O.S.B., A.B., J.C.D., Canonical Norms Governing the Deposition and Degradation of Clerics, XVII-279 pp., 1941.
131. Goodwine, Rev. John, A.B., S.T.L., J.C.D., The Right of the Church to Acquire Property, VIII-119 pp., 1941.
132. Heston, Rev. Edward Louis, C.S.C., Ph.D., S.T.D., J.C.D., The Alienation of Church Property in the United States, XII-222 pp., 1941.
133. Hogan, Rev. James John, A.B., S.T.L., J.C.D., Judicial Advocates and Procurators, VIII-200 pp., 1941.
134. Kealy, Rev. Thomas M., A.B., Litt.B., J.C.D., Dowry of Women Religious, IX-152 pp., 1941.
135. Keene, Rev. Michael James, O.S.B., J.C.D., Religious Ordinaries and Canon 198.
136. Kerin, Rev. Charles A., S.S, M.A., S.T.B., J.C.D., The Privation of Christian Burial, XVI-279 pp., 1941.
137. Louis, Rev. William Francis, M.A., J.C.D., Diocesan Archives, X-101 pp., 1941.
138. McDevitt, Rev. Gilbert Joseph, A.B., J.C.D., Legitimacy and Legitimation, X-247 pp., 1941.
139. McDonough, Rev. Thomas Joseph, A.B., J.C.D., Apostolic Administrators, X-217 pp., 1941.

140. Meier, Rev. Carl Anthony, A.B., J.C.D., Penal Administrative Procedure Against Negligent Pastors, XI-240 pp., 1941.

141. Schmidt, Rev. John Rogg, A.B., J.C.D., The Principles of Authentic Interpretation in Canon 17 of the Code of Canon Law, XII-331 pp., 1941.

142. Slafkosky, Rev. Andrew Leonard, A.B., J.C.D., The Canonical Episcopal Visitation of the Diocese, X-197 pp., 1941.

143. Swoboda, Rev. Innocent Robert, O.F.M., J.C.D., Ignorance in Relation to the Imputability of Delicts, IX-271 pp., 1941.

144. Dubé, Rev. Arthur Joseph, A.B., J.C.D., The General Principles for the Reckoning of Time in Canon Law, VIII-299 pp., 1941.

145. McBride, Rev. James T., A.B., J.C.D., Incardination and Excardination of Seculars, XX-585 pp., 1941.

146. Król, Rev. John J., J.C.L., The Defendant in Contentious Trials.

147. Comyns, Rev. Joseph J., C.SS.R., J.C.L., The Papal and Episcopapl Administration of Church Property.

148. Barry, Rev. Garrett Francis, O.M.I., J.C.L., Violation of the Cloister.

149. Bolduc, Rev. Gatien, C.S.V., A.B., S.T.L., J.C.L., Les études dans les religions cléricales.

150. Boyle, Rev. David John, M.A., J.C.L., The Juridic Effects of Moral Certitude on Pre-Nuptial Guarantees.

151. Canavan, Rev. Walter Joseph, M.A., Litt.D., J.C.L., The Profession of Faith.

152. Desrochers, Rev. Bruno, A.B., Ph.L., S.T.B., J.C.L., Le Premier Concile Plénier de Québec et le Code de Droit Canonique.

153. Dillon, Rev. Robert Edward, A.B., J.C.L., Common Law Marriage.

154. Dodwell, Rev. Edward John, Ph.D., S.T.B., J.C.L., The Time and Place for the Celebration of Marriage.

155. Donnellan, Rev. Thomas Andrew, A.B., J.C.L., The Obligation of the Missa pro Populo.

156. Eltz, Rev. Louis Anthony, A.B., J.C.L., Cooperators in Crimes According to Canon 2209.

157. Gass, Rev. Sylvester, Francis, M.A., J.C.L., Ecclesiastical Pensions.

158. Guiniven, Rev. John Joseph, C.SS.R., J.C.L., The Precept of Hearing Mass on Sundays and Holy Days of Obligation.

159. Gulczynski, Rev. John Theophilus, J.C.L., The Desecration and Violation of Churches.

160. Hammill, Rev. John Leo, M.A., J.C.L., The Obligations of the Traveler according to Canon 14.

161. Haydt, Rev. John Joseph, A.B., J.C.L., Reserved Benefices.

162. Huser, Rev. Roger John, O.F.M., A.B., J.C.L., The Canonical Crime of Abortion.

163. Kearney, Rev. Francis Patrick, A.B., S.T.L., J.C.L., The Principles of Canon 1127.

164. Linahen, Rev. Leo James, S.T.L., J.C.L., De Absolutione Complicis In Peccato Turpi.

165. McCloskey, Rev. Joseph Aloysius, A.B., J.C.L., The Subject of Ecclesiastical Law according to Canon 12.
166. O'Neill, Rev. Francis Joseph, C.SS.R., J.C.L., The Dismissal of Religious in Temporary Vows.
167. Prince, Rev. John Edward, A.B., S.T.B., J.C.L., The Diocesan Chancellor.
168. Riesner, Rev. Albert Joseph, C.SS.R., JC.L., Apostates and Fugitives from Religious Institutes.
169. Stenger, Rev. Joseph Bernard, J.C.L., The Mortgaging of Church Property.
170. Waldron, Rev. Joseph Francis, A.B., J.C.L., The Minister of Baptism.
171. Willett, Rev. Robert Albert, J.C.L., The Probative Value of Documents in Ecclesiastical Trials.
172. Woeber, Rev. Edward Martin, M.A., J.C.L., The Interpellations.

www.ingramcontent.com/pod-product-compliance
Lightning Source LLC
LaVergne TN
LVHW050239080826
844660LV00012B/564

* 9 7 8 0 8 1 3 2 2 3 4 9 0 *